Anyone reading "IN SEARCH OF FOUNDATIONS" will be deeply impressed with the depth of study and thoroughness of research that qualified the author to make a reliable assessment of English Theology during the unsettling years of intellectual ferment that preceded World War I. (His Bibliography, from which he freely quotes, runs well over 300 works dealing with every phase of life in that era)

Unfortunately his learned presentation is so scholarly, and his language so professional, that even a theologian will find himself re-reading paragraphs, (even pages) to make sure that he follows the line of thought. It is difficult reading even for the person interested in that field of research.

And if the whole work is to help a person better understand the turmoil of theological thinking in our day, then the undersigned reviewer shamefacedly admits that he must have missed several connectin links somewhere along the line, as he painstakingly worked his way through the 300 pages of it.

IN SEARCH OF FOUNDATIONS
ENGLISH THEOLOGY
1900-1920

IN SEARCH OF FOUNDATIONS
ENGLISH THEOLOGY
1900-1920

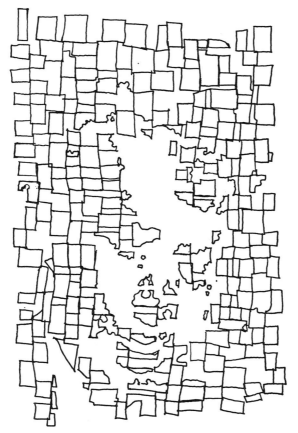

THOMAS A. LANGFORD

ABINGDON PRESS Nashville New York

IN SEARCH OF FOUNDATIONS: ENGLISH THEOLOGY 1900-1920

Seven stanzas of a poem from *Autobiography* by G. K.
Chesterton, published by Hutchinson & Co. Ltd., London, are used by permission of Miss D. E. Collins, owner
of the copyright.

Selections from B. H. Streeter's *Foundations,* published
in 1912, are used by permission of the publisher, Macmillan & Co. Ltd., London.

Quotations from *The Platonic Tradition in Anglo-Saxon
Philosophy* by J. H. Muirhead, published in 1931, are
used by permission of the publishers, George Allen &
Unwin Ltd., London.

Poetry from *My Apologia* by J. M. Thompson, published
in 1940, is used by permission of The Alden Press.

The quotation from "Too True to Be Good" by George
Bernard Shaw (from *The Complete Plays of Bernard
Shaw,* published in 1956), is used by permission of The
Society of Authors, Agent for the Bernard Shaw Estate.

Abridgment of "'Faith" by G. A. Studdert-Kennedy from
The Best of Studdert-Kennedy. Copyright, 1924 by
Harper & Brothers; renewed, 1952 by Emily Studdert-
Kennedy. Reprinted by permission of Harper & Row,
Publishers and Hodder and Stoughton Limited.

Lines from "Recessional" by Rudyard Kipling, from
Rudyard Kipling's Verse. Reprinted by permission of
Mrs. George Bambridge and Doubleday & Company, Inc.

Selections from *Vision and Authority: Or the Throne of
St. Peter* by John Oman, published in 1902, are used by
permission of Hodder and Stoughton, Limited.

Selections from *The Person and Place of Jesus Christ* by
P. T. Forsyth, published in 1909, are used by permission
of the Independent Press.

Quotations from *Conceptions of the Priesthood,* edited by
William Sanday, published in 1900, are used by per-
mission of the publishers, Longmans, Green, and Co.,
Ltd.

SET UP, PRINTED AND BOUND BY THE
PARTHENON PRESS, AT NASHVILLE,
TENNESSEE, UNITED STATES OF AMERICA

TO

MY PARENTS
LOUIE MAE HUGHES LANGFORD
THOMAS ANDERSON LANGFORD
and
MY FRIEND
HOWARD P. POWELL

MENTORS IN LIFE

PREFACE

This book is an attempt to see theological ideas incarnate in their cultural context, an effort to understand religious intellectual sensibilities in living intercourse with their environment. Ludwig Wittgenstein has reminded us that it is only in the stream of life that a thing has significance, so it is the stream of life which we shall attempt to enter in order to understand the significance of English theology in the first two decades of the twentieth century.

The importance of a cultural ethos and the reciprocity that exists between a person and his time make necessary the effort to set theologians into their surroundings and to allow the interplay between intellectual developments and historical events to have its full strength. The era and the men of the era with their ideas and actions, are parts of a single story; each person and each occasion has its own integrity, and yet each is intrinsically related to the others. This study seeks to illuminate the intense struggles, the renewed hopes, the perplexing uncertainties, and the affirmative joys that characterize those who lived in the era.

The order of the book will illustrate the attempt to draw divergent streams together. In the first two chapters, there is a historical introduction that attempts to catch the spirit of the age and thereby set the stage on which the action and thought occur. Into this framework are then fitted chapters that contain more detailed, specific explorations of points that are only mentioned or alluded to in the opening chapters. The themes that are lifted up for special discussion represent issues that uncover the questions theologians were asking, why they were asking these questions, and why they were proposing the answers they gave. Throughout, there is an effort to expose the interrelation of theology and the context in which it lived so that each contributes to the understanding of the other.

A final word is needed. This is a book by an outsider, a non-Englishman. This is a fact that carries certain liabilities but, perhaps, also certain advantages. While recognizing the strong limitations of the former, I hope the contribution of the latter will be more decisive.

In every work one's debts are many and not easily repaid. I mention with special appreciation several persons who read this material while in preparation, Professor Walter E. Hudgins of Greensboro College, Greensboro, North Carolina; Professor John Webster Grant of Emmanuel College, Toronto; Professor James A. Carpenter of General Theological Seminary, New York; Professor John H. Rodgers of Episcopal Theological Seminary, Alexandria, Virginia; and Professor W. Norman Pittenger, now of Cambridge, England. From all these I have learned from disagreements as well as agreements. I only wish my work more adequately reflected the quality of their comments.

THOMAS A. LANGFORD

CONTENTS

I

A NEW TIME

The national election of 1895 brought to office in England a superbly prepared group of patricians. The aristocracy, under the leadership of Lord Salisbury, had given their best and most carefully trained members to continue the right and responsibility of ruling the nation. Queen Victoria still reigned, the Empire was in its fullest bloom, and the landed gentry intended to keep the nation on the course that tradition had set.

On the surface, the waters appeared calm, but surging beneath were undercurrents of different, sometimes surprisingly different, interests and potentially destructive forces. Tokens of transition had been discernible for over half a century; irreversible changes in the pattern of social relations had been effected: enlargement of political franchise; growth in economic class consciousness and mobilization; increasing urbanization; removal of illiteracy; displacement of traditional foundations of social structure, such as the church; and even challenge of the privileges and rights of the aristocracy.

Lord Salisbury, the Prime Minister, with his adamant defense of the established order, was the perpetuator of the grand tradition. Convinced that democracy, which tended to unleash crowd passion, was a threat to liberty, he opposed all proposals to increase the political power of the masses. The natural leaders, those who had inherited the power and responsibility of government and who were possessors of a "superior fitness," were alone to be trusted with the guidance of the nation. Yet, in spite of the high quality of the leadership of both the Prime Minister and his cabinet and in spite of their refusal to listen to the cries for change, the era was a time of transition; one age was passing, and a new epoch was emerging. The catchwords of the period were evolution and change—words that stood for belief in progress and planning. Signs of change were everywhere to be seen: trade unions were talking of representation in Parliament; socialists, some in the form of respectable intellectuals, were calling for nationalization of property; parts of the empire were asking for—even demanding—home rule; and European political struggles were forcing their presence and problems upon the attention of the island kingdom.

Somehow the good Queen's reign had been sundered, much as her heart had been previously torn by the death of Albert. An agricultural economy, with its village life and diversified, family-centered industry, were now only memories, although tenacious and nostalgic memories; pre-industrial England was a time past, a lost world, a way of life that could not be reclaimed. The late Victorians were increasingly aware of an alienation from their fathers: philosophical idealism and a new spirit in the arts were becoming dominant, novelists questioned the criteria which society attempted to impose on the individual, moral standards and social mores were interrogated. Realignment of political allegiance between the Whig and Tory aristocrats in 1886 had been the herald of changing political interests, and the increased size of social and industrial organization required fresh vision rather than appended legislative notes to meet their economic requirements. In theology, as in other areas, there was keen, though sometimes melancholy, awareness of and participation in the cultural transformation. Change was permeative, for the era was in flux, and even the determined resistance of the government that came to power five years before the end of the century evidenced an awareness of the fluidity.

One of the most important background factors in the change was to be found in the seventies and the eighties when Britain experienced the loss of her world trade monopoly and became a world trade competitor. The export of a capital surplus was over by the late seventies, and the nation was living more and more off the income from foreign investments. Concurrent changes in the international balance of power, with Germany becoming territory-hungry and empire-conscious, meant that external relations were as unstable and challenging as the internal life of the country. These newly intruding problems, Elie Halévy has claimed, caused a loss of national confidence and a questioning of national purpose. "Whatever the improvements made in her national institutions, England felt an increasingly powerful conviction that her vitality was less than that of certain other nations. . . . It was the loss of confidence which explains the far-reaching change in her foreign policy which took place towards the end of the nineteenth century."[1] Hence, economic and political turmoil abroad, combined with the social and cultural undercurrents at home, were causes of profound disturbance.

The catalogue of change, however, must no be allowed to detract from the continuity that existed between the early and late Victorian cultures. Concentration upon the transition and upon the threat of even more unsettling changes tends to obscure the interlocking of the preceeding age and the new generation; yet such a continuity was basic, and more comprehensive, than the changes. What had gone before was not simply set aside; the past was not quickly forsaken. The novels of Dickens and Thackeray were still being read, and Wordsworth was an influential spiritual father. There were the parish vicars and the landed gentry who retained a strong sense of social propriety. Above all, Victoria was on the throne (and continued to refuse to look back before sitting down).

It would be misleading and distorting to neglect this coupling of the times. Tradition dies slowly; strong ideas have great persistence;

---

[1] *A History of the English People in the Nineteenth Century: Imperialism and the Rise of Labour*, V, trans. E. I. Watkins (London: Ernest Benn, 1926, 1961), p. viii.

and, in England, to an unusual degree, there remained a profound attachment to the past and a veneration of its values. Nevertheless, the changes are the points of interest that attract the historical interpreter, and this not unnaturally, for they constitute the juncture at which a new reality arises and provide the basis for the awareness of the character of the continuous social ethos, in terms of both its achievement and its residual problems.

The tension between the new and the old that characterized the era is evidenced by the attempts of commentators to evaluate the Victorian period. It is doubtful if any other epoch of English history has been more often reassessed or divergently appraised than that of Victoria's reign. Edward Carpenter, a minor poet, spoke as a participant and provided one perspective.

I found myself—and without knowing where I was—in the middle of that strange period of human evolution, the Victorian Age, which in some respects, one now thinks, marked the lowest ebb of modern civilized society: a period in which not only commercialism in public life, but cant in religion, pure materialism in science, futility in social convention, the worship of stocks and shares, the starving of the human heart, the denial of the human body and its needs, the huddling concealment of the body in clothes, the "impure hush" on matters of sex, class-division, contempt of manual labour, and the cruel barring of women from every natural and useful expression of their lives, were carried to an extremity of folly difficult for us now to realize.[2]

A radically different interpretation is presented by two more recent historians.

. . . during the long and wonderful reign of the good Queen, a little island set the pace for all mankind in industry, in law, in elevating the character and dignity of the poor, in the advance of science, in spreading the Christian religion and Parliamentary institutions in all parts of the earth. Distant lands were peopled with Anglo-saxons, and the dread of war grew less. If one compares representative Victorians with famous Britons of earlier or later times, it is difficult to find in any age in English history a similar galaxy of distinguished men and women; and in view of their

[2] *My Days and Dreams* (London: Allen & Unwin, 1916), pp. 320-21.

14

accomplishments not only in economic achievement but also in literature, in science, in political and social morality, one must give highest rank to the Victorians.[3]

The grandeur and the demeaning of life could both be found. Victoria's reign was one of expansion of empire; enlargement of national hope; and, perhaps more importantly, a time of peace. It was also a period of subliminal doubt, conscious frustration, and vocal challenge. Contrasts were constantly juxtaposed: faith and doubt in religion, *laissez-faire* and socialism in economics, and oligarchy and democracy in politics. For those who loved the period, the Queen herself symbolized all that was good; for those who depreciated the times, the Queen was, again, the symbol of all that was niggardly, prudish, and misproportioned. Victoria was the comprehensive symbol, whether viewed positively or negatively, of the national character.

As the century moved into its last quarter; and in spite of the great Golden Anniversary celebration of 1887 and the Diamond Jubilee of 1897, which attempted to rewed the old Queen and the new time, a fresh wind was blowing through English life. The Victorian era had been split; the late Victorians were increasingly critical of their immediate past; sons were rebelling against their fathers.

Perhaps Rudyand Kipling's "Recessional," written upon the occasion of a naval review, also described the exodus of an age rapidly disappearing.

> Far-called, our navies melt away;
>   On dunes and headland sinks the fire:
> Lo, all our pomp of yesterday
>   Is one with Ninevah and Tyre!
> Judge of all Nations, spare us yet,
>   Lest we forget—lest we forget!

With agitated activity, with expansiveness of wants and fondness of luxury within a context of demands for economic change, the new spirit

[3] W. P. Hall and R. G. Albion, *The History of England and the British Empire* (Boston: Ginn, 2nd ed., 1956), p. 320. For another fervent and eulogistic evaluation of the era see W. R. Inge, "The Victorian Age," which was the Rede Lecture at Cambridge in 1922 and published in *Diary of a Dean* (London: Hutchinson, 1949), pp. 208 ff.

ushered in a new century. "The new century has begun," wrote the editor of the *Church Quarterly Review,* "with an event [the death of Victoria in 1901] which marks, more decisively than anything else could do, the end of a well-marked era in the history of the British power. . . . Already we feel about us the stir of a new time.[4] George Dangerfield has described the change as it was symbolized by Edward VII's visit to Buckingham Palace after his accession to the throne, a palace that the Queen had not visited for more than a day or two at a time since the death of the Prince Consort.

As the King went through its maze of apartments and corridors he came at last—and one can well believe with reluctance—into the private apartments of the Prince Consort. Nothing had been moved since Albert's death: the ink had hardened in the inkstands; intimate letters, yellow with age, lay just as he had left them; chairs, the desk, the carpets seemed to have been waiting for forty years for Albert to return. In one corner stood the organ upon which he had played to Mendelssohn, but it was perished and voiceless. Had the King ever penetrated these rooms before, for some awful interview with that formidable parent? We do not know. He ordered everything to be packed up and put away with care. And then the electrician, the plumber, the cleaner and the Twentieth Century came in.[5]

Edwardian England was the heir of the rich complexity and baffling contradictions of the Victorian era. In a sense, the offspring was, of necessity, different from its parent. But it was different only as the final stage of a process is distinct from its precursory phases; it had its own uniqueness as the twilight has its peculiar place in the day. Edwardian England was Victorian England thinned out and strained; it was wont to exaggerate many of its mother's virtues and vices. A child late come of age whose mimicry tended to mockery, it was Victoria's England with Victoria gone and therefore without its full heart or head.

The new century began with problems and promise. There was what might by this time be called "normal warfare" over economic problems. More than 640 battles in the form of strikes in the first twelve months of the century involved over 180,000 workmen, and although the number

---

[4] April, 1901, p. 1.
[5] *Victoria's Heir* (New York: Harcourt, Brace & Co., 1942), p. 537.

of strikes was reduced from the mid-nineties, their intensity was heightened. The primary cause of this unrest was the fact of poverty, and poverty of a type caused by the Industrial Revolution. The two most distinct features of this economic depravation were unemployment, as contrasted with the characteristic underemployment of earlier periods, and the erosion of family and social structures that previously had supported those in financial distress. It has been estimated that by the turn of the century one person in five could expect to be buried from a workhouse, a poor-law hospital, or a lunatic asylum, and that something like one quarter of the entire population was in dire economic straits.[6] As a consequence, the established social order was being challenged by the laboring class and by the unemployed, who were dissatisfied with their inherited status. The Victorian era had witnessed the birth of a labor party in politics, the germination of socialistic ideology, and a demand for a more equitable distribution of the national wealth. By 1900 there were over two million members of the trade unions; the masses were speaking with insistent voices. With the coming of the new century, the unheeded utterances became impassioned cries for a new society, a new order, a new style of life.

At home the imposing political events were the demands for new social legislation, the growth of the Independent Labour Party, and the challenge to Tory strength. In addition, there were the more visible problems of women's suffrage and educational reform. On the international scene, trade competition, the disintegration of the empire, and the beginning of a new form of alignment importuned for attention. For the first two years of the century the South African (Boer) War dominated international affairs. Newspapers made every battle a crucial test of the Empire, and public meetings questioned the wisdom of armed engagement at all. The war tended to polarize ideologies, so that shouts of Empire and of free nations, of battle and of pacifism were ringing through the land. Finally, in May, 1902, this conflict, which men both praised and damned, was brought to an end, and a settlement was reached. When the war was over Lord Salisbury resigned, and his nephew Arthur Balfour succeeded him to the party leadership. *Le*

[6] Peter Laslett, *The World We Have Lost* (London: Methuen, 1965), p. 200.

Temps of Paris commented on the event, "What closes today with Lord Salisbury's departure is a whole historic era. It is ironic that what he hands on is a democratized, imperialized, colonialized and vulgarized England—everything that is antithetic to Toryism, the aristocratic tradition and the High Church that he stood for. It is the England of Mr. Chamberlain, not, despite his nominal leadership of Mr. Balfour." [7]

If the comment from Paris was extreme, it reflected an awareness of the changes in process. There was peace in South Africa, but the resulting quietness made the clamor from a neighboring island all the more noticeable. The Irish were becoming belligerent; the question of home rule increasingly aroused Irish tempers—and an Irishman in temper is a formidable, unrelenting opponent. As the British eye scanned the globe, it could see disturbing signs everywhere. Russia had expanded southward into China before the turn of the century, and, to protect an "Open Door Policy" for British trade, pacts were signed with Germany (1898) and Japan (1902). By 1904 the country was ready to take a firm stand in European affairs and concluded an entente with France. Problems had evoked pacts. Where all this would lead no one seemed to be sure; but the fact that the nation was now deeply involved in international affairs, and involved not as an invincible power, constituted a cause for pervasive uneasiness.

To cite these political changes is only a means of illustrating the radical movement from a quickly receding past to an uncertain future. There were many other signs of change. Technology was making its contribution with the arrival of the automobile, the motor bus, and moving picture. The modern newspaper and telephone were widely distributed. In 1901 the first trans-Atlantic wireless message was sent from Cornwall to Newfoundland. Travel and talk, mobility and ability to communicate characterized the period. Yet it is easy to exaggerate the importance of these inventions, for in the last analysis the Edwardian period in its daily life was nearer to the age that preceded it than to the age that followed.

King Edward himself, whatever his morals, was a man of impeccable manners who insisted that the proprieties of cultured life be observed.

[7] Quoted in Barbara W. Tuchman, *The Proud Tower* (New York: Macmillan, 1962), p. 59.

Such an external show of order in social life reflected an intense hope and probably a firm expectation on the part of the peerage that they, and Britannia, would continue with the position and *noblesse oblige* they had gained under Victoria. It is, however, apropos to remark that the changes that characterized the Edwardian era must, to a considerable extent, be referred to the loss of a sense of national mission. The power of national purpose was replaced by a bereavement of goals, the Victorian expansion and drive of Empire waned, then died; whether the nation should attempt to revive the dead ideal or search for new goals was problematic. As a result, manners and mannerisms replaced the deeper meaning of national existence. The drive and purpose, of which Victorian manners were an authentic expression, had been lost, and only the etiquette of unrooted mores remained. But manners, if they do not reflect moral force, become the graveclothes of a decaying body. There was reason for concern.

The music of Edward Elgar was born in and characterized the period. On the one hand, there was in his work an opulence, an expansiveness of style, and a full-bodied—even heroic—definition of life. And yet, on the other hand, there was, as E. D. Mackerness has suggested, perhaps a certain vulgarity—a vulgarity that denied the depth of the more obvious and pretentious claims.[8]

C. F. G. Masterman, in his tract for the times, *The Condition of England,* a book that went through six editions in just over two years, diagnosed the situation. The cause of the current social disease, he declared, was to be found in the loss of purpose both as a nation and as individuals. Englishmen had created a nation of public penury and private ostentation, and, consequently, the people of the nation were in mortal struggle. There was conflict between the "Conquerors," persons who tried desperately to make something of life spared the effort of wage earning; the "suburbans," who aped the ruling class and lived in poverty of spirit if not of mammon; and the "multitude," who were economically deprived and atrophied. The tyranny of the present, he cried, denies the past and blocks the vision of a better future.[9]

[8] *A Social History of English Music* (London: Routledge and K. Paul, 1964), p. 206.
[9] C. F. G. Masterman, *The Condition of England* (London: Methuen, 1909), pp. 17, 40, 65, 92.

In spite of its critics' warnings, the spirit of the age was basically optimistic. It is possible to indicate exceptions to this generalization, such as Joseph Conrad, who described man's aloneness, if not lostness; and Thomas Hardy, who contrasted the small pathetic pattern of man's mortal life and struggle against the vast, incomprehensible movements of nature. But one of these men was a foreigner to the land and the other a stranger to the period. Far more typical among the novelists were Arnold Bennett and H. G. Wells, who endorsed and heightened the dominant mood of anticipation and optimism. The age expected a better future—though what a "better" future would be provoked differences of opinion. Traditionalists, for instance, wanted to preserve the social structure and enhance the qualities of the English gentle life. Lord Hugh Cecil, son of the recent Prime Minister, Lord Salisbury, and himself an impeccable traditionalist, called the era a time of conservation and repose, resting only to move forward with more of its inherited strength. The aristocratic vision of what was and what should be still dominated many minds. In the first issue of the *Tatler,* a society news sheet, there was a description of a party given in 1901, a description that characterized the attitude of the established social hierarchy.

Coronets shone on many a stately head. Peer's daughters sold copies of the souvenir at half-a-guinea each. With the artistocracy were mixed other classes. The new-made millionaires and their magnificently dressed wives readily gave 3 gns. for fete and concert in the palace of the Duke of Sutherland. Never can a more remarkable collection of visitors have been seen within the walls of Stafford House; and as the Duchess with a bright smile passed hither and thither she must have been amused as well as gratified by the variety of her guests.

Then the *Tatler* went on to state, "Save on occasions of charitable entertainment such as this, the modern millionaire and *nouveau riche* will knock in vain at the portals of Stafford House."

In a complex manner, the *Tatler* was both right and wrong. The paper was correct insofar as it reflected a regnant mood of the time. Perhaps the most persistent reality in history is the dominance of inertia and somnolent acceptance of what is. Edwardian England had its prophets and its disclaimers, but it, like most other epochs, was dominantly characterized by an inertia that accepted what was as what ought to be. For many people, if not for all, the difference of social status was a part of the order of life, an aspect of existence that was to be accepted. With quiet pulsation, the past pumped its blood into the present, and life with its small pleasures and picayune hurts was quietly endured.

But the *Tatler* was also wrong. The stability of an idealized past was now being seriously challenged. The first voices may have sounded uncouth or boorish; they initially may have given the impression of peevish whining by a disgruntled few, but these voices tenaciously insisted until they were heard, and heard clearly. Not only was the modern millionaire soon to knock again on the door of many palaces and manor houses and expect to be admitted, but also he was taking a new place in politics, as he had already in the economic life of the nation. What is of greater import, those who were not and would never be millionaires were also entering politics; workingmen were becoming well organized with strong political motivation, and common men were beginning to enter the House of Commons. Aristocratic caste had not yet fallen, but by the end of the first decade many of its privileges would be immodestly stripped away.

Lord Hugh Cecil spoke of conservation and repose, but it was a false assessment; perhaps, after all, it had only been a hope. For some, the dominant expectation had a messianic character. The young among the religious still rallied to the challenge to "evangelize the world in this generation." For others, who constituted an increasing number, the evolution of society was toward a more secularist order of life. "Secularism" had been a new word in the 1850's, but as the century matured many made it a part of their vocabulary and became its advocates. G. J. Holyoake, in the nineteenth century, defined the three basic principles of the secularist mood as the improvement of life by material means, belief in science as the available providence for men, and the freeing of morality from religious bases. All the emphases were important. The application of new invention to industrial processes gave prominence to technical reason and to problem-solving. Material transformation of life—especially for the middle classes—now seemed possible. Although the middle class was still a minority of the population, it has been estimated that approximately a million people, or just over one-seventh of the population, could be included in this group by the end of the first decade. To belong to this segment of society was the aspiration and hope of the majority of the population.[10]

Increasingly, the technological achievements that it was daily effecting made science appear a safe, providential guide. Could science save man and his civilization? For some this now seemed a distinct possibility. Planning and careful organization of social relations according to scientific principles seemed to be achievable, individual abilities could be enhanced and social potentiality actualized by the application of these principles and by the invention of technical instruments. Science was giving rise to scientism, and the new faith was exerting its power on the imagination. Finally, the emancipation of morality from religious bases was given prominence. It was not a new theme—not nearly so new as the amazing technological achievements—but it gained fresh force in an age when there were not as many gaps left for God to fill and when religious institutions were identified with the past. Religion and morality might or might not support one another, but the question of their relation was, for many, no longer important. Morality was to be determined by the same rational principles that govern the rest of life. Once and for all, the mood implied, we must reject the escapist tendencies in religion—the desertion of this world for some far-off, distant place that has little relation to the ordinary, mundane, practical concerns of life.

To state the case so starkly is to oversimplify the complexity of the situation. The tendency toward secularization did not, in England, turn into either dogmatic atheism or sharp ideological theorizing. E. R. Wickham has commented, "Sharp lines between fidelity and infidelity cannot be drawn in English society, and one way of stating this is to say that the secular minded outside the churches have a Christian colouration, and that the practising Christians inside have marked secular characteristics." [11] Perhaps the best description of the secularism of the time is to speak of it as a leveling of life, the loss of commitment to any single transcendent goal, accompanied by a concomitant lifting of the

---

[10] *The World We Have Lost,* p. 217.
[11] *Church and People in an Industrial City* (London: Lutterworth, 1957), p. 188.

status of the material environment and an optimism about social amelioration.

The impact of the secularization of society upon the churches formed a strange mosiac. The cultural importance of the traditional religious rituals and beliefs were clearly being challenged. A positive new ideology was replacing the rather passive Christian assumptions of the working class. A strained relation between the working classes and the churches had existed since the beginning of the Industrial Revolution, and as the nation became urbanized the churches lost the population of the cities through their failure to establish effective contact with the economically depressed city dwellers. Reasons for this were multiple. The churches represented conservative support for the *status quo*; they were economically supported by the well-established and administered by the privileged; they tended to represent definite (and definitely not worker) socio-educational-cultural groups; their language, liturgy, and theology were alien; and their interests often focused on the next world. For many of the disenchanted, the labor movement, especially with its ethical stress, seemed to offer an attractive possibility for the transfer of piety to a secular and humanistic movement. In spite of this disaffection, membership in the churches continued to grow in the national scale until the end of the first decade of the twentieth century.[12]

By the end of this decade, however, an attrition in membership had set in, and disaffection with the churches increased. R. J. Campbell in his autobiography ascribed this loss to the spirit of the time, which was materialistic and had no "inclination for the supermundane." [13] E. R. Wickham has attributed the failure to the churches themselves, "The supreme weakness then was a failure to understand the signs of the times, a failure of vision and perception," and this weakness he blamed upon a basic theological error that narrowed the claims of God to the pietistic-religious dimension of life with its tendency to reduce complex

[12] Cf. British Weekly, March 10, 17, 1955, for articles on membership within Nonconformity; also Robert Wearmouth, *The Social and Political Influence of Methodism in the Twentieth Century* (London: Epworth Press, 1957), pp. 46 ff. The Church of England shows a similar pattern. See also Peter d'A. Jones, *The Christian Socialist Revival, 1877-1914* (Princeton: Princeton University Press, 1968). For a synoptic view of the statistics see pages 61-67 and for causes of working class alienation pp. 72-74.

[13] *A Spiritual Pilgrimage* (London: Williams and Norgate, 1916), pp. 163-64.

social problems to the level of personal morality.[14] Perhaps a more judicious assessment of the situation would acknowledge the rightness in both of these claims. The church as a whole had refused to listen with approbation to its internal critics, such as Hugh Price Hughes, John Clifford, Charles Gore, and C. G. Masterman; but neither was society receptive to the message of these socially aware spokesmen. Whatever else secularism meant, it did mean that many of the traditional social supports for religious faith and practice were falling away, and the average person felt little inclined to spend too much time meditating on discarnate realities.

It would be a grave injustice, however, to pass by without mentioning the increased interest and active engagement in social problems on the part of some churchmen. The Tractarian movement, a half a century earlier, with its effort to recover the doctrine of the church had, in some of its representatives, such as Pusey, developed an emphasis upon the social character of man's existence as a member of the Body of Christ and had asserted that bald individualism was wrong in philosophy and practice. F. D. Maurice and Charles Kingsley had performed a prophetic function by setting the stage for Christian involvement in social reform, and by the last quarter of the century, with proper distance being given to the prophets, numbers of churchmen began to follow their lead. In 1877 the Guild of St. Matthew under the provocative leadership of Steward Headlam was facing the problems that social change brought to faith and mission. The subsequent founding of the important Christian Social Union by B. F. Westcott, Henry Scott Holland, and others in 1889, as well as the establishment of the Church Socialist League in 1906, witnessed to the practical implementation of Christian social concerns within the Church of England. Two years after the establishment of this last group, Charles Gore, who was among the most ardent of his time in his desire to relate the sacraments to the slums, reiterated his position, "We must identify ourselves with the ideal of socialist thought."[15] G. K. Chesterton has a delightful description of some of

---

[14] *Church and People in an Industrial City*, pp. 192-93.

[15] G. L. Prestige, *The Life of Charles Gore* (London: Wm. Heinemann, 1935), p. 93. As early as 1891 Gore had spoken in favor of a Christian socialism and claimed for it a significant role as a therapy of society. Cf. *The Incarnation of the Son of God* (London: John Murray, 1891), p. 211.

those who participated in these concerns, as seen from the standpoint
of a Nottingham tradesman.

> The Christian Social Union here
> was very much annoyed;
> It seems there is some duty
> Which we never should avoid,
> And so they sing a lot of hymns
> to help the Unemployed.
>
> Upon a platform at the end
> The speakers were displayed
> And Bishop Hoskins stood in front
> and hit a bell and said
> That Mr. Carter was to pray,
> And Mr. Carter prayed.
>
> Then Bishop Gore of Birmingham
> He stood up on one leg
> And said he would be happier
> If beggars didn't beg,
> And that if they pinched his palace
> It would take him down a peg.
>
> He said that Unemployment
> Was a horror and a blight,
> He said that charities produced
> Servility and spite,
> And stood upon the other leg
> And said it wasn't right.
>
> And then a man named Chesterton
> Got up and played with water,
> He seemed to say that principles
> were nice and led to slaughter
> And how we always compromised
> And how we didn't orter.

Then Canon Holland fired ahead
Like fifty cannons firing,
We tried to find out what he meant
With infinite enquiring
But the way he made the windows jump
We couldn't help admiring.

He said the human soul should be
Ashamed of every sham,
He said a man should constantly
Ejaculate "I am"
. . . when he had done, I went outside
And got into a tram.[16]

The idea of "Christian socialism" was very ambiguous and remains quite impossible to identify in any precise sense. Every spokesman seemed to use the phrase with a different understanding. Religious leaders, for instance, were using the designation for their positions, although the Independent Labour Party was still unwilling to declare itself "socialistic" in its platform,[17] while the Fabians and Social Democratic Federation had no difficulty in proclaiming themselves as such. The main reason for this variegated response was to be found in the fact that in strictly political circles the term had more definite ideological content and intention, whereas for Gore and the majority of religious leaders the term "socialism" was used to indicate a desire for justice, a more equitable (though often unexplicated) distribution of wealth, and a better life for the masses of people.[18] Primarily, what the words indicated was an attitude of willingness to be involved in the social and political affairs of the working people.

The Nonconformist Churches, as well as the Church of England, were being carried in the maelstrom of social change, and among the dissenting churches the Methodists and the Congregationalists were the most intimately identified with the transition. The changes in the social

---

[16] *Autobiography* (London: Arrow Books, 1959, first published in 1936), pp. 153-54.

[17] G. E. Elton, *The Life of James Ramsay MacDonald* (London: Collins, 1939), p. 157.

[18] Charles Gore, *The New Theology and the Old Religion* (London: John Murray, 1907), p. 173. Jones, in *The Christian Socialist Revival*, has forceably illustrated this general ambiguity; cf. esp. his concluding chapter.

structure were forcing these churches with their evangelical tradition to abandon their nineteenth-century individualism. Earlier in the Victorian era, the dissenting churches had had more intimate connections with the working classes. This was due in large part to their common antipathy to the Established Church and to the aristocracy as well as to the dominant economic powers; but it was also due in a measure to the number of their members from among the small tradesmen and the "lower middle class" of the economic order. As the century advanced, the old cooperation was strained, and the older individualistic pietism made it difficult for the churches to find a new role in the developing social and political structure. Calls for a new era of revival and evangelism were raised by many of the leading Nonconformist churchmen, but the response was increasingly meager. More and more, large numbers of the members from these churches became identified with the Liberal Party, and it is not unimportant (although it is not a simple, univocal relation) that the decline of the Nonconformist churches and of the Liberal Party in the second decade of the twentieth century were contemporaneous.

The social dimension of Christian action required attention and forced itself upon the conscience of the leadership of the dissenting churches. By the decade of the nineties, those who were interested in the social condition of the nation had come to the belief that applying Christianity to social situations was a possibility, and this conviction fundamentally changed a number of perspectives: the Christian idea was to be identified not with the salvation of a remnant but with the redemption of the world; hence, churches were not arks of refuge but centers of aggressive activity, and the ideals of the kingdom could be achieved in this world.[19] In sum, brotherhood was a live option for which the churches must decide and upon which they must act.

In 1894, the Christian Socialist League was established and continued until 1898 when it was succeeded by the Christian Social Brotherhood. John Clifford, the stalwart Baptist, was president of the League and led his group in an aggressive campaign of demonstrations and conferences. The vice-president was J. Bruce Wallace, an inveterate liberal,

---

[19] John Webster Grant, *Free Churchmanship in England 1870-1940* (London: Independent Press, 1962), p. 171.

who was a Congregational minister and a supporter of vegetarianism and internationalism as well as the founder of a Brotherhood Trust in 1892 that hoped to establish a cooperative colony possessing its own farms, factories, stores, and homes. The League was only one of the many societies that came into being toward the turn of the century and that expressed a concerted effort to relate the churches to their social environment.

Such a position, either theoretically conceived or practically implemented, was not, of course, universally accepted by all churchmen. The Methodists represented such tensions. Vocal dissent, especially among those who were now respectably middle class, was loud and persistent; but the countervailing voice of Hugh Price Hughes not only carried a great body of Methodists into the mainstream of social concern but also provided the necessary leadership for others in the Free Church tradition. The most concrete illustration of this new mood among the Methodists came in 1907 when the Methodist Union for Social Service was founded under the impressive leadership of S. E. Keeble, W. F. Lofthouse, J. S. Lidgett, J. E. Rattenbury, C. Ensor Walten, S. F. Collier, Arthur Henderson, and W. M. Crook. Parliamentary leaders and churchmen who composed this group were banding together to discuss and publish in order to lead Methodist opinion and, as far as possible, general social consciousness. S. E. Keeble was the most vigorous member of the group in his enthusiasm for socialism, but the entire body was composed of men with great vision and energy, and both qualities were employed in the service of the church and society.

Among the Free Churches, Congregationalism took the lead in social involvement, with the Presbyterians and Baptists following somewhat more reluctantly. In all these bodies the revivalistic and evangelical traditions tended to make for ineptitude in meeting the new social configurations and to some extent precipitated a more direct collision insofar as the individualism of evangelicalism caused basic friction with the newer social or corporate consciousness. The cultural transformation was permeative, however; and no part of society or the church could remain permanently insulated from the new ideas that were at work. In 1908 the prewar enthusiasm for social reform was loudly asserting its interests. John Clifford cried, "The whole sweep and trend of the age is socialistic. . . . The fact is—this is the plan of God. Socialism in the soul of it is Divine. It is of God. The Churches ought . . . to take full share in the gradual reformation and rebuilding of Society, to welcome every practical extension of the Socialistic principle." [20]

The wine was heady. But a caveat must be entered. I have so far been speaking of leaders of the churches; and these were only some, though among the most prominent, of the leaders. They do represent major tendencies in the churches, yet there was always a distance between these leaders and the majority of the churchmen, as the church periodicals of the time reveal. Perhaps the ambiguity of the word "socialism" and its different connotations allowed the oratory and writing to find an acceptance without total agreement; perhaps, as so often, the words were more exhortatory than descriptive; perhaps congregations were willing to hear expostulation without acting. But, whatever the reasons, there was a distance between these leaders I have been describing and the majority of the church membership. It is true that Nonconformity, with its Methodist-Tory and Congregational-radical traditions, supported the Liberal Party, while fewer members joined the Independent Labour Party. In both cases, there was general affinity with a leftward political trend. But the leaders were more vocal and clearly committed than the majority of their followers.

A writer in the *Church Quarterly Review* had exulted in 1901, "How wonderfully the Church adapts her unchanging message to the special needs of every age!" [21] In some cases, and in many ways this periodical never suspected, this was true. But the general picture was uneven. To many others the church seemed out of step with the time. The situation to which the church must now speak had radically changed; the whole tenor of life was different, and the mind of the age reflected a secular disposition. The time when Christian attitudes consciously controlled or

---

[20] Quoted in R. F. Wearmouth, *The Social and Political Influence of Methodism in the Twentieth Century*, p. 241. It should be noted that in spite of the overemphasis that Wearmouth placed on the working-class character of Methodists and of certain persons among the Free Churchmen, an exaggeration that other historians have pointed out (see Jones, *The Christian Socialist Revival*, pp. 305-6), there is still an importance to his study that is to be found in his explication of the effort of many within the dissenting churches to retain their contact with and influence upon the working classes.

[21] July, 1901, p. 455.

basically directed the popular mind was quickly passing. Canon Roger Lloyd has reflected a somewhat understandable exasperation with the age, and particularly with the literate and economically privileged: "There seldom existed a generation of English people which more needed and less desired the Christian Redemption." [22] But how were the need and the message to be brought together? An important assessment was made at the turn of the century by Charles Booth in a prolonged, although poorly controlled, study of religion in the life of economically depressed people in East London. In this study, he found little evidence to support the claim that organized religion was in any degree effective as an agency for the improvement of the condition of the people, except, as he dryly commented, insofar as those who performed the work benefited from so doing. His analysis led him to the conclusion that the churches had so adapted themselves to the class structure that they had become impotent to transform society. In fact, Booth concluded, the politicians had convinced the common people that they were more sinned against than sinners, and evangelical calls for repentance were unheeded if they were comprehended. The problems to which Booth pointed were not confined to that era alone; they were problems of the Twentieth Century, the problems of Christian faith finding its purpose and its appropriate instrumentality in a secular culture.

The church, like the social order, was involved in transition. It would be too much to claim that everyone was aware of the change or that a great majority of the people in the state or the church were keenly concerned about the change. But there were signs that the disturbances were being widely felt; increasingly, people were becoming sensitive to the earth tremors.

The social and political crisis reached its first important peak of the century in 1906 with the general election. For the first time the Independent Labour Party entered its own slate of candidates and won 29 seats, while the Liberal Party was swept to victory with a net gain of 275 Members of Parliament. The people wanted a change, they wanted a government responsive to the issues of the day, and the results of the general election shook the nation. "Unless I'm mistaken," observed

[22] *The Church of England 1900-1965* (London: S.C.M. Press, 1966), p. 54.

A. J. Balfour with his usual philosophical detachment, "the Election of 1906 inaugurates a new era." [23] The transformed character of Parliament may be seen in the number of workingmen and men of small means who were now in the ruling body, as Sir Robert Ensor remarked: "To persons born like Lansdowne and Balfour (and only a little less to Rosebery) it appeared out of the question that a house of commons so composed and led should effectively rule the nation." [24] However this may be, the electorate had called a new Parliament, a Parliament that reflected the frustrations and the hopes of the nation.

---

[23] Quoted in Halévy, *A History of the English People in the Nineteenth Century,* VI, 92.
[24] *England, 1870-1914* (Oxford: Clarendon Press, 1936), p. 388.

II

THE YEARS OF CRISIS

Professor Percy Gardner, a liberal churchman from Oxford, surveyed the cultural situation in the first decade of our century with measured pessimism.

On whichever side we look, we see great changes going on, and still greater upheavals threatening. In politics the state of matters is very unstable. A secularist socialist party is growing stronger and stronger. We see the utmost unrest among the nations of the Continent, and Asia is growing every year more impatient of European predominance. And in religion everything seems to be in a flux. . . . No one who really considers the signs of the times can cherish a light heart as regards the future of the church.[1]

It was not surprising that in the midst of the general transition there was a strong current also propelling the religious communities. Mini-

[1] *Anglican Liberalism* (London: Williams and Norgate, 1908), pp. 136-37.

sters and theologians responded to the new condition with new ideas and fresh strategy, and the most widely publicized of these efforts was the enunciation of "the New Theology" by R. J. Campbell. Campbell was the minister of City Temple, the most prominent Nonconformist Church in London. For over twelve years there had been ferment among certain Congregational ministers, especially in the Midlands,[2] but the cauldron spilled over in January, 1907 when Campbell was interviewed by a reporter from the *Daily Mail*. Violent controversy immediately errupted, but to appreciate the debate it is necessary to state the theses of this New Theology. Campbell was persuaded that the Christian interpretations of life that were most generally rejected were not the Christian faith rightly understood. The spirit of the time, with justice, was in the process of discarding a dogmatic tradition that was dated, overly narrow, and unscientific. On the positive side, he was convinced that the movement toward socialistic forms of government and a corporate conception of society were covert expressions of the Christian spirit, and that they demanded a theology that would root them in the depths of human life, that is, in God.

Campbell held a primary convicton that to explicate the implications of the immanence or the indwelling of God would once again bring the Christian interpretation of life into the arena where thoughtful men lived, and it would once again indicate to men that the good they sought was most adequately embodied in this faith. That all men are religious was axiomatic, and it was symptomatic of the era that he found this belief exemplified in the fact that a vast majority of men demanded democracy and fairness in society. What Campbell intended to show was that this natural religiousness of man has its true source in God's immanence, in his ubiquitous presence. Campbell's style was that of an orator—uncomplicated, rhythmical, and with a good turn of phrase; but it also carried the liability of much public oratory—inexactness and lack of balance in thought. In dramatic language he asserted, "The wagon of socialism needs to be hitched to the star of religious faith. . . . The New Theology is but the religious articulation of the social movement."[3]

Campbell's strength, and he had great strength in spite of his de-

---

[2] Cf. T. Rhondda Williams, *How I Found My Faith* (London: Cassell, 1938), pp. 70 ff.
[3] *The New Theology* (London: Williams and Norgate, 1907), p. 14.

tractors, was that he was empathetically related to his time; both his popularity as a preacher and the success of his writing in the press illustrated his reception. He was also attentive, unfortunately at times uncritically so, to the philosophical discussions and the biblical criticism that emanated from Germany. The philosophical, social, and critical movements taken together, he believed, gave new clarity to Christian understanding. On this basis, he stated confidently, there was not the slightest need for men of thoughtful mind and reverent spirit to recoil from the fundamentals of the Christian creed, for, rightly understood, they were the fundamentals of human nature.

To begin with, the distinction between man and God cannot be drawn in a metaphysical sense: "Humanity is Divinity viewed from below, Divinity is humanity viewed from above." [4] The assertion of the divinity of humanity was not an advocacy of pantheism with its "Fate-God" imprisoned in his universe; rather, he preferred to call his position "monistic idealism" by which he meant that the "fundamental reality is consciousness," with no basic "distinction between matter and spirit." [5] The primordial conformity between God and man was uniquely exemplified in Jesus Christ, who summed up and focused the religious ideal for man. His appearance reaffirmed the spiritual truth that man's higher self is divine and eternal, integral to the being of God. Jesus was divine, as any man may be, simply because his life was never governed by any other principle than that of love. With this paradigm, Campbell was prepared to draw the conclusion that we can think of every human life as a manifestation of the eternal Son and every man as sacred. Further, that which was realized by Jesus is, in essence, realizable for every man.

What then of evil? It was significant that approximately one third of the book dealt with the problem of evil and the atonement. This was a typical concern of the era because, with the demise of biblical inerrancy, there was a reaffirmation of the atonement as one of the most distinctive remaining doctrines of evangelical Christianity. In Campbell's case it was imperative for him to enter the discussion if his interpretation of the Christian faith was to make contact with the evangelical tradition out of which he came and which he still hoped to represent.

[4] *Ibid.*, p. 75.
[5] *Ibid.*, pp. 221-22.

Campbell rejected the doctrine of man's fall in any literal sense, but he maintained that men are captive to the power of sin. Sin he described, in the Socratic manner, as the misdirection of good intentions, a quest for God that has become eccentric. The fall signifies man's misapprehension of his own true good, his false evaluation of values that leads to the substitution of selfish interests for the love of God and the neighbor. The redeeming activity that is appropriate to this view of sin is that of a persuasive power that redirects the mind of man to the true end of life. In the light of this interpretation, the traditional theories of atonement must be rejected, for they perpetuate an immoral conception of God, that is, a view of God as a Sovereign who demands restitution or satisfaction. A "human" or humane view of Jesus' death must be recovered, the redeeming work of Jesus must be understood in terms of providing man with the motive or intentional capacity for loving others. Such a transformation of life is possible because God is continuously present as an indwelling power that breaks man's selfish inclinations and replaces them with attitudes of self-sacrificing love. Ultimately, Campbell contended, since this power is ubiquitous there will be universal salvation in which all men shall be brought together with one another and with God.

The theme of judgment, that is of heaven and hell, was interpreted in terms of the present life. The "last things" take place every moment in the individual's existence, and rehabilitative influences are present that will eventuate in transformed social relationships. "We must," he said, "establish a social order wherein a man can be free to be his best, and to give his best to the community without crushing or destroying anyone else. In a word, we want collectivism in the place of competition, we want the Kingdom of God. . . . This, then, is the mission of the New Theology. It is to brighten and keep burning the flame of the spiritual ideal in the midst of the mighty social movement which is now in process."[6] Christianity had a message; it was an intelligent and intelligible message, and it must be delivered.

Campbell's ideas quickly became the center of raging controversy. Within a week of the *Daily Mail's* interview on January 12, writers

[6] *Ibid.*, pp. 253-54, 256.

in the *Observer,* the *Daily Chronicle,* the *Tribune,* and the *British Weekly* were involved in the discussion. The attackers advanced quickly and thrust at every vulnerable spot. A minority expressed sympathy with the intention of the presentation, but most of the commentators vehemently attacked the ideas and the man who had expressed them. At City Temple the congregation cheered as Campbell responded to his critics in one of his sermons. Catch-names were coined: "Pinchbeck Pantheism," said the *Church Times;* "Passion for Heresy" headlined the *Record.* Advertisements appeared under the title "The New Theology" attempting to sell books ranging from the works of Swedenborg to *The Century Bible.* It was sheer coincidence that in the midst of all the excitement an advertisement appeared in the *British Weekly* for "Guy's Tonic," which, it was claimed, would "positively cure . . . Low spirits, Headaches, Irritability, and Brain-fag" along with "Hesitancy, Noises in the head and General Langour." [7]

But what were the serious reactions to Campbell? Anglicans tended to decry the new interpretation—this heresy had come from City Temple, a place that had always been somewhat suspect. Canon H. H. Henson, a notable disturber of those who slumbered, was surprisingly slighting in his response; when interviewed by the *Daily Chronicle* on January 31 he dismissed the entire business: "Nine-tenths of the New Theology is made up of platitudes, and the remaining tenth is fallacy." There were, however, more substantial rejoiners, especially by Henry Scott Holland and Arthur C. Headlam. Holland indulgently smiled but also seriously attacked the theological position that Campbell represented.[8] In particular, both Holland and Headlam argued that Campbell had not done justice to the distinction between God and nature (Headlam especially criticized Campbell's philosophical assumptions) or to the concepts of sin and authority. Writ small, Holland claimed, the New Theology failed because

---

[7] *British Weekly,* Feb. 28, 1907, p. 580.

[8] "The character of this book carries us back to old days of happy boyish confidence, when we swung along in the flood of our first philosophic raptures, gaily shocking our sisters in the Vacation, and bringing a pained surprise into the sweet, patient face of our Mother. It was all so sure—and we were so pleased with large sweeping phrases—and there was no time to stop and make the necessary qualifications." *Creeds and Critics* (London: Mowbray, 1918), p. 88. Cf. the entire chapter on the New Theology. See also A. C. Headlam, "The New Theology," *History, Authority and Theology* (London: John Murray, 1909).

it did not allow to Jesus Christ the uniqueness and centrality that Christian faith and worship enjoins. The incarnation—as agonized suffering, joyous resurrection, and as new creation—had fallen from the center of theology. And when the heart is gone, the body has no life.

One Roman Catholic historian later remarked cynically, "The Preacher has persuaded himself that he was adapting the Christian message to the minds of the generation which has elected the Parliament of 1906-10." [9] In both the best and the worst senses this statement was true, and the response proved it. For weeks the papers were filled with short, medium, and long letters to the editors; books immediately appeared that took sides in the argument. Most of those from ministers were hostile.

Nonetheless, there were defenders in the land. John Clifford, the courageous Baptist leader, agreed to speak in Campbell's pulpit to indicate, at least, his belief in Campbell's right to theologize in this manner. Among the Congregationalists, T. Rhondda Williams and K. C. Anderson both published books under the same title as Campbell's in the same year, and the books shared the same perspective. From outside the traditional circles Sir Oliver Lodge, the Vice-Principal of Birmingham University and an eminent scientist, published a book entitled *The Substance of Faith* in which he took a position cognate to Campbell's and explicated the substance of religious faith in terms of divine immanence. The most evident fact, which the alacrity of these statements revealed, was the ferment of the era. Large numbers of ministers and serious laymen were no longer willing to remain under the shadow of the old theological tradition; they demanded something new, up-to-date, and relevent.

With all the clamor, G. K. Chesterton could not resist a broadside of his own, appropriately entitled *Orthodoxy,* though in his *Autobiography* he did not directly connect his statement with the arrival of the New Theology. In his delightful style and scathing tone he commented: the whole development of the new theological modes of thought

---

[9] H. J. T. Johnson, *Anglicanism in Transition* (London: Longmans, Green, 1937), p. 70. Cf. Baron Friedrich von Hügel's sustained criticism, "The Relations Between God and Man in the *New Theology* of the Reverend R. J. Campbell," *The Albany Review* (Sept., 1907), pp. 650-68.

constitute a sellout to the non-Christian, materialistic world view of the time; this theology is weak, threatened by every wind of new discovery and liberal thought; altogether and in its several parts it is distinctly sub-Christian and unworthy of the great tradition from which authentic Christian affirmation has sprung.[10]

Among the rejoinders—and one runs across them in almost every publication of the time—the most important were made by two of the truly substantial theologians of the age, P. T. Forsyth and Charles Gore. Forsyth responded first in the pages of the *British Weekly* (March 7, 1907) and then in an article published in the collection by C. H. Vine entitled *The Old Faith and the New Theology*.[11] In both of these articles, he argued that the real issue that was at stake was that of authority. The Scriptures as an infallible sanction for theology had gone, and the question now was: what will replace the Bible? Campbell had attempted to find a new foundation in a vaguely spiritualistic idealism; but this was to move to a wholly unacceptable position, and now Christian faith itself was in question. In a perfect torrent of language, which for Forsyth was quite a current, he struck at the inability of idealism to go to the depths of human sin and gracious redemption (and this in spite of his recognition of its earlier contribution that had rescued Christian faith from deism). Idealistic philosophy, he claimed, destroys the fundamental relation of God to the world as Creator to creature,

[10] *Orthodoxy* (London: Fontana Books, 1908, 1961). The entire book is an attack on this attitude, but see esp. p. 137. Chesterton later converted to Roman Catholicism, but Roman Catholicism was also, to a lesser extent, participant in this moment of crisis. The development of the "modernist" movement within this church was led on the English scene by Father George Tyrrell, S.J. Tyrrell was a complex man—loveable and irrascible, mystical and rigorously intellectual, son of the church who loved and fought his parent. The furor the modernists had caused across Europe was epitomized in Tyrrell's writings. In July, 1907, the decree *Lamentabili* condemned the errors of the modernists; two months later this was followed by the encyclical *Pascendi*, which called the modernists "enemies of the Church." Angered, Tyrrell responded in the London *Times* and *Il Giornale d'Italia*, and his anger provoked action. On October 22 Tyrrell was deprived of the sacraments, and his case was reserved to the Holy See. For further discussion of the Roman Catholic developments see Appendix C.

[11] (London: Sampson Low, Marston, 1907). Among the exponents of the new theology Forsyth was better remembered for his cutting comment about Campbell, who was, he said, "like a photograph over-exposed and underdeveloped." Cf. T. Rhondda Williams, *How I Found My Faith*, p. 94. But it should also be said that in his published responses Forsyth at no point evidences personal disdain or disrespect.

and it is quite irrelevant to the distinctive Christian experience, "which is not concerned as to how we construe God, but how we face him." [12] This present conflict, he claimed, was the most critical since the second century; even the issues raised by the Reformation were small in comparison, for what was really at stake was the whole historical character of Christianity. Forsyth returned to this theme of authority in his later writings, and in this he went directly to the heart of the too often unacknowledged problem that was troubling the age.

Charles Gore responded in 1908 with a book, *The New Theology and the Old Religion,* and Campbell later acknowledged that this book was for him the most persuasive argument against his position. Gore protested that Campbell was really reacting against the aberrations of nineteenth-century Protestantism, not the authentic Catholic tradition. Eight years later Campbell became persuaded, then capitulated and accepted ordination by Gore into the Anglican ministry. For Gore, whose response indicated a redirection in his own theological emphasis, the New Theology was in error primarily because it denied aspects of the ecumenical creeds of Patristic authority. Built upon an immanental bias, such an attempt depreciated the transcendent or supernatural dimension of Christian faith, minimized the significance of evil, and tended to assimilate Jesus Christ to the likeness of other men. "A doctrine which says 'Christ is God' and then goes on to say 'all men are God' is really, I fear, further off the Bible and the creeds than the old-fashioned Unitarianism which said that Christ is not God." [13] Gore sympathized with Campbell's concern to relate the Christian faith to the social situation, but he was convinced that this particular effort to bring the two together had been misdirected.

In opposition to this New Theology Gore spent the major part of his book providing a systematic exposition of the central doctrines of "Catholic Christianity." It was typical of his apologetic approach that he turned immediately to the creedal affirmations of the early church and expounded the reasonableness of its doctrinal affirmations. In these creeds, he argued, we do not have an appeal to the intellectual sensibilities of a particular epoch but to fundamental and universal human needs and religious

[12] *The Old Faith and the New Theology,* p. 50.
[13] *The New Theology and the Old Religion,* p. 87.

longings. Jesus Christ, as described in these creeds, was presented in terms of his whole person and not in terms of his atoning work alone. This is the strength of the Catholic tradition, and it is a strength that must once more be publically affirmed, especially in a time when the creeds were denigrated. As in the case of Forsyth, Gore responded in his characteristic way and in terms of his own strength. And whatever else the public discussion of the New Theology accomplished, it caused these two men to clarify the issue that was at stake both in this debate and in the theological unsettlement of the time, namely the source and nature of authority in Christian life and thought. This issue and the way in which various theologians dealt with it became the pervasive issue of the era and, indeed, of twentieth-century English theology.

The provocations of 1907 and the ensuing theological changes can be understood more adequately if they are once again set within their social and cultural context. The Parliament of 1906 led the nation into five years of rapid social change. The economic policies of nineteenth-century conservatism were frontally attacked, and a large number of strategic battles against the traditional forces were won. In the first year of liberal leadership three contentious bills were proposed: a new education act (which would clarify use of public money in support of religious educational institutions), a Trade Disputes Bill (which removed unions' financial liability for strikes), and a Plural Voting Bill (which would allow a man to vote only in his place of residence, not at each place he owned property). All these bills were calculated to benefit the less privileged citizens. The House of Lords killed the first and the last acts after they were passed by Commons, but the Trade Disputes Bill was allowed to go through. For the most part the activity of the House of Lords may be interpreted in partisan political terms, for the Peers were determined to keep the Liberal government in hand and use their power to support Conservative Party policy. As a consequence, the tension between the Lords and the House of Commons increased and finally issued in renewed demands for a revision of the power of the upper house. In 1908 the Lords once again exercised their prerogative and rejected the most important government proposal of the year, a large-scale alcohol Licensing Bill to combat intemperance. Sir Robert Ensor has described the situation: "The outlook for the government as its third year closed was cheerless. Its members recognized, as everyone must now, that the lords were breaking the spirit, though not yet the letter, of the Constitution."[14] By 1909 the conflict had reached unprecedented heights. On November 4 the House of Commons passed their budget by a vote of 379 to 149, a budget that included a tax on all classes but in which the wealthy would pay more than in the past. Again the House of Lords blocked the way, and the bill was put down on its second reading. This was on November 30. Two days later the Prime Minister, H. H. Asquith, presented a resolution to Commons, "That the action of the House of Lords in refusing to pass into law the financial provisions made by this House for the service of the year is a breach of the Constitution and a usurpation of the rights of Commons." The motion carried by 349 to 134 votes.

The attempt of the Lords to abort the new issue was only a part of the conservative reaction to what many rightly recognized to be a social revolution. The decade had witnessed new legislation that altered the educational system, reset the base of taxation, and in general was responsive to the upsurge of demands by the laboring people. Inevitably, popular movements arose to protect "traditional English values," and Robert S. Baden-Powell, the hero of Mafeking in the Boer War, typified this response. In 1908 he published his *Scouting for Boys,* and a new youth movement was launched. Baden-Powell was determined to prepare the young men of the nation to defend their country against its enemies from both within and without; the causes that brought about the fall of the Roman Empire, he said, would not be recapitulated in Britain. "A Scout," he told his enlistees, "is loyal to the King, and to his officers, and to his country, and to his employers. He must stick to them through thick and thin against any who is their enemy or who even speaks badly of them."[15] The strength of youth was being marshaled to preserve the old social codes of Victoria's era and fend off the death of the inherited economic order.

Unfortunately, international events provided no relief from domestic controversy. In the early years of the century the British had broken

[14] *England, 1870-1914*, p. 409.

[15] Quoted in W. S. Adams, *Edwardian Portraits* (London: Secker and Warburg, 1957), p. 129.

out of their strategic isolation and had entered into international pacts (some of them secret) that fully involved the nation in European life and problems. The diplomats had attempted to keep cordial relations with both France and Germany, but inevitably they seemed to be drawn into alignment with France and into periodic crises with Germany (in both 1905-6 and in 1908-9 there had been naval troubles with the Germans). Throughout the era there were serious questions raised about Britain's armaments, especially about the superiority of her navy over other powers. In addition, the restiveness of some of the empire countries, India as well as Ireland, added to the perplexities.

The year in which the social struggle reached its climax can now be distinguished as the pivotal time when English life was moved from one sociocultural epoch into another. This was the year 1910. And the significance of this year is difficult to overestimate. Politically, the year opened and closed with national elections, and in between there were the uncertainties of unstable government. Further, the year witnessed a change of monarchs. On May 6 Edward died,[16] and the ills with which his reign was besieged now became a violent epidemic. As Sir Robert Ensor sums up the Edwardian era he remarks,

Personal memories of Edward VII have transferred to it something of the king's own character and atmosphere. Men think of the decade as one of calm and contentment, of pomp and luxury, of assured wealth and unchallenged order. Court splendours apart, it was none of these things. It was an era of growth and strain, of idealism and reaction, of swelling changes and

---

[16] Barbara Tuchman has described Edward's funeral in vivid style. "So gorgeous was the spectacle on the May morning of 1910 when nine kings rode in the funeral of Edward VII of England that the crowd, waiting in hushed and black-clad awe, could not keep back gasps of admiration. In scarlet and blue and green and purple, three by three the sovereigns rode through the palace gates, with plumed helmets, gold braid, crimson sashes, and jeweled orders flashing in the sun. After them came five heirs apparent, forty more imperial or royal highnesses, seven queens—four dowager and three regnant—and a scattering of special ambassadors from uncrowned countries. Together they represented seventy nations in the greatest assemblage of royalty and rank ever gathered in one place and, of its kind, the last. The muffled tongue of Big Ben tolled nine by the clock as the cortege left the place, but on history's clock it was sunset, and the sun of the old world was setting in a dying blaze of splendor never to be seen again." *The Guns of August* (New York: Macmillan, 1962), p. 1.

seething unrest. At home, politics had never been so bitter; abroad, the clouds were massing for Armageddon.[17]

Yet all change in England seems to take place within the context of tradition and, in spite of the rebellious spirit, it should be pointed out that 1910 was, of course, a year of coronation. George V came to the throne, and for a moment there was a remembrance of the past and of grand traditions. But, in spite of the pause, events were moving uncontrollably ahead. Even the plea of the new monarch for reason over emotion, for social decorum and national loyalty was little regarded.

Halévy has argued that the struggle over the House of Lords did not bring the country to the brink of revolution; rather, the population was somewhat phlegmatic, and one-half a million fewer people voted in the December election than had voted in the election of the previous January. He even goes so far as to speak of the nation as "indifferent" and "without interest or passion."[18] About the issue of the House of Lords, the judgment may be correct. Even if it be acknowledged, however, that the turmoil may be overly emphasized, it must also be noted that the Independent Labour Party gained more seats than either of the two established parties, and this in itself reflected something of the deep current of political unrest that was flowing through the nation. Certainly, the subsequent events prove that profound dissatisfaction was present. Working people were unhappy with the nuances of change that liberalism fostered; the middle way of gradual change seemed obsolete to an increasing number.

The year 1910 is not just a convenient dividing point for our discussion; it is a landmark in English history that stands out against a peculiar background of struggle. For in this year fires long smoldering in the English spirit suddenly flared up and threatened to consume the nation.[19] There was the anarchist activity of the leaders of the women's suffrage movement, demands for changed conditions by the working classes, political unrest, and the unsettled question of Irish

[17] *England, 1870-1914*, p. 421.
[18] *History of the English People in the Nineteenth Century*, VI, 314, 342, 346.
[19] For a highly readable discussion of the social history of this period see George Dangerfield, *The Strange Death of Liberal England* (London: Constable, 1936).

home rule. Excitement, flaming tempers, grotesque posturing, and physical force became a part of the public scene.

Could the old skins contain the new wine? Some doubted that they could. And to mention only political and social factors does not present the full picture of the cultural mutation. The artistic expressions of the time both exhibited and gave impetus to the transition. Virginia Woolf expressed her conviction about the year in a striking manner, "On or about December 1910 human character changed. . . . All human relations have shifted—those between masters and servants, husbands and wives, parents and children. And when human relations change there is at the same time a change in religion, conduct, politics and literature." [20] This alteration, which was probably precipitated by Roger Fry's London exhibition of post-impressionist painting, resulted, according to Virginia Woolf, in a different perspective from which life was viewed. The Edwardians—Arnold Bennett, H. G. Wells, and John Galsworthy— were interested in externals, they were "materialists" who spent their skill and industry making the surface and trivial appear to be the true and enduring. Life in its essential features and spirit refused to be contained in the "ill-fitting vestments" that the preceding novelists had provided. The unknown and uncircumscribable human spirit must be evoked, suggested, and revealed. In short, authentic literary expression must pierce the flesh and free the inner throbbing of living beings.

In *Howards End,* published in 1910, E. M. Forster depicted the transition in terms of the expansion of London into its rural environs, the contrasts between material concerns and inward spiritual nourishment, the class struggle, and the increasing intimations of fear and panic. The transpositioning of society may be only as soft as a "goblin footfall" but it was audible, and a world in which goblins dwell is a world that harbors deep uncertainty. As Margaret Schlegel, a character in the novel, stands on the Chelsea Embankment, Forster describes her thoughts.

The tide had begun to ebb. Margaret leant over the parapet and watched it sadly. Mr. Wilcox had forgotten his wife, Helen her lover; she herself was

[20] "Mr. Bennett and Mrs. Brown," *The Hogarth Essays* (London: Hogarth Press, 1924), pp. 4-5.

probably forgetting. Everyone moving. Is it worth while attempting the past when there is this continual flux even in the hearts of men? [21]

The Schlegels (the name was German) and the Wilcoxes were the symbols for the clash of tradition and irreverence for tradition, depth and shallowness of feeling, social concern and indifference, love and propriety, culture and boorishness. In the interaction of these two families all the contrasts intermingle, struggle, coalesce, and separate. The flux had attacked the hearts of men, the soul of a nation.

Sir Herbert Read has stressed the importance of this same year. In *Contemporary British Art,* he comments, "The modern period in British art may be said to date from the year 1910." [22] It is, of course, impossible to fix an exact date or a special point of beginning to anything so primitively persuasive as the first growth of an artistic sensibility or style or the setting aside of aesthetic canons. But at the close of the first decade of this century there was a revolutionary spirit in international art and also in British art as a part of that community.[23] Roger Fry, more than any other person, was responsible for this transition. Fry insisted that the artist, in order to express himself, present natural objects in such a way that the emotional elements inhere in them and the plastic form reveal an order and appropriateness that is quite beyond that which nature herself provides. This "transformation," as he termed it, is due to the painter's vision, which is to say, to the total emotion-thought complex that the man of keen sensibilities brings to expression. At the exhibition of 1910, which he entitled "Manet and the Post-Impressionists," the present seemed torn from the past. Amid public perplexity, laughter, and disbelief, the exhibition led some people —Virginia Woolf among them—to a profoundly new sensibility. For this minority, a new renaissance arose as a distinct possibility, even more, as a necessity. A friend, meeting Roger Fry on the street, re-

[21] *Howards End* (Vintage Books; New York: Random House, 1954), p. 137.
[22] (Harmondsworth, Middlesex: Penguin Books, rev. ed., 1964), p. 20.
[23] One need only mention the number of new "schools" that were appearing, such as post-impressionism in France with its explicit development in fauvism and cubism; the Italian futurism of Marinetti and Serverini; dadaism in Zurich, whose further growth brought surrealism in France and Germany; expressionism in Germany and Scandinavia; the Russian suprematists Malevich, Gabö," Pevsner, and Tatlin; Dutch neo-plasticism of Mondrian and Van Doesburg.

marked, "What's happened to you? You look ten years younger." The comment Fry later repeated with the remark that at the age of forty-four he found himself where most people find themselves twenty years earlier—"at the beginning of life, not in the middle, and nowhere within sight of the end." [24]

But there were other opinions, and Walter Richard Sickert, a contemporary artist, typified the negative response. Sickert was a realist. His subjects were portraits, architecture, landscape, and human comedy; his style and intention were to describe what he saw, and he seemed to go no deeper than appearance. In derision, he spoke of the 1910 exhibition as a "spoof" and "a very small and unimportant manifestation." But his own naturalistic style was being called into question, and, indeed, the interrogation seemed to imply a rejection of values that had long been regarded as constituting the foundation of European culture.[25] In contrast, the vorticism of Wyndham Lewis (which began in 1911) was an extreme manifestation of a truculent young man contemptuous of the near past. In his mind, the vocation of the artist was to provide an advanced guard for the civilized intelligence, and in this sense the artist and the intellectual were natural allies. In terms of the content of his painting Lewis was socially aware. The vorticist figures looked like robots, and this may be regarded not only as a plastic experiment but as a comment on modern life; man was being conformed to the pressing uniformities of mass society, a slave to the machine, and was soon to be fodder for the guns. A wedge was being driven through artistic imagination.

Lewis and other post-impressionists expressed a revolutionary spirit, but not, as Herbert Read has remarked, the spirit of revolutionaries who knew where they wanted to go or who carried a "new constitution in their pockets;" rather, it was the revolution of explorers, explorers who had "no compass bearing." [26] This spirit of revolt was not the assured movement toward some utopia or even a step in the direction

[24] Virginia Woolf, *Roger Fry* (New York: Harcourt Brace & Co., 1940), p. 162. See her discussion of this exhibition and its reverberations, pp. 156-57.

[25] Cf. Robert Emmons, *The Life and Opinions of Walter Richard Sickert* (London: Faber and Faber, 1941).

[26] *The Philosophy of Modern Art* (London: Faber and Faber, 1952), p. 46.

of some definite, though temporary, waystation. It was a rebellion against the past, a revolt in the name of authenticity, candor, and integrity. Every nonrepresentational form of art is, to some extent, a denial of the way in which the natural world presents itself, and it is an effort to create a "pure" form, to assert the integrity of the artist's vision, which cuts beneath and re-forms the materials he uses. Mental construction is given a primary place. When, on the English scene, the work of Edwardians such as Walter Sickert was succeeded by that of Wyndham Lewis it was evident that a new attitude was dominant, that one age of artistic style was coming to a close and a new one was emerging.

A transition in poetic style and substance may also be focused at this same time. C. M. Bowra has claimed that the new poetry that began to make itself felt about the year 1910 caused both anxiety and dismay among those who had been bred in a sound Victorian tradition because this tradition had become a hindrance to creativity. The changes Bowra lists are all important: the Victorian vocabulary was rejected because it was adapted to an experience and an outlook that were no longer viable; the new poets saw life in a new way, with extremely realistic eyes, and became passionately concerned to write poetry as purely as possible. Bowra argues that modern poetry shared the same development as nonrepresentational painting where color and line appeal in their own right. There was an attempt to express the essence of the poetic sense and dispense with such addenda as imparting information or stating facts. Significantly, he adds, the modern poets "have no theory of poetry, but believe that they recognize it when it comes and that any explanation of it is irrelevant if not vicious." [27]

W. R. Orage, a literary critic and editor of *The New Age,* which was published from 1908 until 1921, constantly argued that cultural transition, and particularly moral decadence, is revealed in literary style, vocabulary, sentence structure, and manner of treatment. T. E. Hulme, a contemporary and better known person, was arguing before 1912 for the need of precise and concrete word usage, even as he repudiated the primacy of emotion as it was found in romantic poetry. With both of these critics an awareness of a fundamental change in literary style was to

[27] *The Background of Modern Poetry* (Oxford: Clarendon Press, 1954), p. 8, cf. also pp. 3, 5-6.

the fore, and their criticism both recorded and foreshadowed the emergence of a new literary era.

In philosophy, there was also a transition that may roughly be dated with the close of the first decade. In certain ways, philosophy had adumbrated the wide range of sociocultural alteration. For over ten years there had been a growing criticism of idealism spearheaded by G. E. Moore and Bertrand Russell. The Idealists, however, were still around and continued to defend their position, with F. H. Bradley and Bernard Bosanquet shoring the bulwarks of the established position. After 1910, however, they were no longer answered in the extended and serious manner that they had provoked earlier. They still wrote for journals and produced books, but the discussion had been moved to new ground.

Perhaps the most important philosophical publication of the year was *Principia Mathematica* by Bertrand Russell and Alfred North Whitehead. In retrospect, it is possible to see this work as a part of the general cultural shift we have been describing. Although F. H. Bradley had argued that all ordinary language usage needed drastic qualification, there was developing across a wide front an increasing questioning of inherited language as an adequate vehicle for the conveyance of truth. Language was transformed by Russell and Whitehead into mathematically useful symbols so that the ambiguity and inexactness of ordinary language might be overcome. Among novelists and poets who followed shortly, such as James Joyce, T. S. Eliot, and Ezra Pound, the inherited language was also radically strained, then transformed in an effort to express new dimensions of experience and understanding. In each of these cases there may be discerned a new uncertainty about the viability of ordinary language for the expression of what men want to say, either abstractly or with intense personal involvement. Either ordinary language must be carefully, meticulously reclaimed, as G. E. Moore attempted to do, or it must be discarded. The explicit expression of distrust manifested itself at the turn of the first decade, and in this questioning of language was to be found the roots of some of the more significant artistic and philosophic developments of the twentieth century.

Among the novelists, the artists, the poets, and the philosophers there was no prepared constitution, no explicit goal, no carefully defined path; but there was a revolt against the past and a demand for an open future. There were no clearly envisioned ends, but there were explorers, pathfinders, men unable to accept the world from which they had come, men who attempted to find new ways that allowed freedom for their quests.

The issue in all these controversies was that of authoritative tradition. The struggle did not end at this point, but the crucial issues had been laid bare. Could the sanctions inherited from the past any longer be applied to the political, social, religious, and artistic life of the present? With a great surge of conviction, the culture gave a negative answer. A new time demanded new foundations, a new vocabulary, a new sensibility, a new arrangement of power, new political organization, a new literature, and new religious self-interpretation. No one was prepared to indicate what the new forms must be, but that there must be new forms was clear; the time for exploration had arrived.

To lift up the importance of 1910 as a *kairos* in English cultural history is to challenge the thesis that the dividing line between the old ethos and the arrival of a new time was the First World War. Many English cultural traditions were, as a matter of fact, shattered by the Great War; the conflict did mark a transition in the manner of life— and this at its most profound levels. Nonetheless, the issues that gave rise to the cultural mutation had already taken shape prior to the war. What was inaugurated in the prewar era, however, was not completed; the intervention of international hostilities delayed the effect of this reordering until after and with the corroboration of the war.

In 1910 the nation experienced a convulsion, and the following year brought no relief. The summer of 1911 saw labor unrest reach a crisis. Under the impact of the imported syndicalism (trade unionism) a number of labor leaders were convinced that they would have to work outside of and against the government to bring about the democratization of society, and they interpreted all the problems of the nation in terms of a class war. On October 2, 1911 the gathering of all the socialist groups under the leadership of A. M. Hyndman passed a resolution that stated that they were "not a reformist but a revolutionary party." [28] The struggle

[28] *Manchester Guardian*, Oct. 2, 1911.

between the workers and the owners in industry was gigantic. John Galsworthy's play *Strife,* written two years earlier, depicted the struggle in terms of two dominant personalities, one on each side, who seemed fated to fight to the death of both men. To some observers this appeared to be the reality of the situation. In terms of temperature, the summer of 1911 was the hottest since 1868, and the "long hot summer" of labor's discontent became the springboard for union strike action until the beginning of the First World War.

In August of that year the Parliament Act was passed, an act that limited the power of the House of Lords so that no legislation could be stalled for more than one year. This was one of the most significant steps in British constitutional history and certainly the most significant change since the franchise extension of 1867. If there was a transition in terms of the status of the Lords, an equally significant shift was to be found in the status of women. Earlier, in 1903, the leaders of the suffrage movement had made a militant move in forming the Women's Social and Political Union in Manchester under Mrs. Emmeline Pankhurst and Mrs. Emmeline Pethick-Lawrence. This new group was not only militant, but it was also willing to become socially destructive in order to win its demands. Riots, hunger strikes, arson, and fighting were among their methods—and the goal, they claimed, was to obtain full voting rights.[29] It was ironical that the women fought against the Liberal government, which was their best hope, and it is quite possible that their tactics actually delayed the passage of an enfranchisement bill.[30]

The year seemed destined for trouble from every quarter. Before the first month of 1911 was over, the question of Irish home rule once again forced itself on the nation's attention. For over fifty years this had been a continual source of trouble for the political leadership, but at this juncture loudly challenging voices were to be heard from the

[29] H. G. Wells, in his later and not so liberal mood, reflected on their motives, "It became increasingly evident that a large part of the women's suffrage movement was animated less by the desire for freedom and fulness of life, than by a passionate jealousy and hatred of the relative liberties of men. . . . They did not want more life; their main impulse was vindictive." *Experiment in Autobiography* (London: Victor Gollancz, 1934), II, 483. Even if the motives were ambiguous, this in no way detracted from the power and the anarchic tendencies of the movement.

[30] Cf. E. Sylvia Pankhurst, *The Suffragette Movement* (London: Longmans, Green, 1931), p. 338.

neighboring island. To complicate the total situation, Germany was restive and European power was in precarious balance. Sir Edward Grey remarked to Winston Churchill, "What a remarkable year this has been: the heat, the strikes, and now the foreign situation."[31] Parliament had been torn, the populace was in strife, conventions were challenged on every hand, some people went beyond the parliamentarian's comment and spoke of national dissolution.

It is no surprise to find that the general quandary about the past, the present, and the future was also exhibited in the church. In its January issue of 1909 the *Hibbert Journal* published an article by the Reverend R. Roberts of Bradford entitled "Jesus or Christ? An Appeal for Consistency." The article asked simply, should the Jesus of history be equated with the Christ of faith? But the simple question provoked enormous response. Within a week, replies, criticisms, eulogies, and condemnations began to pour in from everywhere. L. P. Jacks, the editor, wrote seven months later that the "stream continues to flow."[32] The question that the article posed was that of the historical trustworthiness of the gospel accounts and the religious interpretation of the person of Jesus. So great was the correspondence that Jacks issued a supplement that contained contributions by leading scholars from every area of British religious life as well as several from Germany, Sweden, the United States, and Switzerland. The precise argument we shall discuss in the chapters on Christology, but to understand the excitement and some of the underlying reasons for the petulant discussion it is necessary to set this event within the framework of the strain of the time. What will become clear is that the crisis of faith was a part of the general crisis in culture. The challenge that confronted the faithful was a part of an awesome challenge that was confronting every institution, every received social form, every inherited presupposition. Culture was in crisis, and the faithful within the cultural ethos shared in the crisis. There is a sense, however, in which the radical questioning of faith was the most primary interrogation, for the basis of the inherited culture was, both consciously and unconsciously, the Christian faith.

When on September 27, 1910 the Annual Church Congress met in

---

[31] Quoted in Barbara Tuchman, *The Proud Tower*, p. 401.
[32] *The Hibbert Journal, Supplement, 1909*, p. 1.

Cambridge the issue of the role of the church was engaged once more. This was the Golden Anniversary for the Conference and a time for recollection and congratulation. But the function of the meetings was to consider the chief social and spiritual problems of the day, and both of these issues seemed to focus in sharp conflict. On the side of social issues there were assembled the people and the issues to make the meeting controversial. On the theological side the discussion came to its crescendo with the papers on Albert Schweitzer's recently translated book *The Quest of the Historical Jesus*. Schweitzer's rejection of the long theological search through the nineteenth-century German studies for the Jesus of history, along with his announcement that the Jesus of the Gospels was not to be understood in modern terms, was heightened by his claim that the apocalyptic character of Jesus' mission and message permanently separated him from modern, progressive, amelioristic thought. Biblical interpretation, christological studies, and the application of Christian faith to social conditions were all thrown into question. The creeds, the Bible, and popular devotion were now being quizzed in a new way; and whatever the future was to be it could not be a straightforward extension from the past. Schweitzer had challenged the church's understanding of its founder.

There was quick criticism, with R. H. Charles the most significant opponent at the Congress. Charles described Schweitzer's work as having a "bizarreness" that was equaled only by "its cocksureness." [33] Even though Charles could speak with unusual technical strength because of his own important study of apocalypticism, his tone was characteristic of the meeting. After the major papers were read, a Canon G. Harford breathed a sigh of relief and expressed his appreciation for "how completely what we call the home product of British scholars has been vindicated before us this evening in comparison with any foreign importation." [34] But in the anteroom (!), where some of the overflow crowd was seated, two Cambridge scholars, F. C. Burkitt and Gordon Selwyn, took the floor to defend Schweitzer. It cannot be claimed that Schweitzer made a permanent, positive impact upon British scholarship, but he did set

[33] *Report of the Church Congress,* Cambridge 1910 (London: George Allen and Sons, 1910), p. 74.
[34] *Report of the Church Congress,* p. 82.

the problems with which British biblical scholars were to wrestle for the next generation, namely eschatology and the kingdom of God.

In the fall of 1912 another sign of change appeared when a group of Oxford friends published a volume of essays entitled *Foundations.* The essays had grown out of a series of discussions and conferences in which the authors had participated. The consultations were stimulated by a common recognition that both the forms and the theology of Christianity had come from an age that was different from the present time. So great were the differences between the past and the present that the very basis of Christian faith had to be reassessed and restated.[35] N. S. Talbot introduced the volume with a description of "The Modern Situation." The present generation, he asserted, was modern precisely in the sense that it was not "Victorian." Unlike their fathers, the contemporary men had never known the world before the "sixties"; that is, contemporary men had not lived before the critical study of the Bible, the immense expansion of scientific knowledge, or the problems of the industrial order and urban life. So thoroughgoing have been the recent changes, he continued, that the resulting insecurity has reached down to the foundations not only of Victorian assumptions, but, indeed, of Christian religion. Consequently, the changes have brought about a different and a difficult time for the Christian preacher and the Christian moralist. Nevertheless, the fact that the age was one of doubt and perplexity should not cause despair. With confidence that it was once again possible to lay the cornerstone for a new building of faith, Talbot asserted that it must be remembered that Jesus himself came into a world with problems not unlike those of this age. He came into such an era, and he was able to minister to its need. Convinced that the light of the world was still shining and would shatter the darkness, he courageously affirmed, "to-day is a day of new hope for the Christian religion."[36] It is not insignificant in this regard that the essay closed with a quotation from Robert Browning, whose optimism saw in every perplexity a sign of hope.

There were reactions, of course. The witty Ronald Knox responded

[35] Cf. B. H. Streeter's "Introduction," *Foundations* (London: Macmillan, 1912), pp. vii-viii.
[36] *Ibid.*, p. 18.

with vigor in *Some Loose Stones,* but the cleverness could not counter the weight of the provocative essays. *Foundations* was an important monument of the era, and not least for the reason that in this volume was to be found an honest acknowledgment of the new situation in which the Christian life must be lived and its faith proclaimed. These essays also displayed the ambiguity of realistic candor and optimistic hope, of change and tradition, of courage and conservation, which characterized so many in the churches. The epilogue set a vibrant, purposeful tone.

And indeed the hour is come; already the armies are arrayed; the battle begun. For all the world is in transformation. . . . Now is the opportunity and the test of faith; and even now in the vision of faith the Captain of the Armies of Salvation goes forth conquering and to conquer.[37]

In theology, as in other areas, prewar England was a time of rapid change, perhaps of mutation; it was a time of excitement, of anguish, of feverish searching, a time of bewilderment and hope and deep involvement in the changing social and cultural life. It was a time for new evaluation, for prophetic voices, and, above all, it was a time for explorers.

[37] *Ibid.,* p. 528.

III

IDEALISM, THEOLOGY, AND CHALLENGE

As theology moved from the nineteenth into the twentieth century, it carried with it a rich and complex inheritance, and it was forced to face the question of its stewardship as an heir living in a new situation. Chief among the legacies were those of idealistic philosophy and the historical, critical methodology of biblical scholars. Both of these gifts, even with their intrinsic values, were cause for perplexity as well as hope: the idealists bequeathed a new philosophical approach that stressed metaphysical and social dimensions of thought along with their practical implications; the biblical scholars, through their newly acquired critical methodology, fostered a renewed interest in biblical research along with its concomitant problem of spiritual authority. In this chapter we shall look at the philosophical inheritance and its contribution to the intellectual milieu in general and to theology in particular.

British thought has always been torn between opposing predilections to Platonism and empiricism, and both tendencies have been claimed as the *philosophia perennis* of the island. But in the last half of the nineteenth century the Platonic tradition, as this was interpreted by Hegelian idealists, regained the ground. The new philosophical thought was swift and thorough in its conquest as the best philosophical minds of the day acted as its knights errant. The particular strain of idealism that flourished in Britain must be interpreted in terms of its own distinctiveness, that is, in terms of its exponents' response to their peculiar context. Hence, while British thinkers shared the general presuppositions of all post-Kantian idealistic philosophy, in its special cultural setting it must be understood as a rejection of the after-currents of the philosophy of David Hume and the contemporary work of Herbert Spencer and John Stuart Mill. Moreover, the new movement represented a qualified repudiation of the regnant individualism of British social theory and practice. Finally, idealism gained unusual strength because it was congenial to the development of the idea of evolution, which Darwin had provided with impressive empirical foundations.

By the sixties the two compatriots of change, Hegel and Darwin, were on the British scene, and the immediate future belonged to them. In some ways it seems strange that men so dissimilar should combine to exert a joint influence. To characterize these two men emphasizes the anomaly. G. W. F. Hegel was completely uninterested in empirical observation, an academician so excessively a philosopher that he became almost the caricature of the philosopher; Charles Darwin was the typical English country gentleman, a possessor of great observational gifts, a lover of the open air life, a scientist who had no metaphysical turn of mind. Yet these two incompatibles joined together and sundered the Victorian era. Both were absorbed with ideas of motion and change; both made evolution or development ingredient to any interpretation of life; and each in his own way reached beyond the empirical data he possessed and propounded interpretations of process that permeated the cultural sensibilities.[1]

---

[1] This contrast is suggested by Baron von Hügel in *The Reality of God and Religion and Agnosticism* (London: J. M. Dent and Sons, 1931), p. 50. The strong movement into idealistic forms of philosophy must not be understood as a complete capitulation of English philosophy to this new style of thought. There remained a persistent tradition that may be designated "realistic." R. G. Collingwood has asserted that realism always remained the most characteristic form of philosophy among the teachers of philosophy at Oxford. But

The fabric of society that surrounded the early idealists and the environment against which they reacted gave their work its peculiar character. They lived in a self-aware industrial society, a time of expansion of democratic rights, educational reform, and trade union organization. In addition, there were changes in the arts and aesthetic theory; international trade and economic conditions at home were in transition. Philosophy was a full participant in this change, responsive to and contributing to the transformation of the national ethos. In one sense, idealism may be understood as an effort to ward off some of the obvious implications of an industrial, technological society. It was humane, spiritual, corporate in its emphasis; and it was of this character in contradistinction to prevalent materialistic and naturalistic interpretations of life. The chief opponents whom the idealists fought were Hume, Comte, and Spencer.[2] The sense of conscious departure from the past characterized the new philosophic effort.[3] It is also significant that it was in this period that philosophy became primarily a university and clerical enterprise. This movement into the relatively isolated confines of the colleges was due in part to the success of Benjamin Jowett in establishing an essential place at Oxford for philosophical study, but the fact that it was idealistic philosophy that grew in the university context may also be symptomatic of a reaction to urbanized, technological, industrialized society.

---

he also admits that the university was "obsessed" with the claims of the "Idealists" (a designation he is hesitant to use). See R. G. Collingwood, *An Autobiography* (London: Oxford University Press, 1939), pp. 15-21. This judgment is a valuable caveat but may be misleading if it detracts from the prominence and persuasiveness of the idealistic school or if it underplays the distinctive character of the new realism of G. E. Moore and Bertrand Russell. The presence at Oxford of contemporaries of the idealists, men who espoused realistic positions such as Thomas Case, John Cook Wilson, H. A. Pritchard, and H. W. B. Joseph, gave strong support to positions that were inimical to idealism. But the newer forms of realism expressed by Moore and Russell must be distinguished from the position of these precursors and contemporaries. For a survey of the positions of those who represented the older forms of realism see Rudolf Metz, *A Hundred Years of British Philosophy* (London: Allen & Unwin, 1938), pp. 479-529.

[2] This was made most obvious in the volume *Essays in Philosophical Criticism,* edited by Andrew (Seth) Pringle-Pattison and J. S. Haldane (London: Longmans, Green, 1883). A group of young dons memorialized T. H. Green with this volume and launched a frontal assault on the bastions of Spencer and Hume.

[3] Cf. comments to this effect by R. A. Wollheim and D. F. Pears in *The Revolution in Philosophy,* ed. Gilbert Ryle (London: Macmillan, 1957), pp. 12, 42. See also Henry Scott Holland's comments, *The Philosophy of Faith and the Fourth Gospel,* ed. Wilford Richmond (New York: Dutton, 1920), pp. 2 ff.

Other important factors were present. Characteristic of mid-Victorian England was a condition of life that Melvin Richter has called "a crisis of conscience," and it was a crisis that demanded answers, even religious answers.[4] J. H. Muirhead, as a participant, summed up the spirit of the movement, "British idealism from the first had been in essence a philosophy of religion. At each stage in its development it has recognized, as the final test of its truth, its power of explaining without explaining away man's religious consciousness."[5] For Hegel, philosophy and religion were formally different but in essence identical. Philosophy was religion in the form of thought with its truth reasoned and explicated; religion was philosophy with all its truth expressed in rituals and rites that symbolically communicated Reality. There can be no doubt that the fusion of philosophy and religion by the Hegelian tradition was one of its attractions on the British scene, especially at this time of crisis for faith and morals.[6]

It is possible to argue, as Melvin Richter has done, that the fortunes of the idealistic movement were in large part determined by the intellectual situation that challenged the grounds for belief in a generation brought up under the discipline of evangelical piety. Supportive of this argument is the fact that "the most prominent spokesmen for British Idealism were all sons of Evangelical clergymen within the Church of England."[7] This was true of Green, Bradley, and Bosanquet; and the emphasis that they drew out of the older evangelical style of life was a strong devotion to ethical duty. Good works, altruism, and amelioration of the condition of men were the marks of this new faith; and to this faith Green especially issued a clear call to the youth of Oxford. Mrs. Humphrey Ward remarked that in the sixties and seventies mem-

[4] Melvin Ritcher, *The Politics of Conscience: T. H. Green and His Age* (London: Weidenfeld and Nicolson, 1964), p. 15. This is a most valuable study.

[5] *The Platonic Tradition in Anglo-Saxon Philosophy* (London: Allen & Unwin, 1931), p. 197.

[6] It is not without significance that Nietzsche spoke of German idealism as theology in disguise or that Heinrich Heine claimed that the open secret of German philosophy was that it was pantheistic. All three of the leading idealists in Germany had started as students of theology—Fichte at Jena, Schelling and Hegel at Tübingen; and, what is of further significance, rather than reintroduce orthodox doctrine these men tended to demythologize Christian dogmas, turning them in the process into a speculative philosophy.

[7] *The Politics of Conscience*, p. 36.

bers of the Balliol College group were "full . . . of the 'condition of the people' question of temperance, housing, wages, electoral reform; and within the university . . . they regarded themselves as the natural allies of the Liberal Party which was striving for these things through politics and parliament." [8]

The importance of such a stance was to be found in its relation to the present devastation of the traditional dogmas of Christian faith. J. H. Muirhead, once again, has left a valuable description of his own experience as a student, "Few of us perhaps had read Hume's *Essay on Miracles* and still fewer Kant's *Religion Within the Limits of Mere Reason,* but the spirit that produced them was in the air and, whether we were empiricists or idealists, we seemed to see that the whole fabric of Christian doctrine in so far as it was based on historical facts had been undermined by it." [9] Darwinism, the development of anthropological studies, especially as these threw light on the history of religion, and German biblical criticism were combining to question the traditional confessions of faith and the role of scripture as the prime authority for Christian doctrine. To many in this generation, idealism provided a spiritual interpretation of the universe that offered a viable alternative to the prevailing materialistic and skeptical mood as well as to the technological preoccupation of an industrial society.

The new philosophy claimed to have another virtue, for not only did it counter the older positivism, but also it offered what its exponents considered a satisfying interpretation of the evolutionary process. For several generations before Darwin the idea of evolution had been an integral part of British thought, but Darwin brought these philosophical ruminations to focus by offering biological evidence that helped to interpret the role of evolution in the world of nature. Hegelianism was also significant at precisely this juncture, for it provided a dialectical interpretation of reality that could subsume such processes under its scheme of overarching purpose. And, of greater importance, Hegelianism provided a means for interpreting the meaning of history that could

---

[8] *A Writer's Recollection* (London: William Collins, 1918), p. 133.

[9] *Reflections by a Journeyman in Philosophy* (London: Allen & Unwin, 1942), p. 42. Cf. also S. C. Carpenter, *Church and People, 1788-1889* (London: S.P.C.K., 1933), pp. 482-83 for the influence of Green.

account for the social and cultural developments that were now vividly in men's minds. "Hegel's method of philosophizing," wrote D. G. Ritchie, an Oxford philosopher, "would adjust itself quite easily to the new scientific method." And to this he added that this method of philosophizing could also use the new science to interpret both man's moral sense and human history.[10]

From a religious perspective, this philosophy could reaffirm what its proponents insisted was the essential meaning of Christian faith, in spite of unsettled questions about historical accuracy, namely, that history was a continuum through which the Divine life and will were manifested. T. H. Green, for instance, saw no need for concrete historical events as a foundation for Christian faith. In fact, he claimed, Christianity is done great harm by "making it depend on a past event."[11] In his specifically theological writings, Green found the essence of Christian faith and life in the notion that within the individual experience there takes place a perpetual renewal of the death and resurrection of Jesus Christ. He was opposed to the traditional creeds and to all dogmatic theology of an orthodox type and was able to ascribe only a symbolic value to historical events, but this symbolism, he argued, was important and helped to retain the imperative of the moral demands in human life.

Following the prescription of Lessing—"Accidental truths of history can never become the proof of necessary truths of reason"[12]—the idealists, with varying degrees of assurance about detail, followed the trail of the Spirit through historical events, but they always insisted that the significance of the concrete events was to be found in their transparency to ultimate and more real ideas. In one sense Hegelian philosophy was preeminently a philosophy of history, taken in the widest sense as a comprehension of both man and nature. But the truth that was manifest in historical events was itself transhistorical, and in this sense all historical events were temporary and partial expressions of the Absolute. Seen *sub specie aeternitatis,* the historical was important as an avenue through which the Eternal Reality makes itself known, but

---

[10] *Darwin and Hegel* (London: Swan Sonnenschein, 1893), p. 56.

[11] *The Witness of God and Faith: Two Lay Sermons* (London: Longmans, Green, 1883), p. 25, see also pp. 67, 73-74.

[12] *Lessing's Theological Writings,* trans. and ed. Henry Chadwick (London: A & C. Black, 1956), p. 53.

no historical event could itself contain the final truth, thus, specific historical events are important only as they function as the media of the rationally true. As Bradley expressed it, although history may express a valid relation or a rational truth, "the principle is there already; and in its reality, the reality of the reconciliation of the human as such, is ideally contained my reconciliation." [13] The question about this method will have to be discussed later, but for the present, the point to be made is that by proposing this way of viewing historical events idealism offered an option that could take the evolutionary process into account in an intellectually acceptable manner.

British neo-Hegelianism also represented a reaction to the individualism of the preceding generations. Most of the members of this group were interested in social and political questions, and their sympathies were primarily in agreement with liberal politics. From the beginning, this interest was evident, as Green had set the example by theory and practice. Others followed in this way: Edward Caird urged his students to find out why so much poverty existed despite the wealth in the nation; Bonsanquet became involved in social work, and *Essays in Philosophical Criticism* explicitly dealt with this concern. This sociopolitical interest came to concrete, corporate expression in 1886 when the Ethical Society was formed in London at Toynbee Hall (which society was an outgrowth of Balliol's involvement with the "condition of the people") for the purpose of systematically discussing the philosophical issues that underlay social change. The reason this group came into being, said one of its founders, was that "social and religious questions . . . were seething from the side of idealistic philosophy," and their scriptures, if it may be said they had any, "were the 'Concluding Remarks' in Bradley's *Ethical Studies*." [14]

At the same time, it should be clear that the awareness of the cohesiveness of community carried the idealists beyond the utilitarians in their understanding of the dynamics of society, but they did not go so far as to conceive society in functional terms as did Durkheim or

---

[13] *Ethical Studies*, p. 325.

[14] J. H. Muirhead, *Reflections by a Journeyman in Philosophy*, pp. 74-75. For a representative set of addresses to the Ethical Society see John Seeley, *et al.*, *Ethics and Religion* (London: Swan Sonnenschein, 1900).

Weber. Noel Annan, who has made this point most emphatically, remarks,

> In England, though weakened by the challenge of Idealism, the old-fashioned positivism remained curiously strong because it had won a spectacular and celebrated battle in the sixties and seventies. The battle between naturalism and religion was fought by both sides almost entirely on positive grounds on the verification of evidence and the credibility of hypothesis —very different ground from that which in Germany the Idealist historian, David Strauss, had chosen in his *Leben Jesu,* which related religious belief to the changing social structure.[15]

IDEALISTIC PSYCHOLOGY

Annan further touches upon a point, although he does not develop it, that is often ignored by commentators—namely, the distinctive psychological interpretation of the idealists. We shall return to this theme in our discussion of Christology because it came to great prominence in theories of the person of Jesus Christ. Experience, or conscious states of intellection and volition, was the starting point for idealistic interpretations of man; at the same time, it must be noted that the unconscious dimension of the human psyche was not of primary importance. Because of the significance of this psychological understanding for all idealistic discussion, we must look at it with some care.

From the time of T. H. Green there had been a strong reaction against the empirical tradition of Hume and the association psychology that resulted from these presuppositions. Green argued that the approach of empirical—that is, Humean—psychology was wholly mistaken, for it attempted to reduce self-consciousness to a series of events, the unity of which could not be shown.[16] This atomism of the mental process, with its consequent description of the human mind as a series of unconnected events, became the target for attack by all of the idealists.

[15] "The Curious Strength of Positivism in English Political Thought" (London: Athlone Press, 1962), p. 10. This essay was originally published by Oxford University Press in 1959.

[16] Cf. T. H. Green, *Introduction to Hume's Treatise of Human Nature, Works,* ed. R. L. Nettleship (London: Longmans, Green, 1885), I, 205-9; and *Prolegomena to Ethics* (Oxford: Clarendon Press, 1883), pp. 79-89.

The single most significant study in the last quarter of the nineteenth century of the role of psychology as an intellectual discipline and of the delineation of the contents of this study was an article by James Ward in the ninth edition of the *Encyclopaedia Britannica*. According to Ward, a person is not a collection of acts, he is the source of activity; there is always a self or subject of experience that can never be explained in terms of atomistic experience, but, rather, is itself the explanation of the unity and continuity of experience. Further, this self cannot be broken down into a set of discrete faculties, and there is no special "inner sense" that reveals the self and its activity; the private ego is known through its public expressions.[17]

Ward introduced the word "subconscious" into the English vocabulary, and it was a more felicitous choice of word than "unconscious," which had been used previously by translators of the German works on psychology. But Ward interpreted the subconscious dimension of the psyche as being a repository of stored-up knowledge, i.e. a type of memory. Although there is some ambiguity in his two illustrations of the soldier who is unaware of his wounds and the scholar who is not consciously aware of all the knowledge he has acquired, the "making" of the subconscious seems to be the result of experience that is consciously received, then stored in such a way that it can be recalled to consciousness at sundry times.[18] The difference between this and the active subconscious of Freud is obvious.

A second major influence upon the developing theory was the work of William James, whose *Principles of Psychology* was widely read in England. James rejected both the associationist and the spiritualistic theories of the mind and wanted to establish a "strictly positivistic" point of view.[19] He claimed that the psychical life is essentially characterized by change (a stream of thought), and consciousness is, therefore, to be understood as a process. The consciousness of the self is

---

[17] James Ward, "Psychology," *Encyclopaedia Britannica* (Edinburgh: A. & C. Black, 1886), pp. 37-38, 84. L. S. Hearnshaw claims that the dominance of Ward's psychology influenced British psychology for sixty years, and it also retarded the growth of behaviorism, experimentalism and physiological psychology in Great Britain for over a generation. *Short History of British Psychology 1840-1940* (London: Methuen, 1964), p. 136.

[18] Ward, "Psychology," pp. 47-48.

[19] *The Principles of Psychology* (New York and London: Macmillan, 1890), p. vi.

the most crucial problem, and this is also dealt with as a stream of thought: each part of the process can be remembered by the knowing subject, "I"; but that which it knows, the empirical self, is designated "me." The knowing "I" cannot itself be an aggregate, but neither for psychological purposes need it be regarded as an unchanging metaphysical entity; rather, "it is a *thought,* at each moment different from thought of the last moment, but *appropriate* to the latter, together with all that the latter called its own. . . . The same brain may subserve many conscious selves, either alternatively or co-existing." [20] Thus the status of the self is established pragmatically, and although his pragmatic philosophy as a whole did not take strong hold in British thought, with few exceptions—most notably F. C. S. Schiller—his study of psychology was widely praised and became quite influential.

F. H. Bradley agreed with the emphasis upon the primacy of experience in psychological study (although he interpreted experience in a more intellectual manner than did James) and, indeed, argued that experience as the conscious state of intellection and volition is the most adequate term for the total activity of the knowing subject. Also in company with James, he disparaged the idea of a substantial self. "Reality is one, and is a single experience," [21] he claimed; but to say this is not to imply a metaphysically primary "self," for the experiencing subject cannot be separated from the Absolute, even though distinctions may be drawn. All experience is "my experience," but it always reaches beyond a singular, isolated context and participates in the Absolute, which includes all "mines." [22] Thus, in the end, experience transcends the self, and it is impossible to know what is meant by "self" in any metaphysically significant way. "Self" is merely an appearance; no doubt it is "the highest form of experience which we have, but, for all that, [it] is not a true form. It does not give us the facts as they are in reality; and, as it gives them, they are appearance, appearance and error." [23] For Bradley, there was a natural movement that started with immediate feelings, in which knowing and being were united;

[20] *Ibid.,* p. 401.
[21] *Appearance and Reality* (London: Swan Sonnenschein, 1897), p. 533.
[22] *Ibid.,* p. 253.
[23] *Ibid.,* p. 119.

proceeded through the stage of relational thinking, which is always unstable and imperfect; then moved to the transcendent state in which all separation of thought from reality was once more abolished. In a sense, it has been claimed, Bradley was sketching in ideal terms a sort of developmental psychology,[24] but at best this may only be claimed in a highly attenuated sense.[25]

One more book must be mentioned because of its influence upon ensuing theology, this was J. R. Illingworth's Bampton Lectures of 1894, *Personality Human and Divine.* A study that imbibed deeply of the idealistic spirit, this book applied the implications of this philosophical position to an understanding of the self. What is striking about the discussion, however, is that there is not a single reference to any psychological study of his day, not even to Ward's article or to the articles that had been appearing for a decade in *Mind.* This is a psychology derived solely from abstract philosophical reflection. For our purposes, the most important section of this book is to be found in Illingworth's discussion of the "Qualities of Personality." The fundamental quality, and the one from which all others are derived, is that of self-consciousness (which is composed of the functions of thought, desire, and will). From man as a self-conscious creature other qualities may be discovered, such as his unity as a self, his uniqueness, his freedom for self-determination, and an irresistible need for communion with others. In other words, the distinguishing qualities of the human personality are reason, will, and love.[26] At no point did Illingworth mention the subconscious dimension of psychic life, nor did he support his description with empirical evidence; but this interpretation of human personhood was so in keeping with the dominant sensibilities of the time that the study became a basic ingredient in theological descriptions for the next generation. As we shall see, these psychological presuppositions were to play an important role in the investigation of the idea of authority, in anthro-

---

[24] Hearnshaw, *Short History of British Psychology,* p. 131.

[25] For reference, it should be noted that the most succinct statement to come out of the idealistic tradition in regard to psychology was Bernard Bosanquet's *Psychology of the Moral Self* (New York: Macmillan, 1897). This was, as the author admitted, simply an attempt to bring together his reflections upon the work of Ward, James, and Bradley, and it does not add to their positions.

[26] *Personality Human and Divine* (London: Macmillan, 1894), pp. 28-38.

pological interpretations, and in christological discussions up to the First World War—and this especially at the point where the various theories agree, namely in their stress upon intellectualistic, self-conscious freedom. This influence was much greater than most commentators have acknowledged, and its effect must be carefully traced.

RESPONSE

The three most important points that arose out of the idealistic discussions, as far as theology was concerned, were the idea of immanence or the presence of God in all reality, the struggle among the philosophers over the metaphysical status of a "person," and the interpretation of history as a dialectical, evolutionary process. The assumption of the immanence of God was the most fundamental of these three issues, and in a sense the other two were implications that resulted from this presupposition; hence, we shall begin with the idea of immanence and attempt to state its meaning and some of its more important influences.

The idea of the immanence of God was one of the most primary assumptions of idealistic philosophy, and in this it was true to its heritage. The philosophical progenitors who lurked always in the background were Plato and Neo-platonists, from the classical world; Berkeley, the Cambridge Platonists, and S. T. Coleridge, from the English tradition; and Hegel, from the continent. In all the predecessors, one can find an insistence upon the "Great Chain of Being" that connected God to man; this continuity between the Divine and the natural, the Creator and his creatures was so essential that the existence of this chain implied a coinherence, a metaphysical interlocking that underlay every interpretation of God, man, and the natural world. But how tightly was the chain constructed? How distinguishable were its separate links? How may the Divine and the human, God and nature be understood in terms of their relatedness and their discontinuity? These were the questions that were forcing themselves upon philosophers and theologians.

By the last decade of the nineteenth century, the idea of immanence had been combined with a type of social Darwinism and an optimistic belief in progress that functioned in many subtly pervasive ways to influence the interpretation of God as Creator and the doctrines of Jesus Christ and the Holy Spirit. In regard to the reinterpretation of the doctrine of creation, immanence was found to be a congenial way of coming to terms with the demands of evolutionary theory, for the mode of God's activity in the world was increasingly interpreted in terms of developmental processes extended over immense periods of time.

From the time of *Essays and Reviews* in 1860 there had been an openness in at least a part of the theological community to Darwin's hypothesis, but the publication of *Lux Mundi* in 1889 provided the crucial point for dating the fusion of evolutionary and immanental themes by theologians in England. *Lux Mundi,* by the order of its essays, suggested that a correlation had been made and that a philosophical, in addition to a biblical and creedal, position had been established as the foundation for theology. In a general way, the writers shared the optimistic and amelioristic outlook of the era. The essay by Aubrey Moore especially reflected this, but the article by J. R. Illingworth along with his book *Divine Immanence* is the best illustration of how susceptible theology was, at least temporarily, to the immanental mode of thought. Illingworth attempted to develop a theology on the evolutionary working of God's spirit that culminated in man's conscious self-awareness of relation to ultimate reality. It is true that there remained a tension with the idea of transcendence, and in less than two decades both Illingworth and Gore felt it necessary to enter certain caveats about overstressing the single theme of immanence; but in part they felt the need for this counterbalancing because of their own ambiguous embracing of the first emphasis.[27]

In spirit, the theologians who were influenced by idealism were more congenial to T. H. Green than they were to Bradley and Bosanquet. C. C. J. Webb has called attention to the distinction that may be made between the earlier idealists, such as Green and Caird, and the later absolute idealists, such as Bradley and Bosanquet, by stating that the

---

[27] The important references are: *Lux Mundi,* ed. Charles Gore (London: John Murray, 1889) and J. R. Illingworth, *Divine Immanence* (London: Macmillan, 1898); and as examples of the counterbalancing, cf. Illingworth, *Divine Transcendence* (Macmillan, 1911), esp. pp. 66-67, and Gore, *The New Theology and the Old Religion.*

latter exhibited a distinct advance in the direction of immanentism.[28] By "immanentism" Webb meant a thoroughgoing identification of the human spirit with the Absolute. T. H. Green, however, is very difficult to interpret in regard to his conception of the indwelling of God, and this lack of preciseness was influential in the ensuing discussion. Although theology at the turn of the century stressed the idea of immanence— and among the New Theologians the capitulation was complete—for the most part, as we have indicated, there was a continued tension between the idea of immanence and the idea of transcendence. Especially in regard to *Lux Mundi* it is necessary to keep this tension in mind, for there has been a persistent overemphasis on the commitment of the contributors of this book to philosophical idealism. As we shall see in Gore, and as was obvious in others of the group, especially H. S. Holland, T. H. Green had contributed primarily a vision of humanized culture and enhancement of personality. From idealism in general they had learned to take God's indwelling seriously. But along with these themes there was the countervailing influence of the biblical and traditional theological insistence upon the necessity of a transcendent God, a God with whom the world may not be identified and who remains sovereign over and separate from his creatures. Faithfulness to inherited convictions about the nature of God meant that while many theologians utilized philosophical categories there were few who totally capitulated to idealism. Even though it was an ardent friendship, theology attempted to keep its independence.

As the theme of immanence took on more concrete form it contributed directly to the understanding of several key issues such as the incarnation, the nature of persons, and the interpretation of history. In the chapters on Christology we shall discuss the implications of this doctrine for the understanding of Jesus Christ; for our present discussion it is necessary to follow the idea as it developed in regard to the relation of finite personhood to the Absolute and to the understanding of history.

To set the stage for our discussion of the problem of the nature of personhood, we shall look at its clearest and most important pre-

[28] *A Study of Religious Thought in England from 1850* (Oxford: Clarendon Press, 1933), p. 87.

sentation in the period, namely, that of F. H. Bradley. This position establishes the foundation for our discussion because it was quickly countered by the personal idealists, who had been influenced by Lotze. A clear indication of the divergent developments within the idealistic tradition over the metaphysical nature of persons may be seen in the argument proposed by Bradley and the reactions of Pringle-Pattison and Hastings Rashdall. Bradley stated the problem in a radical manner because of his apparent willingness to threat all finite entities, including persons, as attributes or adjectives of the Absolute. A thoroughgoing criticism of the notion of "self," he contended, reveals non-adjudicable contradictions; consequently, such a notion cannot be correctly used in the elucidation of the nature of ultimate Reality.[29] The argument that all idealists accepted—namely, that it is impossible to make any affirmation in respect to an object without implying its relation to a subject —implies that we cannot stop short of carrying the logic of this necessary interrelationship to its final conclusion. Hence, for Bradley all relations are "internal," that is, everything is logically connected with everything, and "understanding" comes by the explication of these relations.[30] Therefore, in regard to the discussion of the "self," an individual personality has meaning only in relation to its total context. On this basis, if personality is attributed to God he would of necessity have to be regarded as an entity with a total configuration of relationships and not as the Supreme Being in whom all finite beings, individuals and communities alike, "live and move and have their being." Thus, Bradley

[29] Once again, Green's ambiguity caused perplexity, this time in regard to the personal nature of God. Arguments by Arnold Toynbee (the first) and W. D. Lamont claimed that Green did believe in a personal God. But A. W. Benn pointed to the vagueness of this idea in Green's writing. For a discussion of this see Richter, *The Politics of Conscience*, pp. 116, 184-85. Certainly, Lamont's comment seems correct when he says that the transcendent and pantheistic ideas "which struggled in his mind never quite fought the battle to a finish." *Introduction to Green's Moral Philosophy* (London: 1934), p. 190, as quoted in, *The Politics of Conscience*, p. 183.

[30] A. C. Ewing has suggested a clear statement of the meaning of "internal relations": "If any terms are in fact related by any relation, the relation could not have been different without the terms also being different in some respect or respects . . . and from this it is concluded that knowing must make a difference to the object known." *Idealism: A Critical Survey* (London: Methuen, 1934), pp. 45-46. In short the theory of internal relations means that a subject can only be known in terms of the totality of its relationships, including its relationship to the knower, and all these relationships are essential to the particular subject and to an authentic knowledge of that subject.

argued, personality must be denied to God. In addition, as we have seen, Bradley disparaged the idea of a substantial self for man since the individual person is an aspect of the world of appearance. The person, even as an experiencing subject, cannot be separated from the Absolute, and we cannot know what selfhood means in any metaphysically significant way. In sum, from Bradley's perspective, it is impossible to attribute selfhood to either God or man in an intelligible manner.

Opposed to this position were the personal idealists, and one of the most forthright statements was that of Andrew (Seth) Pringle-Pattison, who had contributed the leading article in the symposium *Essays in Philosophical Criticism* (1883). At this time, because of his suspicion that the idea of the Absolute was a menace to individuality in general and human personality in particular, Pringle-Pattison argued that absolute idealism was not valid. In his work *Hegelianism and Personality* he expressed with great vigor reasons for moving in the direction of personal idealism and for stressing the metaphysical distinctiveness and integrity of the individual person. Pringle-Pattison maintained that Green's entire system centered in the assertion of a unique self or a "Spiritual Principle," which was his favored nomenclature, as necessary to knowledge and morality. It is the presence of this principle that renders the world intelligible (a cosmos) and provides the explanation of ethics as a system of precepts. Nevertheless, as regards the nature of the spiritual principle in Green's thought, "almost everything is vague." The result is that the nature of both man and God is left inexplicit, and the ensuing interpretations of English philosophers (as with Hegelianism in general) tended more and more to identify "the human and the divine self-consciousness in a single self." [31] But this, he contended, is exactly what a religious interpretation cannot allow, for only an independent person who is a self-contained (i.e. free) being can be related to God in a religiously significant manner, that is, in a relationship of genuine reciprocity. To unify the Divine and the human in a single consciousness, he concluded, is ultimately destructive of both.

Pringle-Pattison's criticism did not halt the interpretation of God and

[31] Pringle-Pattison, Andrew (Seth), *Hegelianism and Personality* (Edinburgh: Wm. Blackwood and Sons, 1887), p. 215; cf. also pp. 3-4.

man in absolute idealistic forms, and of special importance in this debate were the Gifford Lectures of 1902-3 by Lord Richard B. Haldane, *The Pathway to Reality,* and the same lecture series of 1911-12 by Bernard Bosanquet, *Principle of Individuality and Value* and *The Value and Destiny of the Individual.*[32] Haldane went further than any of his predecessors in denying the metaphysical distinctiveness of the individual person. Especially in his first series of lectures he was little concerned with the types of argument that had been brought against this position and simply stated his conclusion in a dogmatic fashion that men are adjectival expressions of the Absolute. But Bosanquet is even more significant in this regard because he was aware of the importance of this problem. He introduced his lectures by reaffirming his conviction that "the things which are most important in man's experience are also the things which are most certain in his thought."[33] Was man's experience of himself as possessor of discrete personhood to be included in this certainty? Bosanquet wanted to give adequate allowance for the truth to be found in this awareness, but his main effort was to show that in the ultimate, metaphysical sense "there can be only one individual, and that, *the* individual, the Absolute."[34] Human beings were accorded a special status, but there was no metaphysical distinctiveness, and the value of individual persons is to be understood in a derivative sense. Thus, it is in the ultimate or absolute Reality that the individual person finds his own meaning and his ultimate goal; in consequence, no importance is to be attached to the permanence or survival of specific personalities.[35] Soul-making is the *raison d'etre* of finite existence, which ultimately means, in this system, that the finite individual finds his purpose in identification with the universal purpose of the Absolute. The seeking after a consummate unification of finite individuality with the Ultimate, he argued, is a part of all human consciousness, whether it is so recognized or not; and in the end the *summum bonum* is to be found in conscious awareness of participation in the Absolute. At the same time, he was exceedingly reluctant to identify the God of

[32] Cf. also D. G. Ritchie's critism of Pringle-Pattison in *Darwin and Hegel,* chapter II.
[33] *The Principle of Individuality and Value* (London: Macmillan, 1912), p. v.
[34] *Ibid.,* p. 68.
[35] *Ibid.,* p. 20 n.

theology with the Absolute; the unitive experience carries man beyond every limitation of finite explanation or indication. He wrote,

> The conclusion is, in a word, that the God of religion, inherent in the completest experience, is an appearance of reality, as distinct from being the whole and ultimate reality; a rank which religion cannot consistently claim for the supreme being as it must conceive him. But this conception, which finds him in the greater self recognition by us as present within the finite spirit, and as one with it in love and will, assigns him a higher reality, than any view which stakes everything on finding him to exist as a separate being after the model of man. Religion establishes the infinite because it is continuous with and present in the finite—in love and in the will for perfection. It does not need to appeal to facts of separate being, or to endeavor to demonstrate them. It is an experience of God, not a proof of him.[36]

Hastings Rashdall of New College, Oxford, took up the battle in defense of personal idealism and thus sided with Pringle-Pattison. Under the influence of Berkeley, who was his most direct philosophical forefather, and Lotze, who was the most significant recent philosopher for the personal idealists, Rashdall developed and defended his point of view. He was convinced of the idealistic starting point, which he stated in Berkeleian manner, that there is no such thing as matter apart from mind or that things cannot be conceived as existing by themselves since they exist only for mind.[37] But he was equally convinced that there is a plurality of minds or identifiable selves who know and experience reality. The crux of his presentation is found in his definition of personality as a thinking and feeling consciousness that has a permanence through time, that distinguishes itself from objects of its thought and from other selves, and, most important, is possessor of a consciousness that is directed by will (i.e., the person knows himself to be a volitional *arche,* beginning.) Thus there is an absolute exclusiveness of the individual consciousnesses; "A person is a conscious, permanent, self-distinguishing, individual, active being." [38] Yet, here, Rashdall maintained,

---

[36] *Ibid.*, p. 255.

[37] Cf. *Personal Idealism: Philosophical Essays by Eight Members of the University of Oxford,* ed. Henry Sturt (London: Macmillan, 1902), p. 370; and *Contentio Veritas* (London: John Murray, 1902), p. 7.

[38] *Personal Idealism,* p. 372.

we face a paradoxical situation: on the one hand, an imperfect personality is the most that we can attribute to even the most richly endowed of human selves; but, on the other hand, we do have a conception of perfect personality that is not derived from our self-knowledge. If this is so, then our conception of true personality leads to the conclusion that there must be some ultimate Person who is perfect and from whom our final criterion is derived, and such a Person is God. God is, in the most complete sense, a Person, *the* Person; it is in this ultimate Person that the norm of all personhood is to be found. Moreover, it is God's perfect knowledge (omniscience) that sets the valid context of man's fragmentary, sporadic awareness, for God in his unique consciousness holds all reality together. God is not identified with all reality in a pantheistic or absolute sense; but reality exists in the all-comprehensive mind of God. The distinctive emphasis in Rashdall's conception of God was that he clearly attributed will as well as thought to God, as opposed to some of his predecessors, especially Green, and he also emphasized the existence of other wills or other individuals with metaphysical integrity as finite persons. Thus Rashdall defended, against "almost every Hegelian I read," [39] a pluralism that allowed for ontological independence of individual selves. This can be taken to mean that God is limited by other selves, but, Rashdall argued, he is limited only by that which proceeds from his own will and power. What is more significant is that God wills other selves with whom he may have fellowship. This is important, for, in the final analysis, reality is a community of persons.

The last person in the period of whom we must speak was C. C. J. Webb; and for this we may look especially at his Gifford Lectures of 1918-19.[40] Webb came out of the idealist background, and he specified two themes from that tradition that he wanted to retain. First there was the Hegelian insistence that the Christian revelation manifests a unified or holistic view of the world, a unity that is to be found in spite of the widest differences. This Webb took to be an authentic assertion of monotheism, which denies that "there is any reality in which God is *not* immanent and which, in the last resort, can claim to exist

[39] *Ibid.*, p. 382.
[40] *God and Personality* (London: Allen & Unwin, 1919), and *Divine Personality and Human Life* (Allen & Unwin, 1920).

independently of his immanence therein." [41] Second, the elimination of sheer arbitrariness from the doctrine of revelation must be emphasized, for Christian faith is not irrational and Christianity may be envisaged as the culmination of a universal process that was at once God's revelation of himself to man and man's discovery of God.

In his Gifford Lectures, Webb began with the topic of personality in God, and the discussion of this theme led him to the interpretation of personality in man. The basic argument was that historically the development of the concept of personality has been profoundly influenced by the discussion of the nature of the Trinity in Christian theology. Though Webb, more than the other idealists, searched for the unique in history his argument from history was still fundamentally dependent upon his philosophical interests. He wrote,

Personality is not merely something which we observe in men; rather it is something which, though suggested to us by what we find in men, we perceive to be only imperfectly realized in them; and this can only be because we are somehow aware of a perfection or ideal with which we contrast what we find in men as falling short of it. *In such cases we rightly begin with thinking out the ideal and then considering the experienced facts in the light of it.*[42]

In his discussion, Webb provided an historical interpretation of the meaning of the term "person." The Greek word *persona,* which originally meant mask and/or the actor in a play, came to be used legally to mean "party," and, more important, came to define the uniquely human possibility for social intercourse. Nonetheless, he argued, the appropriation of the word to signify the dignity of a person in relation to his fellowman would probably not have taken root in the modern languages of Europe had *persona* not come to be used by the Latin-speaking theologians of the Christian church as the equivalent of the Greek *hypostasis. Hypostasis,* which originally meant "a standing below" in the classical Greek, came later to mean "real, concrete existence," so that the distinction between *hypostasis* and *ousia* (substance) is difficult to make. The con-

---

[41] *A Study of Religious Thought in England from 1850,* p. 166.
[42] *God and Personality,* p. 21. (italics mine), also p. 175, and *Divine Personality and Human Life,* p. 19.

sequent use of the terms in the formulation of the doctrine of the Trinity, which makes *hypostasis* and *persona* equivalent expressions, determined the use of the word "person" in the modern period. The continued discussion of this concept comes to its most adequate definition in the Western tradition in the thought of Boethius, *"Persona est naturae rationabilis individua substantia"* ("Personality is the individual subsistence of a rational nature").

Webb claimed that the term "personality" had not traditionally been associated by theologians with the idea of "the personality *of* God" Rather, interest was centered upon the dialectic between the distinctions and equality of the Trinity; thus the term was used primarily in the sense of "personality *in* God." God was first spoken of (in the sixteenth century) as one Person, even though Trinitarian theology had made this difficult if not impossible. But Webb maintained that it is necessary to speak of the personality *of* God if we are to do justice to the biblical message and to man's relation with God.

It is also at this point that the cruciality of the incarnation becomes clear. He said succinctly, "The success of Christianity in maintaining a doctrine of Divine Personality is due to its peculiar doctrine of Divine Incarnation." [43] Personal religion is secured by the experience of encounter with God through Jesus Christ, for it is the incarnation that protests against the dissolution of reciprocal relations into pantheism or mystical monism. Webb's understanding of the incarnation was that it is to be identified with the historical depiction of Jesus in the Gospels as one whose moral and spiritual supremacy, combined with "an exceptional personal charm," is so great that it arouses a profound personal love and devotion. [44] While this description reflected little critical historical analysis, the assumption is that the revelation of God in Jesus Christ is the illuminating fact that manifests concretely what has been vaguely residing in the mind. Insistence upon the historical fact of the incarnation, Webb claimed, separated his thought from that of Hegel precisely because this single event becomes the necessary criterion by which all other religious significance is evaluated. At the same time, there remains a mutual corroboration between the concrete event and

[43] *God and Personality,* p. 82, cf. also pp. 213, 272.
[44] *Ibid.,* pp. 81-82.

the ideal conception. Jesus is redeemer because he fulfills the demands of the religious consciousness by overcoming man's spiritual alienation.[45]

It is time to pause and draw together the lines we have just been pursuing. The theme of the immanance of God had its primary impact upon theology in terms of the understanding of personhood. Theologically this implication was important because it reverberated through the discussions of the nature of God, of Jesus Christ, and of each human person. It is not insignificant that the attempt to reestablish the centrality of personhood in its most distinctive spiritual and metaphysical character was undertaken at a time when biological, evolutionary thought tended to emphasize the primacy of man's continuity with the natural order. As a consequence, this movement must be understood as a protest against a reductionistic materialism and an all-encompassing naturalistic evolutionary theory. In distinction, idealist philosophers stressed the ultimacy of spirit. But this general position was open to diverse explication. For the absolute idealists, such as Bradley, Haldane, or Bosanquet, that which gave significance to the human person was his intrinsic participation in the Absolute, a relationship that was to be located in the continuity of man's mind with the all-encompassing Spirit. Man's dignity was to be found in the fact that he was a reflection of Ultimate Reality. For the personal idealists, such as Pringle-Pattison, Rashdall, and Webb, this was not dignity enough, for man must be understood in terms of his inviolate metaphysical integrity. Hence, rather than interpreting each human individual as a fragmentary expression of the Absolute Spirit, they insisted upon the ultimacy of each human spirit. The commitment to idealism remained, but a pluralistic view of the nature of ultimate reality was a primary presupposition.

The importance of this discussion for the interpretation of the nature of God, Jesus Christ, and man is evident and will be described as our discussion proceeds. Is God to be interpreted as the Absolute Spirit, as a limited expression of that Spirit, or as a metaphysically distinct Person who is related to other metaphysically distinct persons? Is Jesus Christ, like all other men, a concrete expression of the all-inclusive Absolute, does he have a unique status as an exemplification of the

[45] *Ibid.,* pp. 179, 245.

Absolute, or does he possess a distinctiveness as a person among other persons—both God and men—that preserves his metaphysical integrity? How does the person of Jesus provide an interpretative key for the understanding of the nature of all men? And what are men? Are they partial and temporary expressions of the Absolute Spirit? Do they have an inviolate nature that may not be absorbed into the single unifying Spirit? These were the issues that the idealists bequeathed to the theologians of their day. Among the philosophers who were also theologians in terms of primary intellectual and vocational commitment, such as Rashdall and Webb, the choice seemed clear; the alternative of speaking of God as a Person who is distinct from although also related to men seemed to preserve best both the glory of God as well as the dignity and perplexity of human existence.

By focusing his attention upon the historical event of the incarnation, C. C. J. Webb lifted up the question of the role of history in idealistic thought, and to this third area we now turn. A number of questions clustered around the discussion of the meaning of history: what is the significance of history and, consequently, of the historical Jesus? Does world history have any metaphysical reality in distinction from the Absolute Spirit? Does history make a difference to the Absolute? In what sense is Christianity a historical religion? Interestingly, these problems were not immediately taken up as such by theologians; and although they play a significant part in mid-twentieth century discussions, it is true to say of British theology, and especially of English theology, that the nature of history was never as central an issue as it was for German or American theology.

Edward Caird in his Gifford Lectures, *The Evolution of Religion,* made it plain that the core of Christianity lay in the idea it conveys, not in any single historical person, and the fruition of this idea had come with the resurgence of an idealistic philosophy in which "the principle of Christianity has come to self-consciousness." [46] Pringle-Pattison, in spite of his other differences, agreed at this point. Even more directly than Caird, he found the central truth of Christianity in the dogma of the incarnation as this was philosophically interpreted; consequently, he

---

[46] *The Evolution of Religion,* 2 vols. (Glasgow: James MacLehose, 1894), I, 316, cf. also 291.

warmly protested against the orthodox tendency to limit the incarnation
to the particular person Jesus. He did not claim that the life of Jesus
was nonessential to an incarnate manifestation of God, but rather he
stressed that the life of every man is, in principle, an expression of
the incarnation and that it is misleading to attribute to Jesus some
distinctive metaphysical status. " 'Man,' " he quotes from Chrysostom
with approval, "is the true 'Shekinah'—the visible presence, that is to
say, the divine." [47]

Hastings Rashdall, who remained one of the most consistent of the
personal idealists, also was ambiguous at the point of the significance
of the historical Jesus. He began on a positive note and attempted to
counter the idea that the incarnation did not occur in a particular person.
Against Pringle-Pattison he argued that if we acknowledge that it is
especially in the moral consciousness of man at its highest that God
is revealed, then it is possible that a single human life is such a medium.
Or, if we believe that every human soul incarnates God to some extent
and acknowledge that there are spiritual leaders of mankind such as
heroes, prophets, and saints, then it is at least possible to believe that
in one man the self-revelation of God has been most adequately expressed.
Rashdall then concluded his argument by stating his thesis that "in the
life and character, the teaching and Personality of Jesus Christ the world
has received its highest revelation of God." [48] This revelation, he continued, is still being developed by the work of God's Spirit and especially
in the society of Christ's followers. In spite of his attempt to give
the historical Jesus a clearly defined place in his thought—and this under
the influence of Ritschlian theology as we shall see in our discussion
of Christology—there remained a certain ambiguity in Rashdall's position.
In an earlier statement, he had argued that the truth or value of the
Christian ethic does not depend upon its having been taught by Jesus.

---

[47] *The Idea of God in the Light of Recent Philosophy* (New York: Oxford University
Press, 1920), p. 157. Lowes Dickinson, one of the most distinguished humanists of his era
and a man who often reflected the contemporary ethos at its best, wrote on this problem
a succinct statement that characterized the doubts of many, "My difficulty with Christianity
is and always has been, that Christians make the center of their faith the historical existence
of a man at a certain age, I daresay he *did* exist, though that has been doubted. But if he
did, what was he really like? I cannot think that religion can depend upon such uncertainties." E. M. Forster, *G. Lowes Dickinson* (London: Edward Arnold, 1934), p. 212.

[48] *The Modern Churchman* (Sept., 1921), vol. XI, nos. 5-6, p. 286.

"If it could be shown that the sayings which we have been in the habit of regarding as most characteristic of the historical Jesus were in reality none of His, if it could be shown that there never was an historical Jesus, or that we know nothing to speak of about His teaching, the truth and the value of the teaching attributed to or Lord in the Gospels would not be one whit diminished." [49]

If these two statements are taken together it is evident that the particular historical person is significant because he revealed a universal truth that was already partially known; he brought to concrete expression an eternal verity. History remained the stage upon which the Ultimate Spirit expresses its character—although Rashdall insisted that this is manifested only through the interaction of persons who possessed individual metaphysical integrity.

By the end of the period of the dominance of idealism in English philosophy, the question of the relation between the idea of history and the status of individual historical events had not been adjudicated, and certainly not for the theologians. Oliver Quick challenged the idealists and the Ritschlians at the close of the era and argued that they simply did not take history seriously.[50] Once again I must mention the name of C. C. J. Webb, for although he delayed his primary concentration upon this problem until after the first two decades of the century, there were already indications of his interest as we saw in his discussion of personhood; and, more than any other idealistic theologian, he recognized the cruciality of the problem and worked to find a viable solution.[51]

If idealism was to bequeath problems in terms of the evaluation of particular historical events, it, through many of its representatives, made common cause with evolutionary theory to reinforce a belief in progress. Faith in progress became the dominant historical expectation of the late nineteenth and early twentieth century. Advances in technology, medicine, and charitable concern, as well as the increased recognition of the value of human personhood, seemed to reflect a progressive

[49] *Conscience and Christ* (London: Duckworth, 1916), pp. 274-75.

[50] *Liberalism, Modernism and Tradition* (London: Longmans, Green, 1922), p. 24; also *Catholic and Protestant Elements in Christianity* (Longmans, Green, 1924), p. 112.

[51] Cf. esp., *The Historical Element in Religion* (London: Allen & Unwin, 1935), and also his earlier book where he preliminarily explored this issue, *Studies in the History of Natural Theology* (Oxford: Clarendon Press, 1915), esp. pp. 22 ff.

development that portended a better future. In the culture at large, ameliorism became the watchword; the past was past, the future beckoned.

The interpretation of life was now forward-directed. Frustrations were caused by not achieving new goals as much as by inheritances from the past. Energies were expended in changing the *status quo* and in bringing in the world that ought to be. Idealism did not create this belief or this hope, but it did help to reinforce and in some ways direct the hope to ends worthy of rational man.

REACTION

But idealism did not go unchallenged, and whatever the ultimate outcome, the place of idealism in the history of philosophy had become problematic by the end of the first decade of the twentieth century. "Must philosophers disagree?" F. C. S. Schiller, himself a philosopher, asked in an essay. Perhaps philosphers must disagree if they are to be philosophers, for the searcher for truth is a wanderer always seeking a new home and fresh air to breathe. There had been a presistent dissent by contemporaries of the idealists, such as John Cook Wilson and H. A. Pritchard, but at the turn of the century something more than an intramural philosophical discussion of the nature of truth was involved, for this time philosophy was a participant in the larger sociocultural transformation that took place around 1910. In some ways a new philosophical challenge was the herald of the other impending changes. In this instance, at least, philosophical ideas provided the seed that germinated, developed, then bore fruit in the rest of culture.[52] Post-idealistic philosophy reflected a new spirit, was expressed in a new literary style, utilized a different vocabulary, and held a different world view from its predecessor.

Rivals often fight hardest when they share common assumptions and are concerned with common problems, and most philosophical debates are carried on within a tacitly, if not consciously, agreed upon arena. To a significant degree this was also true of the idealists and their

---

[52] It is not insignificant that G. E. Moore, one of the principal figures in this transition, was the philosophical father of the Bloomsbury group of which Virginia Woolf was a key figure.

opponents, for they did share many common assumptions, and questions of metaphysics and ethics remained at the center of the discussion. Some recent commentators have stressed the continuity of thought between the two positions. Thus D. F. Pears emphasizes the fact that

. . . both theories are of the same type: both operate with the same set of philosophical concepts—object, particle, division, and synthesis—and, although they give these concepts a logical interpretation, nevertheless they say things which are fully intelligible only if we visualize them in physical terms . . . [then Pears goes on to claim that Russell produced] a theory which is, in the deepest sense, Platonic.[53]

There were also basic changes, however, for none of the questions was approached in the same way, nor was there any agreement as to the type of results desired. With G. E. Moore, who was the initial spokesman for the new challenge, philosophy became more restricted, privatistic, technical, and tentative. And nothing exemplifies this better than his autobiographical statement, which throughout exhibits these characteristics.[54] In this account Moore evidenced a technical and sharply focused attitude toward philosophy; and he revealed much less interest than his immediate predecessors in the practical implications of his moral theory in terms of religion and social or cultural problems. The compartmentalization of knowledge that was increasingly characteristic of university life in the late nineteenth century was now even more sharply expressed. Philosophy was declaring its autonomy, and the changes this effected were of the first importance. In terms of style, the idealists were generally unrestrained, exuberant, like a surging river often overflowing its banks. Moore's style was much more restricted and precise, comparable to a carefully cut canal that moved in the shortest and neatest manner from one point to another. Rigorous control and technical exactness came to the fore; cautiously, Moore confined his philosophical interest to a better defined, more manageable area. From one perspective, this restriction could be seen as a truncation of the spirit, a withdrawal from a full-orbed involvement in life; from another point of view, it could

---

[53] Gilbert Ryle, ed. *The Revolution in Philosophy,* p. 55.

[54] P. S. Schilpp, ed. *The Philosophy of G. E. Moore* (New York: Tudor, 1952, 2nd. ed.), introductory autobiographical statement.

81

be seen as a liberation—that is, as a withdrawal—from truant, wasteful wandering over the landscape of human affairs and as a more profound probing of the individual—his sensibilities; his language; his logic; and his personal, rational encounter with the world.

In Bertrand Russell, the other major progenitor of the new philosophical style, we have, in terms of his person, an entirely different and much more complex man. Russell persistently confessed that he did not know what philosophy really was, which was probably a way of saying that what he was interested in doing was not what his predecessors had usually done. As a consequence, he gave free rein to his diverse interests and under the rubric of "philosophy" engaged in interests as variant as highly technical mathematical-logical inquiry, epistemological studies, analyses of the nature of mind and matter; and he spoke on almost every political, educational, and moral issue that confronted the era.

In April 1899 G. E. Moore's "The Nature of Judgment" appeared in *Mind*. This was the first attack on idealism, and, in a precursory manner, it represented the new philosophical attitude and method. In this article he attacked a basic idealistic assumption by declaring that fact is independent of experience and has a status of its own. For several years Moore continued his offensive in various publications;[55] and then in October, 1903, he issued his famous article on "The Refutation of Idealism."[56] In this essay he argued that the most that a "spiritual" universe can mean is that it is "intelligent" and "purposeful" and not "mechanical." But the idealists fail to show that this is the case by means of rigorous and viable philosophical method. Consequently, all the senses ever given to the proposition *"esse est percipi"* (the touchstone of idealistic epistemology) are false; and to demonstrate this Moore turned to a close analysis of the use of language. His argument may be stated as follows: the sensation of blue admittedly differs from the sensation of green, but both are nonetheless sensations; therefore they have (1) something in common, which he calls "consciousness," (2) something

[55] "The Nature of Judgment," *Mind*, April, 1899; "Necessity," *Mind*, July, 1900; "Identity," *Proceedings of the Aristotelian Society*, 1901; and "Experience and Empiricism," *Proceedings of the Aristotelian Society*, 1903.

[56] *Mind*, vol. XII, no. 48, pp. 433-53. For further comment on this see *The Philosophy of G. E. Moore*, esp. pp. 653 ff.

in which they differ, which he calls the "object" of this consciousness. Thus every sensation has two distinct elements, and as a result three different assertions about the elements of sensations are possible: (a) that one of them exists, (b) that the other exists, (c) that both exist. From this it follows that if anyone tells us that to say "blue exists" is the *same* thing as to say that "both blue and consciousness exist," he is making a mistake and a contradictory mistake, because the *esse* of blue is something distinct from the *esse* of the perception of blue, and there is no logical difficulty in supposing blue to exist without the consciousness of blue.[57] Later Moore acknowledged that a distinction may be drawn between the use of "blue" as a property (such as the blue tie, which certainly may exist without being perceived) and the use of "blue" as a quality (that is, as a sense datum). And while this forced him to admit that no sense datum exists unperceived, it is still necessary to distinguish between the sense datum and any physical surface to which it may be "attached" in perception. If this is the case, then idealism failed to prove that *esse est percipi*. But it should also be noted that Moore was not wholly negative; he commended the idealists for distinguishing sensation and thought and for emphasizing the importance of thought. But he was convinced that the questions to be raised and answered needed far more careful analysis than was commonly devoted to them.

In the same year that Moore published his attack on idealism he also published *Principia Ethica* with its argument in support of intuitive, nonanalyzable awareness of "good." Metaphysical philosophers had continually attempted to root ethics in the ultimate nature of reality, and Bradley had only lately attempted to establish such a relationship. Moore, for his part, maintained that the characteristic good must be clearly distinguished from things that are good, or from "the good." The distinction must be maintained even if it should happen that some other characteristic were invariably present when good was present. Failure to make this distinction leads to the "naturalistic fallacy," i.e., a false identification of good with some property of that which has goodness. This book *Principia Ethica* had an immediate impact, at least upon certain

---

[57] The presentation of this argument has followed the discussion of C. J. Ducasse in "Moore's Refutation of Idealism," *The Philosophy of G. E. Moore*, p. 226.

intellectual groups, and opened new vistas for many who had found idealism completely unsatisfying. John Maynard Keynes described his own reaction, as well as that of his intimate group of friends, in exuberant language, "The influence [of *Principia Ethica*] was not only over-whelming, but also . . . it was exciting, exhilarating. The beginning of a renaissance . . . we were the forerunners of a new dispensation." [58]

The high evaluation made of Moore by certain persons among the Cambridge undergraduates is indicated by Leonard Woolf in his recol-lection of a conversation with Mrs. Sidney Webb. Beatrice Webb re-marked, "I have known most of the distinguished men of my time, but I have never yet met a great man." Woolf responded, "I suppose you don't know G. E. Moore." [59] This esteem was not lightly conferred. Moore's commitment to truth, the integrity of his person, the im-pressiveness of his ability—in sum the combination of his mind, char-acter, and behavior—made him profoundly influential upon some of the most promising young intellectuals in England at the turn of the century.

Bertrand Russell, a defected Hegelian, aligned himself with Moore, although he distinguished the attitudes and motives that each of them had. "Moore was most concerned with the rejection of Idealism, while I was most interested in the rejection of monism." [60] Russell concen-trated his main attack on the notion of internal relations, which Bradley had argued was logically the prius out of which all understanding must arise. Against this position Russell maintained that the fact that a thing has relations does not prove that the totality of its relations are logically a part of its nature, or that for an entity to be understood one must understand all of its logical relationships.[61] If all relations are not to be understood as "internal," so that the totality of necessary logical interrelations is prior to interpretation and to its ontological character, then—and this is the important point—pluralism rather than monism is a possiblity. It is significant that Russell had reached this

---

[58] *Two Memoirs* (London: Rupert Hart-Davis, 1949), p. 82.

[59] Leonard Woolf, *Sowing: An Autobiography of the Years 1880-1904* (London: Hogarth Press, 1960), p. 131.

[60] *My Philosophical Development* (London: Allen & Unwin, 1959), p. 54.

[61] Cf. esp., *Problems of Philosophy* (London: Williams and Norgate, n.d.), pp. 222-23, 231.

point after a serious, "almost religious" search for some truth that was more than human, that is, independent of the minds of men and even of the existence of men. Not finding this type of certainty in religious affirmation he hoped to discover it in pure mathematics, although once again he was forced to acknowledge the impossibility of this alternative. In spite of failure of this final hope, his release from idealism was a great liberation. "I felt . . . as if I had escaped from a hot-house on to a wind-swept headland. I hated the stuffiness involved in supposing that space and time were only in my mind. I liked the starry heavens even better than the moral law, and could not bear Kant's view that the one I liked best was only a subjective figment." [62]

J. H. Muirhead has provided a good indication of the reasons for the shift in philosophical interest, as seen by an idealist.

There was much in the temper of the time that favoured reaction. Idealism had had a long innings, owing partly to the great ability of the group of thinkers who had initiated the movement on both sides of the Atlantic and the inherent weakness of the form of empiricism which in those days was its chief opponent; partly to its success in vindicating, amid a general dissolution of traditional beliefs, the reality of the objects from which what was best in religion, art, ethics, and politics drew their nourishment. But new forces were at work. It was not only that old beliefs were undermined, but men were ceasing to be interested in the background of experience on which they rested. New interests concerned with the science and art of human life filled the horizon. Even in the physical sciences, where the mind in search of the permanent had seemed to find this in atoms and the laws of their interactions, a revolution was taking place which seemed to involve everything in movement and relativity. Under these circumstances it was not surprising that philosophy weary of grappling with metaphysical conceptions of an Absolute, which seemed not only remote from the actual everyday world, but to have been invested by writers like Bradley with a certain ghostliness, should have been tempted to turn to methods more in harmony with the modernism of the time.[63]

Opponents of idealism, however, found more strictly philosophical reasons than Muirhead mentioned for rejecting its major premises. Pri-

---

[62] *My Philosophical Development*, p. 61, cf. also p. 11.
[63] *The Platonic Tradition in Anglo-Saxon Philosophy*, p. 279.

marily these were to be found in the ambiguity of their use of terminology, especially such words as "conceive," "concept," "relate," and "in the mind," for all of which two or more distinct meanings can be found. In addition, they claimed that cognition is better understood if it is discussed in terms of finding rather than making and that a theory of the physical world existing apart from experience is at least reasonably defensible.[64]

Yet, it must be made clear that the alternative philosophical position, as this was represented by G. E. Moore, was not a return to a "hard," concrete world. Moore at no point held that metaphysics was nonsense, but he did attempt to show how complex were the questions of metaphysics and how difficult it was to make clear, unambiguous metaphysical claims. Further, he argued that unless better, more careful reasoning was provided by metaphysicians, then philosophy would have "as little claim to assent as the most superstitious beliefs of the most ignorant savages."[65]

Moore was not an idealist, although he was interpreted by some to possess a certain unworldliness. J. M. Keynes points to this aspect of Moore's thought, "It is remarkable how wholly oblivious he managed to be of the qualities of the life of action and also of the patterns of life as a whole. He was existing in a timeless ecstasy." Then he added, "The New Testament is a handbook for politicians compared with the unworldliness of Moore's chapter on the "Ideal' [*in Principia Ethica*]."[66] But others, such as Leonard Woolf, challenged Keynes' description of Moore's influence at this point (on good grounds, in terms of the content of *Principia Ethica*). Woolf claims that Moore had a strong, concrete moral influence that was expressed in his employment of common sense.[67]

In an unambiguous manner, Russell was directly involved in practical ethical issues. Both as a philosophical principle and as a guide to action, Russell maintained that we can understand the ordinary world and that it is the height of folly not to embrace this world. At the level of

---

[64] A. C. Ewing, *Idealism: A Critical Survey* has a careful and extended discussion of these objections.

[65] G. E. Moore, *Philosophical Studies* (London: K. Paul, Trench, Trubner, 1922), p. 4.

[66] *Two Memoirs*, pp. 92-93.

[67] *Sowing*, p. 147.

philosophical method, this meant that Russell was convinced that if we could succeed in understanding our everyday beliefs there is the possibility that they are intellectually satisfying, and, further, what is required is that we carefully analyze these mundane beliefs. At the level of ethical involvement, this meant that moral qualities could be discerned by such a method of analysis and put into practice if one possessed the courage to apply his convictions.

The impact of this new mood was indicated by Leonard Hodgson who was a student at Oxford at the time,

When I was beginning my studies in Oxford in the years before 1914, philosophy was emerging from the dominance of Hegelian idealism and theology was nearing the end of a period mainly devoted to the literary and historical criticism of the Bible. The revolt against Hegelian idealism seemed to mark the end of four centuries of devotion to the study of the theory of knowledge; Cook Wilson and Pritchard were recalling us to the pre-Cartesian sanity of the assumption that knowledge means knowing a thing as it is, not altering it.[68]

By the end of the first decade of the twentieth century the revolt against idealism was in full array. Many of the strongest leaders among the idealists were still actively engaged in the discussion of philosophy, including both Bradley and Bosanquet, but they seemed to be men who were bypassed in their own time. Perhaps some retained a hope that there would be no eclipse. Idealists still held important teaching posts, they were selected for the Gifford lectureship, and they still valiantly defended their position; but the hope was vain, and what internecine philosophical battles left unfinished the cultural transformation accomplished. Even before the Great War had started this smaller conflict had already been decided, and idealism was rudely taken from its throne.

[68] Leonard Hodgson, *Towards a Christian Philosophy* (London: Nisbet, 1943), p. 7. Gilbert Ryle remarks about another aspect of the change, "Between the time when Bradley was an undergraduate and the time I was an undergraduate the population of intellectuals, and particularly of academic intellectuals in the British Isles had changed from being a predominantly clerical to an almost entirely lay population. . . . This laicizing of our culture and this professionalizing of philosophy together explain much of the change in style and direction of philosophy in (roughly) the post-Victorian English-speaking world." *The Revolution in Philosophy*, pp. 2-3.

IV

AUTHORITY: NONCONFORMITY AND THE BIBLE

The word "religion" comes from a root that means being bound or tied; originally it meant being bound by vows to a particular way of life, to accept a definite authority, to be disciplined by and obedient to a specifiable source credited with sanctioning power. But the new century brought to the religious communities of England, even as it confronted the social and political life of the nation, a dubiety about the primary sanctions of life and thought. This problem has continually haunted modern history, and no one era has an exclusive claim to its presence; in the early years of the twentieth century in England, however, this issue came to undeniably clear focus. We have already attempted to show how the question of authority was ingredient to the profoundly disturbed cultural and social upheaval of the early twentieth century, an upheaval that came to its climax in the years 1910 and following when fundamental political, aesthetic, economic, philosophical, and social transformations were effected. Within this broad background we must now set the problem of sanctions in the theological tradition. Before we turn to a historical account of the development of this problem, it may be well to pause and attempt to clarify the ensuing discussion.

Authority, descriptively speaking, represents power or force (whether personal or institutional, whether received as a command from the past, a present reality, or an end to be achieved), the exertion of some compelling sovereignty. To define authority in this general manner still leaves open the specification of its mode of expression. At one end of this spectrum, compulsion may be exerted by an outside force that requires conformity to its laws or intentions, sometimes quite apart from responsible personal concurrence. Thus an ecclesiastical organization, for example, may be authoritative in the sense that it capitalizes upon its status to evoke obedience or utilizes its power to enforce its prescriptions and require concurrence with its traditions. This type of force is always present to some degree in community existence, and the very presence of authoritative power always carries with it the possibility of tyrannical exertion. Perhaps as close as one can come to a concrete illustration of this concept is to be found in John Henry Newman's eulogy of John Keble,

who guided himself and formed his judgments, not by processes of reason, by inquiry or by argument, but to use the word in a broad sense, by authority [conscience, Bible, Church, antiquity]. . . . It seemed to me as if he ever felt happier, when he could speak or act under some such primary external sanction . . . what he hated instinctively was heresy, insubordination, resistence to things established, claims of independence, disloyalty, innovation, a critical, censorious spirit.[1]

At the other end of the spectrum, authority is often conceived in terms of autonomous power; that is, the only recognized sanction of thought and action is that of the independent, unique person, although the seat within the individual where this power is resident may be variously described as conscience or reason or free will. One illustration of this view is given by L. P. Jacks in his autobiography when he described the Uni-

[1] *Apologia Pro Vita Sua* (London: Sheed and Ward, 1946), p. 194.

tarian understanding of authority, "My teaching is to be that which the development of my own mind may commend itself to me, and that I am to conform to no other standard than that of my own conscience." [2] In studying the period, it is evident that some expression of autonomy was an ingredient in nearly all uses of the idea of authority.

A third discernible use of the concept of authority may be described by the term "theonomy," that is, a law that has its roots in an acknowledged transcendent ground but that expresses itself through the conformity of the mind and spirit of an individual with this ground. Thus, although authority is the expression of the will of a sovereign power, the mode of that expression is not inimical with free decision for and participation in the purpose of that Reality. P. T. Forsyth in *The Principle of Authority in Relation to Certainty, Sanctity and Society* represents this perspective when he writes, "This authority [of Jesus Christ as expressed in his cross] so super-rational in its nature and action, is yet in its method so rational that it emerges only amid psychological conditions [i.e. it respects man's integrity as a human being]. It is not magical." [3]

Often the discussion of authority was confused in the English historical development by the lack of clarity as to how the concept was being used. Hence, a distinction such as "external" and "internal" authority is sometimes drawn without further clarification as to the nuances of the concepts. As the discussion came to fruition at the turn of the century, however, one presupposition remained constant: whatever authority was acknowledged had to be consciously recognized and assented to. Idealistic psychology, with its emphasis upon conscious rationality, dominated the conceptualization of the nature of religious authority: Whatever sanction was accepted had to be consciously apprehended and affirmed, be in keeping with man's self-directive rationality, and respect his free moral agency. The description that Newman gave of Keble was more and more looked upon as unsatisfactory; the integrity of man, as this was understood in the idealistic descriptions of man, must be protected. No one in the era entirely escaped this assumption or sought to overthrow it completely,

---

[2] This is a statement he took from the Reverend Richard Armstrong. *The Confession of an Octogenarian* (London: Allen & Unwin, 1912), p. 91.

[3] (London: Hodder & Stoughton, 1913), p. 300.

although several spokesmen were to stretch it in an effort to be more inclusive and adequate in their description of human nature and its dynamic psychological functioning.

Perhaps the person who most directly brought the issue of authority to the fore and pressed home its challenge in the last decades of the nineteenth century was the distinguished Unitarian James Martineau. Working within the context of the revived idealism, and with a particular indebtedness to Immanuel Kant, Martineau arduously sought to find the sure ground of religious sanctions. To establish such foundations, he explored the realm of human experience and claimed that every man was possessor of a sense of a "nobler claim" that is placed upon him. That is, every man has a residual awareness of a binding moral authority to which he is responsible and to which he is called to give faithful obedience. This authority, he argued, is transcendently grounded, and it reaches across to man and makes contact with the human spirit at the points of "conscience" and "reason" (by which he meant something akin to Kant's "moral reason"). The presupposition that underlies this discussion is that man and God are inseparably related in such a manner that religious experience is "like a single drama of two authors." [4] This theme of synergism runs throughout the discussion and is the basis for Martineau's discussion of the coimplication of God's command and man's response in every valid description of authority. In the act of acknowledgment of a primal sanction for life, God has come to man immediately and is recognized in a direct fashion that negates the need for any intermediate channel of communication. Man becomes aware of God's presence and claim by an intuitive apprehension that is authenticated in an immediate experience in which man knows himself to be bound by this authority. Authentic religious experience, on this basis, is that act in which man responds positively and willingly to this transcendent authority. When he distinguished between conscience and reason, Martineau used the example of conscience as the seat of immediate awareness or discrimination and reason as reflective judgment upon this intuition and its implications. Such a use of Kant to explicate the understanding of religious au-

[4] James Martineau, *The Seat of Authority in Religion* (London: Longmans, Green, 1890), p. 290.

thority set a line of development that was to become increasingly influential in twentieth-century English theology.

Martineau helped to specify the problem of sanctions for Christian faith, but other events were making the need for reevaluation urgent, indeed imperative. The matter of enabling power was no longer simply an interesting philosophical question, it was being forced as a practical issue upon the whole Christian community. Chief among these other forces was the critical study of the Scriptures. At the basic level, Martineau's development was a response to this fact. His primary service was to make the cardinal issue clear. But what was the background of this problem? The nineteenth century had witnessed an increasing application of critical methodology to biblical study. The radicalness of the questions asked of the canonical materials and the originality of the answers suggested by German scholars led the way, but as early as the first quarter of the nineteenth century English scholarship was also responding to this lead through the pathbreaking work of such figures as Herbert Marsh, Professor of Divinity at Cambridge; Thomas Arnold, Headmaster of Rugby School; and Connop Thirlwell, a Fellow of Trinity College, Cambridge. In distinction from German scholarship, English scholars moved more slowly, and at many points more carefully, through the lower critical problems—such as questions of textual reconstruction and exegetical investigations—before embarking upon a full-fledged engagement with higher critical problems. In the process of transition the contributions of Brooke Foss Westcott, Joseph Barber Lightfoot, and Fenton John Hort stood out in terms of both their immediate relevance and continuing importance.[5] Whatever the strength of the later impact of higher criticism, the work of this group of Cambridge divines was to act as a filter through which the new issues would have to pass. By the last quarter of the century, however, the problems of higher or historical criticism in biblical study were imposing themselves in an unmistakable manner and demanding candid answers. English biblical study moved at a quickened pace, and the nation's religious thought was forcefully shaken.

Among Nonconformist scholars, the revolutionary force of higher

---

[5] For a comprehensive account of this development see Stephen C. Neill, *The Interpretation of the New Testament* (London: Oxford University Press, 1964), esp. pp. 4 ff.

criticism was a quick and commanding power. The inroads of doubt about biblical authority and its implications for Christian faith were temporarily fended off for the Anglicans by the persistent authority of the creeds, but in the dissenting churches, for whom dogmatic theological authority had been identified with the biblical content, the question of the possibility and status of theology had to be raised and was raised in a provocative manner.

We are primarily concerned not to trace the history of the development of biblical criticism but to delineate its impact upon theology. For the churches that came out of the Calvinistic tradition, the Scriptures had provided the primary authoritative base for theology, and built upon this foundation was their other most distinctive emphasis, namely the doctrine of the atonement (which was coupled with personal religious experience). For Free Church scholars (here I refer primarily to the Congregationalists, Presbyterians, and Baptists who shared a common Reformed background) the acceptance of the implications of higher criticism shook the roots of Christian life and thought. Primarily, the critical studies had called into question the infallible authority of the Bible and necessitated a reinvestigation of the sources and sanctions of theology. If the Bible in its totality, which had served as a trustworthy foundation, was no longer stable as an infallible document, upon what base could theology be established? The investigation of the life of Jesus seemed to promise a viable alternative.

Although the new interrogation of the Scriptures was disturbing for many, the first impact came as a signal of hope to a significant portion of the theological leadership. This hope was built upon the belief that careful explication of the Scriptures would in the long run make its inherent nature and therefore its true authority open for all to see. In part, this was a sharing in the scientific frame of mind that permeated the period— if one conscientiously sorted out the facts, these facts would exhibit their own truthfulness and give rise to valid hypotheses. A significant aspect of this hope was centered in the historical Jesus. With confidence, many commentators looked forward to the illumination that would come as Jesus was removed from his dogmatic swaddling clothes and revealed in his concrete existence in terms of his teaching, his social and cultural situation, and his unique personal qualities.

One of the clearest indications of the affirmative attitude toward higher criticism was to be found in the manifesto published in 1893 by eight Congregationalist ministers entitled *Faith and Criticism*. W. H. Burnett, writing about the Old Testament, spoke primarily of revelation as the "Divine Education of Man" and of critical studies as revealing the process by which revelation had been both deepened and extended. "It is hard to believe," he said, "that the pruning knife can cut so deeply and freely, and yet leave the life not only untouched and unimpaired, but purified and strengthened." [6] W. F. Adeney, in commenting on the New Testament, also argued that different stages of development were to be found in the New Testament, and thus differing emphases are understandable (such as between Paul's early and later epistles). But the importance of the New Testament, as historical criticism has also made evident, is that it points beyond itself to the authority of Jesus Christ. Adeney decisively located Jesus' authority primarily in his teaching, that is in his conveyance of truth, so that "His disciples are persuaded to repose confidence in His grasp of the subject." [7] Another contributor was the well-known Hampstead minister, R. F. Horton, who supported a critical approach to the Scriptures because, he held, it revealed even more plainly the intrinsic difference between the Bible and other scripture. [8] In spite of conservative protests to an earlier book he had written to defend this same stance, he now explored the doctrine of the atonement in the light of developing critical attitudes and found it to retain its central place in Christian experience. The most important contribution to the collection was the article by P. T. Forsyth, "Revelation and the Person of Christ," in which he radically disagreed with the effort to identify revelation with Jesus' verbal expression of truth (such as Adeney had done). As we shall see in more detail later, Forsyth contended that revelation is not of truths, but of persons and personal acts, and preeminently the person of Jesus Christ, who is met as crucified-redeemer. The movement of authority is from Christ to the Bible; from certainty of his redemptive power to the historical assessment of Jesus' life. [9]

---

[6] *Faith and Criticism* (London: Sampson, Low, Marston, 1893), p. 6, cf. also p. 46.
[7] *Ibid.*, p. 72.
[8] Cf. *Inspiration and the Bible* (London: T. Fisher Unwin, 1888), pp. vi, 15.
[9] *Faith and Criticism,* pp. 99, 101, 111, 139. Among the English Presbyterians William G. Elmslie was taking a similar positive attitude toward the new studies, and his biblical

In the same year, 1893, A. M. Fairbairn characterized the transition as a movement from an old theology that was "primarily doctrinal and secondarily historical," to a new theology that was to be "primarily historical and secondarily doctrinal."[10] The foundations of authority were clearly changing, and Fairbairn focused the issue sharply when he argued that both Evangelicals and Anglicans had up to now agreed in their method of evidential proof—a simple appeal to inerrant authority. The Evangelicals had appealed to the Bible, and the Anglicans to the Patristic period. In both cases they had been uncritical and unhistorical, for even though they differed in the authority to which they appealed, they were agreed that their particular authority was the purveyor of the very truth of God.[11] Fairbairn himself moved in a Ritschlian direction and argued for the authoritative character of the God-consciousness of Jesus, which has the power to come from the past into the present and to invigorate a similar consciousness in men of every age. Now, he claimed, this can be asserted with a fresh power, for the historical study of the Scriptures had so unshrouded the historical Jesus that today "we stand . . . face to face with him in a sense and to a degree unknown in the Church since the Apostolic Age."[12] He also, at this point, reasserted the centrality of the doctrine of the Holy Spirit and the Calvinistic theme, *testimonium Spiritus sancti internum,* so that the biblical portrait and the direct reinforcement of the Spirit were combined. Crediting of Christian faith, therefore, was not to be located simply in the Bible, essential as this may be to depict the historical figure of Jesus; rather the sanction for Christian thought and life was to be found in God's gracious speaking to the conscience and mind of each man through the agency of the Holy Spirit, who may use both the Bible and the church.[13]

Now, all these elements . . . are necessary to the being of a living revelation and with its authority in religion. Without the living and incorporated unity,

---

lectures were applauded for the new insight that they provided. See W. B. Glover *Evangelical Nonconformists and Higher Criticism in the Nineteenth Century* (London: Independent Press, 1954), p. 142. Cf. also the draft form of a new creed, 1888, pp. 197 ff.

[10] *The Place of Christ in Modern Theology* (London: Hodder & Stoughton, 1893), p. 3.

[11] *Ibid.,* pp. 10-11.

[12] *Ibid.,* p. 295. For the same emphasis by another Congregationalist see Alfred E. Garvie, *Studies in the Inner Life of Jesus* (London: Hodder & Stoughton, 1907), esp. the Preface.

[13] *Ibid.,* pp. 498, 509 ff.

realized in and through the Holy Spirit, of a satisfied reason, an inspired society, and a living God seeking the living soul, the written revelation will not reveal. And without these there can be no reign of authority in religion, while with these authority cannot but reign.[14]

The first impingement of biblical criticism, which we have just assessed, did not bring distress, at least not for many among the theological leadership. Indeed, there was an element of optimism that was wedded to the anticipation of the clearer understanding of the historical Jesus. This positive aspect, even though it was ultimately disappointed, was of profound value as the full impact of biblical criticism was felt. Such a reaction merits clear recognition, for the optimism that was brought in by the first wave of critical study allowed opportunity for transposing the locus of authority from the biblical words to the person of Jesus Christ, even though this was understood in a variety of ways. However, on the whole, the removal of the biblical base for dogmatic theology did seem to cause a demise of interest in traditional theological issues—this was the second wave created by historical criticism of the Scriptures. John Webster Grant speaks of "The Revolt against Dogmatic Theology" as one of the most pronounced features of Nonconformity at the turn of the century. Traditional Calvinism, with its doctrinal conservatism, already seriously eroded by the revivalistic tradition in which it was participant, was further discredited by the new questions about both theological foundations and doctrinal formulations. There was an impatience with concentration upon inherited dogma, and "the challenge to faith presented by science and criticism, the new interest in the history of religion, and the demand for the reform of the life of England left little room for the pure theologian." [15]

Thus, if some, such as the contributors to *Faith and Criticism* and Fairbairn, wanted to redirect theological work, others were prepared to ignore it as uncertain in its formulation and relevance. The struggle for equal rights with the state church, particularly in education, absorbed much of the interest and tended to reaffirm the principle of freedom, including that of individual right to interpret Scripture. D. W. Simon

[14] *Ibid.,* p. 511.
[15] John Webster Grant, *Free Churchmanship in England, 1870-1940,* p. 115.

described the condition of English Nonconformity in 1891 at the First International Congregational Council meeting in London,

The first thing that calls for notice is the pronounced and widespread distaste, not to say aversion or hostility to the theological or scientific treatment of Christian truth. Lack of interest in systematic theology is not, indeed, a very recent phase of Congregational life. . . . What used, however, to be lack of interest has largely deepened into positive dislike, not to say contempt. When prominent ministers refer in tones of mock humility to their ignorance of Systematic Theology, or earn cheap applause by denouncing dogma and contrasting it with life, when ministerial associations gaze wonderingly at a man who takes a deep personal interest in its study and thinks a knowledge of it necessary to true ministerial efficiency; when journalists rarely let pass an opportunity of flouting doctrine and dogma; when leading laymen explain impatiently, "We want practical teaching, not doctrine"; when the fact of a candidate for a pulpit having a sound knowledge of theology counts, as a rule, practically for little or nothing in his favour; and when it is easier to get a thousand pounds to build a college than a hundred to provide adequate teaching—what else can one say? [16]

In spite of the fact that this statement was by a man who was rowing against the stream and was tempted, for that reason, to overstate his position, on the whole it was a correct description of the situation. Even though there were exceptions to the movement away from biblical authority, especially among the Baptists, a changed attitude toward the Bible and theology among the Nonconformists was evident. Yet in some sense the Bible, of necessity, had to remain at the center of Free Church interest, for an appeal to its authority was the historical foundation of their distinctiveness; and if its former authoritative function could no longer be maintained then a new understanding of its role became a necessity.

Among the most outspoken Congregationalists who demanded that the church face its new situation forthrightly was K. C. Anderson. Anderson described with verve the manner in which the twentieth century was finally breaking the shackles that had bound the church since the Middle Ages,

[16] As quoted in *ibid.*, pp. 116-17.

That there is a new spirit in the world interpreting afresh the great doctrines of the Christian faith must be evident to the most unobserving. . . . It is affecting not only our religious beliefs, but the whole structure of our traditional ideas in society, in government, in literature, and in art.[17]

This statement indicates a recognition of the radically new situation with which the church was faced, and it looked at the changing scene with clear vision as to its inexorable transition. A much more careful and balanced statement was made by John Oman, who was later to remark that in Western cultural history the Enlightenment was more important than the Reformation, for while the Reformation brought about important changes within the inherited and accepted religious context, the Enlightenment called every authority into question—even God himself—in the name of man's autonomous rationality. Consequently what we are witnessing in the twentieth century, he implied, is the working-out of the delayed impact of the Enlightenment.[18]

The evidence of this change was also to be found within churches of Methodist heritage. The Methodist movement represented an evangelical tradition, concerned with the moral and practical life of its adherents and with gaining and expressing a social conscience. The most significant figure in Methodism was Hugh Price Hughes who spoke to and for Methodism as editor of *Methodist Times,* which had been founded in 1885, and it was the founding of this magazine that, Maldwyn Edwards says, "is in fact a convenient date for marking the beginnings of a dominant Liberalism within the Methodist Church." [19] Although the expression of this liberalism was primarily directed toward concern for the social condition of the nation, it also evidenced an openness to the new critical studies of the Scriptures. Two Methodists who were even more significant for Methodist theology were John Scott Lidgett, who has been called "the greatest Methodist since John Wesley," and A. S. Peake, a Primitive Methodist, who was the first Rylands Professor of Biblical Criticism in Manchester University. These two men were among the intellectual leaders who, by their own positive appropriation of the critical

[17] *The Larger Faith* (London: A. & C. Black, 1903), pp. v-vi.
[18] John Oman, *Grace and Personality* (Cambridge: The University Press, 2nd ed., 1919), p. 3.
[19] *Methodism and England* (London: Epworth Press, 1943), p. 168.

method and its results, prepared for the transition of attitude in regard to the Bible within the Methodist communion. Of these two Lidgett was the more significant systematic theologian and one of the most important church leaders in England in the first quarter of this century. A man of wide interests and abilities he was active in social reform, a leader of his own denomination, friend and adviser of men in power, and also a thoughtful and creative theologian. Lidgett was rooted in evangelical Christianity, but he was also cognizant of newer philosophical and social movements and attempted to combine the two streams. His primary commitment was clear, however, and the acceptance of themes from these latter areas was fitted into his received theological framework; thus, though he reflected elements of both idealism and evolutionary theory, they were always of illustrative and extrinsic value and never became controlling in his thought.

With the demise of verbal inspiration and the refocusing of attention upon the person of Jesus Christ, the Nonconformist theologians increasingly emphasized the doctrine of the atonement. The outburst of writing about this problem is not only impressive but also instructive; the authority of Jesus Christ was identified with that power to create new life through his saving work. If valid sanctions for Christian life and thought could no longer be secured in an infallible Scripture, they could be grounded in the reciprocity between the Savior and his redeemed people, in the personal, reconstituting engagement of Christ and man.

Lidgett, who had a remarkable awareness of recent and contemporary theology for such a busy man, spoke of the doctrine of atonement as being neglected in immediately preceding theology, although he also mentions some striking exceptions, such as Frederick D. Maurice, McLeod Campbell, and R. W. Dale. He undertook the rectification of this situation by setting the doctrine clearly within an ethical and personal context.[20] Above all, he claimed, the atonement must not become a legal device of "divine politics," rather, it is essential to understand it as the bestowal of God's love that is efficaciously expressed in the death of Jesus Christ, a self-donation that restores a man to fellowship with God and sets man upon the path of spiritual growth.

[20] Cf. *The Spiritual Principle of the Atonement* (London: Charles H. Kelly, 1898); *The Fatherhood of God* (Edinburgh: T. and T. Clark, 1902).

Unwilling to accept the tendency to say that the atonement is a mystery that defies interpretation,[21] Lidgett hoped to provide a rationale that, though not exhaustive, might be a true guide. Everything, he argued, centered in God's nature as Father, for thus it was that Christ primarily revealed him. This emphasis preserved both the personal and the moral relations that must be maintained, and, consequently, it made possible a viable interpretation of the dynamics of the relationship between God and man. (It must be remembered that Lidgett was using the paradigm of a Christian Victorian father who combined authority, as becomes a patriarch, with love, as becomes a Christian man.) Further, the concept of Father has primacy both in the interior life of the Godhead and in the exterior action of the Godhead; that is to say, it is proper for theology to give primacy to that which already claims primacy in God's self-revelation. At every point in his discussion, Lidgett intended to keep God's action and man's response in reciprocal relation, for it is in such reciprocity alone that atonement and the authority it conveys can be understood.

The Atonement is not an ordination of the bare will of God without intrinsic relation to the salvation which is effected by it. It is not a satisfaction to the personal rights or to the affronted majesty of God. The fundamental condition of fatherly satisfaction is, that it shall satisfy the fatherly by perfecting the filial. By virtue of his fatherhood, the father is the guardian of the law of righteousness, which protects the family bond of love and fellowship. And this principle, as we have seen, has its supreme exemplification in God's dealings with mankind in the cross.[22]

For the mainstream of Nonconformist scholarship, the problem that the waning of biblical authority brought was fundamentally important, and among those who recognized this issue and its ramifications the person who saw it with the greatest clarity was P. T. Forsyth. Forsyth insisted that the primary question that theology must resolve was that of the rootage of Christian faith. "As soon as the problem of authority really lifts its head, all others must fall to the rear,"[23] he wrote, and

---

[21] A position that was taken by men as widely different as Dean Church, an Anglo-Catholic, and R. F. Horton, the liberal Congregationalist.

[22] *The Spiritual Principle of the Atonement*, p. 301.

[23] *The Principle of Authority*, p. 1.

his concentration upon this problem indicated that he believed what he wrote. In Forsyth we have a unique figure, a man of single and, because of that, penetrating insight. It may be claimed that Forsyth, preeminently among the Nonconformists in the first quarter of the twentieth century, attempted to meet this problem systematically by investigating both the source and the nature of normative Christian thought.

The richness of Forsyth's thought is difficult to capture in short compass. He was occasionalistic in his writings and lived in constant engagement with his time. The best read theologian of his era in German theology—and it was an age that read German theology—he spoke directly and relevantly, if also aphoristically and provocatively. For Forsyth, "the principle of authority is ultimately the whole religious question." [24] The loss of authority in both religion and society had brought contemporary English life to the point of anarchy and breakdown; there seemed no point from which leverage could be applied to establish a stable social order. Forsyth was convinced that the interrogation of spiritual sanctions posed the basic issue, and until some answer could be given at this point the church could not serve society. But how can one state the nature of spiritual authority? He proposed what he took to be the most significant answer. Authority, he wrote, "lies in the absolute right of the new Creator of Humanity. . . . That is to say, the work of Christ's person must be taken into prime account, His power not only to know and show His perfection, but to perfect His perfection in the new history of a sinful race." [25] And again, in the *Cruciality of the Cross* he stated, "A true grasp of the atonement . . . meets the age in its need and impotence, its need of a centre, of an authority." [26] Thus Jesus Christ, as both Christ and Lord, has absolute authority in the Christian's life and in the life of the Christian community. The ultimate sanction for Christian living and thought can be acknowledged only within the movement of faith; and for this reason the person and work of Jesus Christ took central place in Forsyth's theology.

The Lordship of Jesus, he insisted, should not be confused with a sub-

[24] *Ibid.*, p. 3; cf. also *The Work of Christ* (London: Fontana, 1965, first publ. in 1910), pp. 38-40.

[25] *Ibid.*, p. 13.

[26] (London: Independent Press, 1909), p. ix.

jective authority such as could be equated with religious experience; on the contrary, it is an objective authority that provides a new life and not simply a new truth. The ultimate criterion of all living and thinking is the One who has brought man to his new way of existing. This norm is found to be true not *by* experience but *for* experience; it is the ground of experience, not the consequence of it.

Moreover, the authority of Jesus Christ is not to be located in some single aspect of his life and teaching—it is impossible to fall back upon Jesus' words or his example; the authority of Christ is to be found in his total self-donation. Consequently, revelation cannot be construed as some truth Jesus came to teach or illustrate; it is to be found in his making man "true," that is, in the reconstitution of lives in conformity with his own.[27] "Truth" as used in this context has an existential significance and does not apply to ideas except—and this is a major qualification—as "true" thinking or reflection arises out of the new way of being.

Forsyth was the clearest of all the writers of this period as to the nature of authority. It is, as he expressly said, "a source of power,"[28] and this power is the authority with which Christian life is invested by the redemption of Jesus Christ. It is a power that resides not only in the life of the individual believer but also, and preeminently, in the life of the church. In addition, the sanction of theology, because it is the source of Christian life, is the power of God that underlies the transformation of one's existence and initiates a new life that is built upon a new base and moves toward a new purpose. Such authority is not imposed by an institutional or legal or impersonal power; rather, there must be reciprocity, for the gospel of Christ "speaks of a God to whom we are reconciled in a mutual act which he begins; and not of an order or process with which we are adjusted by our lonely act, or to which we are to be assigned."[29]

To express the nature of authority in this manner is to say that the final authority is founded upon the work of God in Christ and in the Holy Spirit, which gives us "God's self-certainty . . . in faith."[30] The validating power of Christian living, therefore, is found in the event of

---

[27] *The Principle of Authority*, p. 30; *The Work of Christ*, p. 67; *Cruciality of the Cross*, p. 16.

[28] *The Principle of Authority*, p. 15.

[29] *The Work of Christ*, p. 82.

[30] *The Principle of Authority*, p. 44.

salvation. Since authority is rooted in the work of God for man, it is God who authenticates himself in his redemption, who provides certainty. Hence, assurance is founded in the objectivity of God's gracious activity, not in the strength of the believer's faith; God alone creates the choice and guarantees our communion with him. Christian truth, and the convincing force that flows from it, is a new life, a new way of being that is established and nourished by God.

To follow Forsyth in his elucidation of this principle, we must turn directly to the work of reconciliation that God performs through Jesus Christ and the Holy Spirit. The objectivity of the work of atonement is found in the fact that Jesus Christ through the Holy Spirit creates the possibility of man's response. There is no tapping of a natural reservoir of human desire for God; on the contrary, God himself must create even the capacity for response.[31] Consequently, there must be a new creation, for such a reconstitution of life is impossible for man since even the desire for it is alien to his spirit. The objectivity of God's atoning work is, then, found precisely in this act of new creation which is redemption. The authority to which one must surrender is that power which has invaded his life in such a manner that it provides a new power and a new direction for living. The Lordship of Christ is not, therefore, a goal that he sets for us; it is an empowering that enables one to live in obedient faithfulness.

Everything in Forsyth's analysis depends upon the cross, upon the gracious reconciliation that has given man a new nature. The authority is the Redeemer, and acquiescence to this authority is the free, responsible act of the redeemed. To make the point as clear as possible, we may say that for Forsyth God gives to man the response-ability, and this provides man with the freedom to become the creature that his Creator intended.

Throughout the discussion it is evident that the themes of truth and authority have been redirected by Forsyth. He was not primarily interested in "truths" about God nor in authoritative statements, creeds, or hierarchical systems. In opposition to such traditional representations, he emphasized the mode of being over thought, existence over intellectual reflection; his concentration was upon the way in which man is related

---

[31] *The Work of Christ*, p. 47.

to God at the primary base of life. As a consequence, theology was reflection upon the Redeemer who effected this new life and the resulting
redeemed selfhood. His emphasis upon the atonement is evidence that
Forsyth remained in the evangelical tradition; but because he recognized
the theological task as the structuring of the order of values between redeemed existence and thought and because he followed with care the
elucidation of the elements of this structure, he went beyond most
evangelical theologians and won a distinctive place among the Christian
thinkers of the era.

The setting of Forsyth's discussion was to be found in the crisis in the
social and intellectual life at the turn of the first decade of the twentieth
century. Forsyth was keenly aware of the environing social turmoil, and
he often argued that his understanding of authority had implications for
society outside the church. In caustic language, he criticized those within
the church, namely the New Theologians, who identified religion with
social evolution. The Free Church, he claimed, was in danger of becoming
absorbed by its engagement in the social and political life of the nation
and of identifying itself as the religious side of democracy. Vigorously
he maintained that Christian faith is not socialism seen in its depth; it is
not a means of baptizing the national ego; the church is not a troop of
scouts who look for good deeds to do, nor is it simply a ministering community to a sick world. The church is dominantly defined by its divine
worship and by its obedience to God. Not only as a matter of theological
principle but also as a matter of evangelical strategy, the desire for political
strength is eccentric. The Free Church has attempted to become a parliamentary influence, but in losing its center in the holy grace of God it has
lost its influence with the leaders of public affairs and has not gained it
with the working classes.[32] The authority with which the church approaches the world is the authority of God's word; a word that confronts
the world with the demand of holiness. Christianity faces the world
with demands; it approaches the secular order with a word of warning
and a gospel of redemption. The Cross of Christ brings with it a clear
sense of the God's controversy with man, of the sharp issue between
Christ and the world, the church and civilization. The church should

---

[32] *The Church and the Sacraments* (London: Independent Press, 1917), p. 21.

speak with the voice of a prophet; it should express God's righteous indignation and his redemptive love; it should demand that every social structure (*laissez faire* or socialistic), every political organization, every human relationship be judged by its conformity to God's purpose of redemption and the implications of that redemption for the world. Christ stands over culture in judgment because he came into the world as Redeemer. A tension between church and culture remains, and should remain, for its very retention is the one sign of Christian hope.

A prophet voice was sounding. The question of the foundations of Christian thought and action had been brought center-stage. In retrospect it is difficult to conceive a tepid response, yet, the majority of churchmen as well as the populace remained unconvinced that there was a momentous transition or that the inherited faith was radically challenged. Forsyth issued a call for renewal and the reestablishment of viable foundations, but most of his contemporaries listened with detached or quizzical spirits. A few, however, were aware of the same issues and attempted to make their own contribution to analysis and answer. Of primary significance among these was John Oman.

A Presbyterian theologian of Westminster College, Cambridge, John Oman published in 1902 his provocative discussion of *Vision and Authority*. Arguing against the foolishness of attempting to establish religion upon an infallible church or an infallible scripture, Oman claimed that true freedom and true authority arise simultaneously when a person is captured by a vision that calls forth the full-orbed possibilities of human existence. "[Jesus] invokes the good offices of the Church, not its authority. He appeals to the testimony of Scripture, but never offered a word of it as a final reason for belief. His final appeal is always to the heart taught by God." [33] In 1911, at the time of national crisis, Oman published a series of articles in the *Expositor,* which were later rewritten and entitled *Grace and Personality,* a book that was a major contribution to theological literature. With unusual clarity, Oman documented the demise of traditional authorities, and not least those within the church. Under the solvent of the historical method, he argued, "all of the in-

[33] *Vision and Authority: Or the Throne of St. Peter* (London: Hodder & Stoughton, 1902), p. 181. The influence of Martineau upon Oman is not explicitly acknowledged, but there is a continuity of emphasis and an indebtedness is almost certainly there.

fallibilities began to crumble. An infallible Orthodoxy, an infallible Christ, an infallible Scripture." [34] All the accepted foundations were eroded. Nonetheless, men continued to feel that God's truth ought to be infallible, and they feverishly looked about for the exercise of God's irresistible grace. But there were questions that had to be asked and especially in the present situation when the foundations were shaking: How is God's authority expressed? What is the manner of God's relating to man? What is the assurance of Christian faith?

In the new, post-Enlightenment situation in which external, authoritarian structures have fallen away, Oman maintained that man is forced "to look at life and try to understand what it would say to us, without any fixed prejudice regarding the answer." [35] No longer can it simply be assumed that God's omnipotence is directed in a straight line by his omniscience; what is required is a careful analysis of how religious men have described his manner of activity. On philosophical as well as theological grounds, Oman rejected the dominant Hegelian forms of idealism and moved in the direction of Kant. "Our knowledge," he wrote, "cannot be a purely mental creation; and . . . it cannot be a mere effect of an outward cause." [36] Rather, knowledge is to be found in the coinherence of givenness and reception; "We are nothing except what we receive, yet we can receive nothing to profit except as our own." [37] These two dimensions of man's epistemic existence—that of his environment and that of his own activity—are focused in man's ethical and religious experience. His thesis may be stated trenchantly: in morality, freedom is emphasized; in religion, dependence is primary.

To get out of the impasse between moral action and religious trust, an impasse that traditional discussions of freedom and determinism had maintained, Oman found it necessary to set the issues in a fresh context.

[34] *Grace and Personality*, 1st ed., p. 4; 4th ed. p. 6. Cf. also *Vision and Authority*, pp. 173-77.

[35] *Grace and Personality*, 4th ed., p. 25. Further references to this book will be to this edition, which is the most available.

[36] *The Natural and the Supernatural* (Cambridge: University Press, 1931), p. 102. Although this book is written later, the philosophical position of Oman is consistent throughout his writing. For a discussion of his epistemology see, Thomas A. Langford, "The Theological Methodology of John Oman and H. H. Farmer," *Religious Studies*, Winter, 1966, pp. 229-40.

[37] *Grace and Personality*, p. 33.

The proper question to ask is, what end does grace seek to serve? And the only sufficient answer is that grace leads men into mature moral selfhood. But what is the nature of a "moral person"? Significantly, Oman combines a phenomenological description of moral and religious awareness with a nonempirical philosophical psychology in which he closely follows J. R. Illingworth. The tensions between these two diverse elements in his thought create frictions, but first it is necessary to follow his description of man's moral character.

To be a moral person is to be autonomous, self-consciously self-determined. This is his definition, but it needs explication. In the first place, there is self-determination that is found in the fact that man is conscious of being a responsible person. If it were not for this awareness of man's own power and obligation, there would never have arisen either a consciousness of the self in tension with the world or the sense of self-identification or self-continuity. Responsibility, consequently, indicates a power that the individual has for action, that is, for self-determination. Secondly, the moral person is self-determined according to his own self-direction. Only that action which is based upon self-legislation is of moral importance and can express moral personhood. Unless there is an independence of judgment, there can be no basis for discussion of right or wrong, good or evil, and man would be an automaton. "An order imposed by God otherwise than through our own sense of right, however exalted its demands, would be no moral order." [38] Thirdly, the final characteristic of the moral person is that self-directed self-determination is within the sphere of self-consciousness. This is to claim that every genuinely personal act is based upon a conscious, rational evaluation of oneself and one's context and what is required in a specific context, and it is only as events are brought under the judgment of these intersecting factors that one's acts are truly responsible and authentic.

In distinction from such a moral person is the religious person, for religion claims that man is completely dependent; it speaks of man as being captive to God. Immediately the possibility of contradiction arises; is man to be understood in terms of his moral freedom or in terms of his religious dependence? With this interrogation we are brought, once

[38] *Ibid.*, p. 54.

again, to the perennial problem of predestination and freedom, and such a problem drives to the heart of the meaning of grace and faith. In any description of religious experience, ascription of everything to God must be given primacy; "Faith must rely, not partially, but utterly upon God." [39] Yet, such a description must not be set in opposition to man's moral freedom; rather, it points to the interaction between the self and its world.

If, however, our world is not of our making, we may not isolate our personal independence, as though it were of no consequence what kind of world we live in, and it did not matter what meaning or purpose it manifests or of what manner of fellowship it admits. Seeing we need a moral world to act in, moral truth to walk by and a moral fellowship in which to serve, to divide moral independence from religious dependence is merely to dissect living reality in order to make explanation easy. [40]

On this basis, man's moral independence and his religious dependence are recognized to be different strands of the same cord, moral freedom and religious dependence are brought together. The insight of faith provides for an understanding of the world as a place that "succors moral persons." But such an evaluation depends, for the religious man, upon the finding of God who is worthy of trust. Morality points beyond itself and has its ultimate basis in the constitution of the world. The primary trustworthiness of God, as Oman saw it, is to be found in the fact that he does not work with a high-handed indifference to the natural order or the integrity of the individual person. Classical supernaturalism, which described God's activity as an intrusion into the natural order, must be set aside. The whole creation is so ordered as to develop, try, mature, and enrich man's self-determination and the fulfillment of his moral personhood. Such an expression of God's grace is not limited to any special, sacred sphere of life or single historical event; it is to be found in the whole range of experience in the natural world that witnesses to God's gracious activity. In the light of this teaching, it is not surprising that Oman has a very undeveloped Christology.

[39] *Ibid.,* p. 35.
[40] *Ibid.,* p. 62.

With very subtle analysis Oman investigated the relation of man's moral agency to God's grace. Faith, he argued, is not spiritual unless it is won by man's own insight into truth; that is, it is not a truly personal act unless it is an act of self-determination by conscious decision. There is no solution to be found by resort to explanations of subconscious or nonrational grounds for action, for this is only another way of removing the distinctively personal quality of man's activity. The insight that the religious man has is one that deals with the reality that is presented to him; he does not create his world, but he does come to evaluate it, and his peculiar religious evaluation consists in the fact that he takes the world to be trustworthy in the enhancement of the values of moral personhood. Consequently, "no truly religious and moral person is ever tempted to compromise between his own will and God's or to consider them alien or opposite." [41] To stop with self-determination ends in individuality and independence, but it does not issue in moral personhood. For that which makes a person a center of value is responsible interaction between the self and its world, and to divide moral fellowship from religious dependence is to sunder a living reality.

Religious assurance comes when one is convinced that his appropriation of the significance of the world is actually true of the world, that his insight is not private but a valid perception of the nature of reality. The validation of the insight is to be found not by comparison with some third perspective or some standard that is *ab extra* but in the fact that this view of life makes sense of the dual dimensions of moral and religious experience.

Man's environment stands over against him and is known only as it crosses his mind as meaning; and the interpretation of that meaning, or perhaps more exactly, the apprehension of that meaning, is the contribution of the observer. What must be made clear is that Oman is not suggesting that religious awareness is response to any special object, but rather is constituted by a special type of awareness of all objects taken as a whole. The universe is sacramental, the divine purposes are written into the fabric of the world, so there are moments when the environment is received with a sense of holiness and is evaluated as sacred. And man,

[41] *Ibid.*

moral man and religious man, has his distinctive place within this sacred context.

John Oman was distinct from his contemporaries in several significant ways. Unlike Forsyth, he concentrated upon man's unique place within and his contribution to his total environment. Oman built his theology upon a "natural" morality and a general analysis of religious experience. He did not share the realistic epistemological conviction of Forsyth, which stressed the initiating and dominating force of God's unique redemptive act in Jesus Christ. In distinction, he emphasized the phenomena of man's universal, yet seemingly contradictory, moral and religious awareness, an awareness that arose only in the constellation of givenness-reception that characterized man's relationship to his environment. Insight, personal commitment, and loyalty were the distinctive qualities of man's moral and religious stance. The complementarity of morality and religion was to be found only as man recognized that autonomous, self-conscious self-determination were not contrary to God's mode of operation but were the very channels that he used to instruct and enliven. In the final analysis, God is "the strength of all our doing." [42] Thus, the further side of moral action continues over into religious trust. Only belief that one lives in a moral universe that is supported by God's providence can underlie an authentic moral commitment.

Once again, the question of authority is placed within a new context. True freedom and true authority arise simultaneously; they are, at their base, interdependent; and the coming to life of man's freedom and his acknowledgment of authority occurs when he is captured by a vision of himself and his world that calls forth a full response to his total environment.

AN OVERVIEW

In retrospect, the last decade of the nineteenth century and the first decade of the twentieth century may be seen as the era in which the question of authority in Nonconformist theology was relocated; from the time when the biblical authority was called into question, the need

[42] *Ibid.,* p. 37.

to reestablish foundations for Christian faith and thought became acute. The theological leadership moved in concert away from a plenary view of biblical inspiration, but their alternatives were radically varied. "New Theologians" looked to the philosophical base provided by idealism and adopted an immanental beginning point. Others sought the source of authority in the person of Jesus. Among these, some, such as Adeney, tended to fasten upon such facets as the teaching of Jesus; but others, such as Lidgett and Forsyth concentrated upon the work of Jesus Christ as expressed in his atoning grace. In neither of these latter two cases was there any primary dependence upon idealistic philosophy. The very fact that the atonement was emphasized implied a radical separation of God and man. Also, in neither case was there a strong amelioristic expectation, though all these men were concerned to speak relevantly to the social and cultural condition. When these responses are viewed together, it is evident that Nonconformity was torn by divergent reactions to contemporary philosophy and the societal ethos as well as to the Bible and traditional theology. R. J. Campbell and the New Theologians concentrated upon the doctrine of God, Forsyth and Lidgett upon the doctrine of Jesus Christ and especially upon soteriology. The New Theologians stressed God's identification with the world; their rivals, his unique presence. The New Theologians sought their authority in God's ubiquitous, indwelling Spirit; their rivals, in the unique work of Jesus Christ. The New Theologians identified Christian faith with a belief in progress; their opponents questioned this assumption.

The primary concern of the New Theologians was to express the meaning and truth of Christian faith in the changed conditions of a distinctly modern situation. Aware that the Enlightenment had challenged the orthodox creeds and the authoritative base upon which they were built, they attempted to formulate Christian belief in such a manner as to make relevant contact with the philosophic, social, and scientific mood of the era. Their opponents replied with the contention that in the reformulation that the New Theologians espoused, they had uncritically failed to respect the distinctive claims of Christian faith. In contrast the centrality given to the atonement was an effort to reaffirm the most definitive aspect of a specific faith. Standing within the Reformation tradition, the Nonconformists who were zealous to maintain the unique character of Chris-

tian faith found the essential aspect of that faith in the atoning work of
Jesus Christ, and it was upon this event that they focused their attention.

John Oman, in company with Martineau and the New Theologians,
sought for the source of authority in a dimension of experience that was
common to all men. He, too, moved from a general philosophical position to the special claims of Christian faith, but the philosophical commitment that he represented was distinct from the idealism of Campbell
and his followers.

Oman developed an epistemology that combined elements of idealism
and realism, and in this sense he provided a *via media* between Forsyth
and Campbell. But in terms of the search for sanctions his methodology
placed him on the side of the New Theologians. Man's universal moral
awareness provided Oman with the base for his discussion of authority,
for men act morally out of a conviction about the moral meaning and
worth of life. When this confidence is pressed to its foundations, it implies a trust in the providence of God, who has created and sustained
his world to "succor moral persons." Thus, authority is not given in
some single and singular event, it comes into being as one probes the
depths of his moral commitment and finds that his autonomous, self-
conscious self-determination has its roots in an absolute dependence upon
God. Autonomy finds its true depth and therefore its authentic existence
in a system of reality that seeks and enhances the development of free
self-realization. Freedom is rooted in the acceptance of an authority that
gave man the vision of what he could be and the courage to express his
potential selfhood. Authority was internal, germinative, and teleological.

Once again, in distinction Forsyth was intensely concerned to emphasize the essential and distinctive marks of Christian life and its ultimate
sanction. He was convinced that this unique quality was being compromised by every attempt to establish a natural theology or a valid, universal, authoritative foundation. Such approaches, he believed, failed to
recognize the seriousness of the problem and, consequently allowed the
issue to remain unsolved. Authority, for Forsyth, was established by the
unique and particular redemptive work of Jesus Christ; only in the condition of new-being could one speak of the sources and assurances of Christian life, and it was precisely this sort of assurance that was required in
the maelstrom of cultural transformation.

Oman was aware of the opposition and the reasons that gave rise to the different approach. But he was also convinced that the integrity of human personhood required that God's mode of activity be in keeping with man's rational, moral nature. There was no possibility of returning to a supernaturalistic position that describes God's activity as an irruption into the natural order. God works through the channels of his own created order, and for Oman the doctrine of creation always stands at the base of any valid theological system. In an elucidation of man's relation to his environment he rooted religious-moral experience and authority in man's evaluation of his world as sacred.

Awareness of the need to establish a viable authority was clearly recognized by both Forsyth and Oman, though one based his claim upon the redeeming work of Jesus Christ and the other upon the doctrine of creation. No concensus was reached. The search for authority was to con tinue.

V

AUTHORITY: ANGLICANISM, THE BIBLE, AND THE CREEDS

The base upon which Christian faith was understood to be built, as this developed in Anglican theology, had three foundation stones: Bible, tradition (creeds), and reason. Not unnaturally, one or another of these underpinnings had been given a primary place by various theologians in the past, but the foundation stood most solidly when the joint strength of all three supports was utilized. The history of twentieth-century Anglican theology is the story of the reassessment of these foundation stones, the questioning of their continued strength, and the attempt to reset them so they could support the weight of the building. By the last quarter of the nineteenth century, the first of these supports, the Bible, required reinspection, for to some, at least, it appeared to be of dubious strength. The reassessment of Scripture issued in disquieting findings, findings that soon led into a reevaluation of the creedal traditions. Finally, by the fourth decade of the twentieth century the confidence in reason was also weakened. Insistently, two questions presented themselves: Were the tra-

114

ditional supports unstable? If so, would faith fall? We shall, in this chapter, trace the challenge to the authority of the Scriptures and the creeds.

The effect of higher criticism upon theology was more delayed in Anglicanism than it had been in Nonconformity. In part, this was due to the internal condition within Anglican biblical scholarship, and in part it was the result of the established relation of biblical authority to the other foundations of Christian thought. Internally, Anglican biblical scholarship had not been unaware of the development of the critical study of the Scriptures, as indicated in the last chapter. Even in the early part of the nineteenth century there had been pioneers, such as Herbert Marsh, Thomas Arnold, and Connop Thirlwell, who explored historical, critical problems. After midcentury there were other pathmakers like the writers of *Essays and Reviews* and Bishop Colenso who had explored Old Testament problems. In response to these latter developments, tension and struggle quickly emerged. The volume *Essays and Reviews,* which appeared in 1860, caused a storm of protest because of its authors' refusal to countenance plenary inspiration, and the two writers, who were subject to ecclesiastical courts, were tried and sentenced to two years suspension, although they were exonerated by the Privy Council in 1864. Samuel Wilberforce demanded Synodical condemnation of the volume and in 1864 won this plea. Pusey led an effort to force the church to reaffirm the authority of the whole canonical scripture and obtained the signatures of 11,000 clergy and 137,000 laymen in support of his move. Bishop John William Colenso also caused an uproar. Colenso, who was an energetic missionary bishop in Natal, Africa, published studies of Romans and the Pentateuch and Joshua in the 1860's in which he expressed doubts about the infallibility of Scripture.[1] Bishop Gray of South Africa condemned him and asked the English bishops to do likewise. They agreed to censure Colenso and asked him to resign his see; when

---

[1] Colenso was a mathematician from St. John's College, Cambridge, and had used his mathematical ability to figure that if one were to take some of the priestly legislation literally then each priest would be required to sacrifice from 400-1,500 lambs a minute and eat 88 pigeons daily. He also derived that each Hebrew mother averaged 30 children and that Moses had an army almost nine times as large as Wellington's at Waterloo. He concluded that the Old Testament could not be taken in a literal sense. In his third volume he also used the theory of the Jehovist and Elohist sources of the Pentateuch. *The Pentateuch and Book of Joshua Critically Examined* (London: Longmans, Green, 1862), 3 vols.; *Romans* (Cambridge: Macmillan, 1861).

he refused, they condemned his book. Thus, although there was openness on the part of some, the second half of the century witnessed a continuing opposition to liberal biblical scholarship.

Another important factor was present. The most important biblical scholars in the second half of the century were the Cambridge trio of Westcott, Hort, and Lightfoot, men of undisputed scholarly eminence. Their work with textual problems and their generally reserved conclusions in regard to higher critical issues tended to direct the attention of English scholarship to linguistic and exegetical problems and hence delayed the impact of the more radical studies from the continent. To mention this fact is intended to detract neither from the significance of their scholarly achievement, which was exceedingly impressive, nor from the decision of their students to follow these careful, surefooted guides. It was true, however, that the very greatness and success of these men did, for good or ill, delay the impact of the more radical higher critical studies in Anglican biblical scholarship. Externally, the authenticity of the biblical record was reinforced by the corroboration that it received at crucial junctures from the patristic creeds. The Bible did not stand alone, nor was the student dependent only upon its internal evidence, supplementing and supporting the historicity and validity of the Scriptures were the creedal references to its general trustworthiness and especially to the New Testament testimony to Jesus Christ.

Scholarly probing of biblical documents continued, though with usual English reservation, and by the last two decades of the nineteenth century those who were most intellectually aware were convinced that they could no longer deny the importance of these studies. The watershed was the publication of *Lux Mundi* and particularly the article by Charles Gore, then Principal of Pusey House, Oxford. In a long and careful discussion, Gore argued that many of the scientific conceptions about the world and some of the historical statements in the Old Testament could no longer be regarded as literally true. The recorders of Israel's history were subject to ordinary laws in their estimate of evidence, and critical study rendered impossible any continuation of claims for Old Testament infallibility. But reservations about the Old Testament did not affect his conviction about the validity of the New Testament depiction of Jesus. The most striking aspect in this essay was Gore's admission that given the environmental circumstances, there was a limitation to Jesus' understanding of scientific and historical phenomena; although he quickly went on to say that this lack of omniscience in no way affected his fully valid revelation of God. A distinction must be drawn between that which was revealed in Jesus Christ and the vehicle which was used for that revelation; hence, to take the incarnation seriously, Gore contended, it was necessary to speak of God's self-emptying (*kenosis*) of his glory in the revelation of himself through the limitation of human nature. "Thus He *used* human nature, its relation to God, its conditions of experience, its growth in knowledge, its limitations of knowledge."[2] For Gore, the foundation stone of Scripture, though somewhat weakened, posed no immediate threat to faith; for, in addition to the remaining validity of this support, faith could still confidently depend upon the firmness of the other two stones.

The three supports sustained one another. It was this fact which separated Anglicanism from the Nonconformists, whose theological tradition had always stressed the primacy, and often the exclusiveness, of the biblical foundation. If the higher criticism of the Scriptures should, however, begin to carry implications that undercut the strength of the creeds this would be, and indeed soon was, cause for concern. Gore himself remained firm, in spite of the anguish that his concession over biblical infallibility caused some of the more orthodox, such as H. P. Liddon. In his own mind, Gore never doubted that Scripture, creeds, and reason all witnessed to the same truth, and that the authoritative foundation of the Christian faith was unshaken. In a moving passage he described his struggle with this issue.

I speak the honest truth, I can hardly tell you how often, with the whole sincerity of which I am capable, I have asked myself that question [of the relation of the New Testament message to the creedal affirmations], and reinvestigated it anew to the very utmost of my power, and always with a renewed certainty of assurance that the humanity of our Lord, as you find it recorded in the Synoptic Gospels is not capable of any other interpretation, if you are fair to the evidence, than that which the first Christian Church gave it.[3]

---

[2] *Lux Mundi*, p. 360, cf. also pp. 351-52. for Gore's treatment of Old Testament content. We shall discuss Gore's Christology in a later chapter.

[3] *The New Theology and the Old Religion*, p. 88.

There is some difficulty in assessing how a single attack upon any one of these three supports affected Gore's thinking, since he was so convinced of their combined strength that attacks upon one or another of their credentials carried very little weight. Some critics accused him of giving the creeds an independent authority,[4] but always, it appears clear, Gore returned to the combined strength of the supports. He expressed this clearly in his book *The Creed of the Christian*.

The truth which, as Christians, we value, does not rest upon one foundation, but two: not on tradition *and* scripture; nor on two foundations only, but on three, for I must not forget the "unction of the Holy Ghost"—the personal illumination given to each Christian. Here are three supports, no one of which is sufficient by itself—the Bible, the Church, the individual mind and conscience.[5]

Gore's reference to the "unction of the Holy Ghost" implies a view of reason that is more than man's natural rational ability. This is in fact so, but it must also be understood that because of his stress upon a *logos* Christology, which we shall discuss later, there is a sense in which man has natural resident possibilities for cognition. Every man is endowed by his Creator with rational competence to some degree, and while his rational insight may be enhanced by the informing presence of the Holy Spirit, this is an enhancement of an ability that is already present in man.

The very strength and uncompromising character of Gore's response

---

[4] Cf. Carpenter, *Gore: A Study in Liberal Catholic Thought* pp. 136-42.

[5] (London: Thomas Hibberd, 1896), pp. 65-66. The fact that Gore sometimes stressed one and then another of these criteria has also given rise to the contention that Gore often shifted the grounds of his argument and that ultimately he was unsure of the primal ground for the authority of faith. There is some evidence for this. For instance he continually appealed to the *Commonitorium* of St. Vincent of Lerins, but he was unwilling to press this in disputes where division of opinion was evident, and his interpretation of *kenosis* clearly went against the traditional and the most widely held doctrines. He could move from almost unbridled faith in reason to dubiety about its power. In criticizing Roman Catholic theories of authority he exalted the Scriptures, but for other purposes, such as establishing Apostolic succession, he assigned to tradition the primary place. There was inexactness and a variation of emphasis. But, from Gore's perspective, this was due only to a willingness to see all three strands as bound together; sometimes it was proper to emphasize one, at other times another, but always they provided joint strength. Cf. Carpenter, *Gore: A Study in Liberal Catholic Thought,* Chap. V, which is the best statement on Gore's understanding of authority.

to the question of authority may itself be indicative of the inroads of the interrogation of the church's sanctions. Gore understood the seriousness of the challenge. He was clear as to his own faith and its bulwarks, and he zealously spoke to an uncertain age from the vantage point of his own certainty. It is impossible to study Gore's biography without respecting him. He was sincere, intelligent, and disciplined, outgoing yet contemplative, a generous and genuinely humble man; he fought hard for what he believed, always with candor and courage. He could also be irrascible and demanding, tenacious and unrelenting. Perhaps Gore's strength, and his liability, was the fact that every quality that he possessed stood out in stark relief. What he was, he was; and the many-sided facets of his personality all shone with luminous unmistakability. We shall return to Gore later in this chapter, for because of several events at the turn of the first decade of this century, he moved into the middle of a sustained controversy.

Anglicanism was broad, Gore was not its only theologian, and other figures arose to give different and distinctive answers to the question of authority. W. R. Inge indicated that it was this problem which prompted him to offer "a third way" for the grounding of religious truth. In *Christian Mysticism* published in 1899 he wrote,

At the present time, the greatest need seems to be that we should return to the fundamentals of spiritual religion. We cannot shut our eyes to the fact that both the old seats of authority, the infallible Church and the infallible book, are fiercely assailed, and that our faith needs reinforcements. These can only come from the depths of the religious consciousness itself; and if summoned from thence, they will not be found wanting. The "impregnable rock" is neither an institution nor a book, but a life or experience.[6]

In response to this call for an assured foundation upon which Christian faith might be built, Inge turned to the study of mysticism. This study, he confessed, was of personal importance as he sought to find deep, firm roots. Having found such roots he became a spokesman for a type of experience that he believed provided a therapy for the modern soul.

[6] *Christian Mysticism* (London: Methuen, 1899), pp. 329-30. Cf. also *Christian Ethics and Modern Problems* (London: Hodder & Stoughton, 1930), preface.

Positively, the vision that he encouraged men to share was an awareness of unseen reality, an acknowledgment of eternal values that persist through every change and sustain men in every social condition. In one sense, this concentration upon ultimate reality led him to an aloof stance in regard to the social and cultural turmoil of the period, and it is arresting that in his diary, which includes the years 1911-1914, there is a remarkable indifference to concrete political events, and this at a time when he was in daily contact with prominent public figures. In another sense, he felt that he was speaking most pertinently by looking beyond these ephemeral events and recalling men's attention to eternal verities.[7]

Explicitly, on the subject of authority, Inge delivered a lecture in Liverpool in 1912 entitled "Authority and the Inner Light." In this essay he defined his own position clearly. By "authority" he meant the communication of a higher power, a voice that speaks with compelling force and to which the correct correlative is humble and grateful submission. But no authority is infallible, and the category of infallibility is not one that men or a church can use. Thus whatever is spoken to man with authority still addresses man in such a way that he is called upon to exercise his own judgment. True authority, on this argument, is founded upon a correlation between the commanding word that has been received and conscious obedience.

What we call authority is pedagogic, propaedeutic; it is the way in which we begin to learn. For the only real goodness and wisdom are free and autonomous, resting on an inner consent to a law understood and accepted as the true law of our own being, the service of God which is perfect freedom.[8]

In Inge we find an effort to meet the threat to the foundations of Christian faith by a new exploration of mystical awareness. This immediate, primary awareness of the fundamental ground of reality provides a sure base upon which one may stand in spite of rapid change or

---

[7] Sidney Dark's mawkish, harsh essay on Inge exaggerates the first aspect of his attitude (namely, his indifference to social events) because Dark refused to recognize the second element as having any importance. Cf. *Five Deans* (London: Jonathan Cape, 1928). Adam Fox in his biography, *Dean Inge* (London: John Murray, 1960) is too uncritical and does not directly raise the questions that were involved in Inge's attitude.

[8] *Authority and the Inner Light* (London: J. A. Thompson, 1913), p. 32; cf. also *Christian Mysticism*, p. 331.

moral ambiguity in any social situation. In following this way, Inge embraced a view of authority that stressed autonomous reflection reaching its depth by immediate engagement with the Divine. These fresh studies of mysticism are intrinsically significant, and throughout his learning and insight are impressive; but it is even more significant that this particular interest should come to the fore at a time when the cultural supports of Christian faith were giving way, and men were searching for an anchor. Look inward! Inge called. Look deeply inward! For here is the true anchor of the soul.

Another response within Anglicanism was represented by the liberal or modern churchmen; typical of this group was Hastings Rashdall, the Oxford scholar. In 1903 a group of theological compatriots issued a group of essays entitled *Contentio Veritatis.* Although there was a variety of views represented in the book, there was common agreement that a new interpretation of the Christian faith was required. Rashdall contributed to this volume, and he continued to express his opposition to creedal subscription, either for Christian belief or for ordination in the church. A liberal in spirit, Rashdall was opposed to all restrictions upon thought and remained suspicious of the exercise of ecclesiastical power. In regard to revelation, he maintained, it has authority only as it is verified independently by reason and conscience. Participation in the spirit of Christ, not confession of his name, is the hallmark of faith; thus the attempt to impose dogmatic formulas or creedal definitions as the criteria for discipleship is abortive and gives rise to ecclesiastical tyranny. In a typical statement he described what Christian discipleship means.

A man who believes what Christ taught about God's Fatherhood, about human brotherhood and human duty, about sins, the need for repentance, the Father's readiness to forgive, the value of Prayer, the certainty of immortality —the man who finds the ideal of his life in the character of Jesus, and . . . strives to imitate him . . . he is a Christian, and a Christian in the fullest sense of the word . . . and such a man will be saved, and saved through Christ; even though he has never heard of the Creeds, or deliberately rejects many of the formulae which the Church or the Churches have "built upon" that one foundation.[9]

[9] *Philosophy and Religion* (London: Duckworth, 1909), p. 173.

In spite of the rather imposing list of things a man should believe in the preceding quotation, it is clear in Rashdall's writings that it is not intellectual assent that is important; what does count is the active acceptance of Christ's example as the guide for one's life. Rashdall refused to fall back upon either the Bible or the creeds as the final authority in the Christian life. Intellectually, rationality is the only valid norm; practically, Jesus as the chief example fulfills our moral ideas and ideals and thereby calls for obedience.[10] In 1911 a group in general agreement with such views inaugurated a periodical, *The Modern Churchman,* as their medium for continued expression of their persuasion.

The Church of England was a cathedral with many rooms, and within its fellowship was a compartment that contained a strong evangelical, Protestant voice. The most consistent and prominent expression of this position was to be found in the monthly periodical *The Churchman* (possibly this title gave rise to the naming of their journal by the liberal Anglicans, *The Modern Churchman*). Starting a new series in 1899, this magazine held a conservative but not a plenary view of scriptural inspiration; its basic themes were the Protestant and scriptural foundations of the Church of England. This group faced the same problems as the Nonconformists in regard to the threat to biblical sanctions.[11] Since their theology was rooted in the Scriptures, and since the experience of redemption continually reaffirmed the validity of this interpretation, this group was unwilling to release their moorings. In defense, they reiterated their belief in biblical authority, denounced liberal tendencies, and continued to affirm the full validity of biblical Christianity. The changes that the twentieth century brought did not significantly affect this group, and its position remained basically unchanged. What constituted a problem with this position was the imprecision about the hermeneutic principles that should govern the interpretation of Scripture. What was assumed was that the Bible "properly" interpreted would yield the positions on redemption and personal holiness that they espoused. This group was the

---

[10] Throughout Rashdall's exposition there are obvious points of indebtedness to Ritschlian theology and particularly to Adolf von Harnack. We shall explore this dimension of his thought in our discussion of Christology.

[11] For a representative statement see Henry Wace, "Modern Criticism and Inspiration," *The Churchman* (Sept., 1902), pp. 637-45. Wace was the editor.

least sophisticated in their awareness of the presuppositions that governed their exposition of Christian faith, presuppositions that were themselves at stake and that required careful delineation and support. Commonly, they reiterated their belief in biblical authority at the same time they depreciated critical scriptural studies and the changing cultural ethos.

It is difficult to indicate exactly when the influence of biblical criticism first exerted its influence on the interpretation of the creeds, but certainly by the turn of the century the questioning of the miracle stories—which would directly involve the Virgin Birth—was evident in a number of writings. In July, 1901, a review in the *Church Quarterly Review* of the *Encyclopaedia Biblica,* edited by T. K. Cheyne, dealt critically with the issue in an article by Professor Paul Schmiedel of Zurich in which a number of the miracles were questioned, including the Virgin Birth and the resurrection.[12] That the influence of negative assessments was felt by a number of the clergy was evident in William Temple's pre-ordination struggles with parts of the creeds and in Hensley Henson's questioning of the need for subscription to the creeds as a requirement for ordination.[13] Throughout the first decade of this century the tension increased as a number of books and articles took sides on this issue. Intra-church struggles between the high churchmen, the modern churchmen, and the evangelicals added political and personal dimensions to the unsettlement.

The year 1911 saw the temperature reach crisis level, and this especially at Oxford. Once again, it was evident that theology, with all its peculiar issues, was participant in the general cultural struggle. In that year J. H. Skrine delivered the Bampton Lectures on *Creed and the Creeds;* this turned out to be a liberal interpretation that reflected a pragmatic attitude toward the formation of the creedal statements. The function of the creeds, he argued, is to give definition to the faith of the church at a specific time; as the situation of the church's life changes, so must her creeds. Affirmations that once were valid can become obsolete and fail to elicit an honest response of the whole person. A creed is true only if there comes with its confession "the reciprocation which makes life for the soul of the confessor." [14] In order to provide most adequately for this

---

[12] Vol. LII, pp. 261 ff.

[13] Cf. *The Value of the Bible and Other Sermons* (London: Macmillan, 1904).

[14] *Creed and the Creeds* (London: Longmans, Green, 1911), p. 112; cf. also pp. 33-38.

possibility of honest confession, a church may, as need demands, revise or reformulate her creeds. The criterion that is applicable in such a re-statement is that the creed must continue to provide the church with the power to transmit the life of God.[15]

Such a position, though it was much discussed, was obviously un-acceptable to the high churchmen, and it is not strange that in the same year J. R. Illingworth brought out his book *Divine Transcendence,* which was an effort to reassert the authority of the creeds and of the church in spite of and in recognition of the growing opposition to the traditional sanctions for faith. Although he opened his discussion with an acknowl-edgment of the difficulties and perplexities that faced those living in the contemporary situation, he gave no ground to the attempted encroach-ment of a less explicit standard; as he brought his argument to a close he asserted that the episcopacy is the most direct expression of God's sov-ereign rule and that episcopal authority is still "identified with that of old, and wholly unaffected . . . by any advances of criticism or fluctuations of popular prejudice." [16] Consequently, the creeds stand secure, and for "Christians" there can be no question about the facts of the New Testa-ment as these are corroborated by the mind of the united church in the creeds. What the age demands, he contended, is not new creeds but a new emphasis upon the authority of the episcopacy, which alone guaran-tees the full validity of the teaching of the catholic tradition.[17]

The controversies reached their climax with the publication in May of J. M. Thompson's book, *Miracles in the New Testament.* In 1910, Thomp-son had published two books, *Jesus According to St. Matthew* and *Synop-tic Gospels.* These appeared to be orthodox; consequently the appearance of *Miracles in the New Testament* was all the more shocking. For Thompson, a radical restatement of the place of miracles in the life and ministry of Jesus was made mandatory by three considerations: Christian faith must be intellectually convincing to the modern, educated man; criticism deserved a fair hearing; and it was necessary to make clear that the power of the gospel was to be found in the cross, not in miracle

[15] *Ibid.,* p. 139.
[16] *Divine Transcendence,* p. 110.
[17] *Ibid.,* p. 194.

stories.[18] His conviction and his courage were expressed in lines from his autobiographical poem.

> Yes, I would stand or move, defend or strike
> In company of allies I dislike,
> Face the impoverishment of life, the losing
> of all I valued, . . .[19]

In his last book, Thompson, who was a Fellow and Dean of Divinity at St. Mary Magdalene College, Oxford, openly questioned the possibility of miracles *per se,* and in the course of his argument rejected all the miracle stories in the New Testament. At the same time, he did not question the uniqueness or Lordship of Jesus as the Christ. In a short paragraph, he summarized his own position in terse, unambiguous language.

Though no miracles accompanied His entry into, or presence in, or departure from the world; though He did not think or speak or act otherwise than as a man; though He yields nothing to historical analysis but human elements; yet in Jesus Christ God is incarnate—discovered and worshipped, as God alone can be, by the insight of faith.[20]

God was present in Christ in an immanental fashion; God was in Christ incognito—visible only to the eyes of faith. Such a straightforward, unequivocal presentation caused consternation and challenge in the Oxford community. Edward S. Talbot, Bishop of Winchester, acting as Ordinary for Magdalene College, withdrew Thompson's license to exercise his prerogatives for the cure of souls in the College (though he did not inhibit Thompson from preaching or officiating in the college), and

---

[18] On Thompson see esp. A. Goodwin, *Reverend James Matthew Thompson 1879-1956* (London: Oxford University Press, 1957; taken from the Proceedings of the British Academy, XLIII, 278-79).

[19] J. M. Thompson, *My Apologia* (Oxford: Alden Press, 1940), p. 89.

[20] *Miracles in the New Testament* (London: Edward Arnold, 1911), p. 217. Cf. also pp. 160 and 211 for his summaries of the meaning of the Virgin Birth and the Resurrection.

Gore, as Bishop of Oxford, went further by refusing him permission to officiate in any manner in his diocese.[21]

William Sanday was the first to respond publicly to the position of Thompson. In a sermon before the University of Cambridge on May 7, 1911, Sanday took a moderate line and suggested that Thompson had lifted up a central problem that required new interpretation of the creeds. Others entered the fray: Kirsopp Lake, Hastings Rashdall, C. W. Emmett, and Hensley Henson defended Thompson; B. H. Streeter and A. E. J. Rawlinson (both of imminent *Foundations* fame) sympathized but had reservations; A. C. Headlam, Principal of King's College, London, and Henry Scott Holland opposed him. Thompson had brushed a hornet's nest.

To further compound the issue and increase the tension, the Thompson episode was followed by insistent voices and new events that reflected the general unsettlement. J. N. Figgis, a high church Anglican and a man who won the attention of many of his generation, looked at contemporary civilization and found it to be at a crossroads. The church and the world, he claimed, are standing in radical opposition to one another. On the one hand, there is the church with its mystery, its truth, and its authority. On the other hand, there is the modern world with its trust in intellectualism and its non-supernatural interpretation of life. The conflict has brought the age to Armageddon. The progress of which the modern world boasted was a hollow sham of materialistic conceit; outside the church, men do not know where they are—they are lost, searching for sure foundations, for life itself. Men are confused and unable to arrive at a "knowledge of reality." The only answer, Figgis maintained, was a return to the church with its firm anchors and its sure hope—and

---

[21] Gore succeeded Thompson's uncle Francis Paget as Bishop of Oxford in August, 1911. For a short, interesting recounting of this debate by one of the participants see H. H. Henson, "Preface" to *The Creed in the Pulpit* (London: Hodder & Stoughton, 1912). Henson pleaded for patience and open-mindedness, and stated his own position as a middle way. "On the one hand, I approach the discussion of the Creed from the point of view of one who himself accepts the traditional theology as the necessary basis of teaching; and, on the other hand, I acknowledge that this traditional theology has in many respects fallen out of accord with modern knowledge, and needs to be cautiously but frankly revised, This attitude of acceptance with reservations is not likely to be welcome . . . to many people." P. ix. It was not.

these are to be found in the creeds as they are maintained and interpreted by the true Catholic Church.[22]

In 1912 *Foundations* was published, and N. S. Talbot, son of the Bishop, introduced the volume by announcing that the era was witnessing a fundamental change from reliance upon to criticism of its inherited assumptions.[23] *Foundations* was a remarkable book in that its authors brought forth a luxuriant growth of interpretation from a commonly shared base. The presupposition that informed the discussions was the conviction that experience is primary to intellectual interpretation, and on this presupposition they developed theology as an interpretation of religious experience.

Such a view of theology was not unique with these writers; it was in the air, and a number of thinkers were showing an affinity to this mode of thought. In part, this type of interpretation was dependent upon the influence of the German theologians Friedrich Schleiermacher and Albrecht Ritschl, an influence that was crossing the channel as a fresh wind. In part it was the outgrowth in interpretations of religion, such as that of James Frazer, who stressed the universality of religious experience in his study of the history of religions. In part, it was an outgrowth of the theme of immanence and the developmental theory. It was also indebted to the developing interest in idealistic psychology, so that throughout concentration was upon conscious experience. In no other writings of the time, however, were all the cultural influences brought together in such a thoroughly eclectic and explicit manner as they were in *Foundations*. And, once again, it must be noted that the emphasis upon religious experience was, as in the case of Inge, an effort to find an authoritative source of Christian affirmation and a point of reference that would stand in the midst of doubt and change.

The essay on "The Bible" by Richard Brook of Merton College clearly stated the perspective. "The Bible is God's book," he wrote, "because it is

---

[22] Cf. *Civilization at the Cross Roads* (London: Longmans, Green, 1912). See also, David Newsome, "The Assault on Mammon: Charles Gore and John Neville Figgis," *The Journal of Ecclesiastical History*, Oct., 1966, pp. 227-41 for a discussion of the relation between these two critics of twentieth-century British society.

[23] Thompson was not invited to contribute to this volume, although he had been closely associated with the other contributors for some five years. This was a keen disappointment for Thompson, but it reflected the more moderate path of these friends.

in a unique and universal sense Man's book. It is the record of and the vehicle for transmitting a great human experience—an experience of God, of human need, and of God's response to that need." [24] Then he continued his discussion under the subtitles: "The Content of the Religious Experience of the Biblical Writers," "The Origin of the Religious Experience of the Biblical Writers," and "The Permanent Value of the Religious Experience of the Biblical Writers." It was because the biblical writers possessed a special genius for religion that they were thought of as being inspired in a special sense. Thus, the Bible not only reflects men's experience of God, but it is also the record of a specially qualified group of men who have perceived the deepest aspects of the meaning of relationship with God and who have recorded their experience in such a way that it speaks authoritatively to other men. "The Bible is for religion what the great masters are for art. It is, as has been well said, like 'a picture gallery of the old masters.' " [25] It is not for theology but for religion that we go to the Bible, but in finding the meaning of the religion of the Bible we have the foundation for theological reflection.

In Brook's essay we have the boldest and baldest statement of the role of experience in religious life and theological activity. All the other contributors followed in this way, but there was an increasing subtlety of their interpretation. B. H. Streeter's essay on "The Historic Christ" was a scholarly and suggestive interpretation of the synoptic view of Jesus Christ. After noting the critical problems involved in attempting to establish anything like a complete biography of Jesus, he nevertheless affirmed that there is a "strong presumption in favor of the substantial reliability of the general impression given by them of the life and teaching of our Lord." [26] On a number of specific issues he made important comments, not least of which was his insistence that a view of the synoptic conception of the kingdom of God must emphasize both its present and its future dimensions. Constantly aware of the work of Johannes Weiss and Albert Schweitzer, he was also convinced that if one remained faithful to the gospel account then both the realized and the expected dimensions of the kingdom must be kept in balance. The part

[24] *Foundations*, p. 30.
[25] *Ibid.*, p. 64.
[26] *Ibid.*, p. 83.

128

of Streeter's exposition that provoked the most comment was his discussion of the resurrection, a discussion in which he denied both the orthodox position, which stressed the physical resurrection, and a modern view that conceived of the resurrection appearances as a series of "subjective visions." In contradistinction to both of these positions he affirmed what might be called an "objective vision" theory, and he commented, "On such a view, the appearances to the disciples can only be styled 'visions,' if we mean by vision something directly caused by the Lord Himself veritably alive and personally in communion with them."[27] Once again the underlying presupposition was that of the primacy of religious experience, but now this view was expressed in a much more carefully balanced and subtle manner. Streeter was a biblical scholar and a theologian of a high order, and he judiciously worked through the nuances of the interrelationship of objectively given historical events and the response to these facts by a sensitive interpreter.

After Streeter's article there followed several other essays, all of them revealing this same starting point and all of them important contributions to the areas that they covered. A. E. J. Rawlinson and R. G. Parsons explored various theological interpretations to be found in the New Testament; William Temple wrote essays on "The Divinity of Jesus Christ" and "The Church," both of which we shall discuss in detail in other chapters; W. H. Moberly contributed discussions on "The Atonement" and "God and the Absolute"; Rawlinson made his chief contribution in a chapter entitled "The Principle of Authority." It is this essay which is most important for our present discussion, and to it some consideration must be given.

Rawlinson was irenic in spirit and, perhaps because of this, his investigation of authority is one of the most balanced contributions on this topic to be found in the early years of this century. He began his discussion with an etymological study that provided a definition, "Authority signifies primarily a statement or an opinion for the truth of which somebody is prepared to vouch: more particularly an expression of responsible and competent opinion." Then he went on to explicate his meaning, " 'Authority' attaches in general to the utterances of 'authorities,' that is to say,

[27] *Ibid.*, p. 136.

of persons of wide experience and expert knowledge in the spheres, of whatever kind, in which they *are* 'authorities.' " [28]

This definition sets the discussion of authority in the context of statements or expressions of truth and as such is more intellectualistic than his ensuing discussion supports; but if this definition is taken to be normative, then several implications immediately follow. First, authority does not mean infallibility, and it is not only a distortion but also a dangerous and tyrannical possibility to endow any authority, either of the individual or the institution, with infallibility; this is true whether the authority be the Pope or the Bible or the spiritual insight of an individual believer or religious teacher. What is needed in the present situation, he claimed, is a restatement of the principle of authority that will avoid "either confusing it with infallibility or legalizing it as despotism." [29] After assessing typical expressions of authority in both the Protestant and Catholic traditions, Rawlinson asserted that the best way to restate its meaning is to follow the natural development of a person from childhood to adulthood, to recognize that different types and expressions of authority are valid for different stages, and to support a fully mature recognition of the interplay between tradition and responsible consent. Modifying the appeal to experience as an isolated guide to truth he argued for a recognition of the necessary tension and interaction between fact and interpretation, theology and religious experience. He sums up the first stage of his discussion, "The function of authority in religion [is] neither to compel assent nor to override reason, but to testify to spiritual experience. Its province is not to define truth for the intellect, but to guide souls into the way of peace." [30]

Again his original definition must be remembered: authority is a statement or opinion about truth that someone is willing to vouch for. And now to this must be added the further aspect that authority is the statement about the truth that someone else is willing to acknowledge as having validity and to which he is willing to offer his obedience. Such obedience is not blind or uncritical, at least not for the mature adult; it is based upon the perception that the authority deserves obedience because it is true. Within the community of the church, the concept of authority

[28] *Ibid.*, p. 366.
[29] *Ibid.*, p. 373.
[30] *Ibid.*, p. 380.

is closely bound with the recognition of the validity of the spiritual experience of the saints and the validity, but not the infallibility, of their interpretation of the source and meaning of that experience.

Consistently in *Foundations* the effort was to free the idea of authority from identification with either an external institution or with autonomous experience. Experience is primary, but each writer attempted to relate individual experience to the experience of the wider Christian community, both past and present, and affirmed his belief that by going to the school of the saints and by growing in responsible personal interpretation the believer finds an authority that is trustworthy as a guide to his own experience and theological interpretation. The interplay between individual and community, between the past and the present, between obedience and reason, between receptivity and activity was carefully maintained and insightfully developed. Questions about the way in which each contributor worked out this interaction varied; but in Rawlinson's study there was a strenuous effort to keep these themes together and to establish a creative tension between them. Such a balance was difficult, especially in a precarious era when extremes seemed more appealing than such careful mixing, but it is the virtue of this volume and especially in Rawlinson's essay, that it attempted to strike such a balance and to keep it steady.

Whatever its intrinsic value, *Foundations* added to the perplexity of the time. Charles Gore was incensed at the article by Streeter; Ronald Knox counterattacked; and W. R. Inge commented that the Archbishop's control of the threatening disruption seemed uncertain.[31] Perhaps such strong reaction surprised even the contributors themselves; but it was in keeping with the inflamed mood of the time.

The furore over the publication of *Foundations* had not settled when, in 1913, there came Kikuyu. In June of that year, a conference of Protestant missions along with the Church Missionary Society (Church of England) took place in Kikuyu, East Africa. This meeting was held in the wake of the Edinburgh Conference on missions (1910) and the heightened interdenominational enthusiasm of that conference. At the

---

[31] Cf. Ronald Knox, *Some Loose Stones* (London: Longmans, Green, 1913); and W. R. Inge, *Diary of a Dean*, p. 18.

ensuing Kikuyu Conference the Anglican Bishops of Mombasa and Uganda, along with several priests from their church, committed themselves to a temporary federation of mission societies, with a view to establishing a new, united church of East Africa and Uganda. When the conference concluded there was a united communion service in the Presbyterian Mission Church with the Bishop of Mombasa celebrating and giving communion to the representatives of the other groups—Presbyterian, Baptist, Methodist, and Friends.

Beginning in August, 1913, the Bishop of Zanzibar, Frank Weston, demanded some official action against the Bishops, wrote an open letter, then finally demanded concerted episcopal effort to bring the case before the Provincial Court to obtain a judgment. After talking with both the Bishop of Zanzibar and the Bishop of Uganda early in 1914, Archbishop Davidson stated that there was no precedent for the trial of a Bishop outside a Province by a Provincial Court, but intimated that he would submit the matter to the Consultative Body of the Lambeth Conference (a body of Bishops that had been appointed in 1910) and that after receiving their advice he would make a statement on the matter.[32]

The question of the authority of the church and its creeds, especially for the ordained clergy, touched a tender spot in the ecclesiastical body.[33] In the midst of the controversy Gore wrote an open letter to his priests. This letter was an important document of the time, for in this communication Gore deplored the "drifting" and "tumbling along" of the Church of England in regard to its doctrinal base. While he still wanted to allow scope for liberty of opinion, he was convinced that the time had come for a strong reaffirmation of the creedal principles that had framed the church's life. The truth of the Christian faith, he was persuaded, was definitely expressed in the creeds, and to these any minister of the church

---

[32] For an account of these events see Clifton Kelway, *The Story of Kikuyu* (London: Cope and Fenwick, 1915); Randall Davidson, *Kikuyu* (London: Macmillan, 1915); Frank Weston, *The Case Against Kikuyu* (London: Longmans, Green, 1914); J. J. Willis, Bishop of Uganda, *The Kikuyu Conference* (Longmans, Green, 1913); Frank Weston, *Ecclesia Anglia: What Does She Stand For* (Longmans, Green, 1913); Cyril Emmett, *Conscience, Creeds and Criticism* (Macmillan, 1918).

[33] H. H. Henson wrote, *"Foundations* offended the belief and Kikuyu compromised the discipline of the Church of England as these were understood by the new party of Neo-Tractarians, who had increased rapidly in numbers and importance." *Retrospect on an Unimportant Life* (London: Oxford University Press, 1942-50), I, 155.

must subscribe. It was this issue of ministerial subscription which most concerned Gore. In typical fashion he acknowledged, indeed insisted, that patience must be shown to those who are unsure and want time for reflection and study of these matters; "but a man after a time must make up his mind," and if he concludes that he cannot accept the creeds then he should resign his position in the church. The church, and her Bishops who are entrusted with discipline, cannot blink at this present challenge to her authority, to the creeds, and therefore to the Christian faith. The episcopacy must act with firmness in a spirit of love; they must reaffirm the catholic tradition in which Anglicanism inhered.[34]

Gore's message was a challenge to the Anglican Church as a whole, and it was not allowed to pass unanswered. Immediately, the issue was joined, and scholars of every persuasion entered the list. W. R. Inge complained that the modern Ritualist (Gore) was quite ready to surrender the old theory of inspiration as regards the Bible but only because his "oracle" was the church. "The Bible may be thrown to the critics, but the creeds are inviolable."[35] J. F. Bethune-Baker from Cambridge also entered the field and struck forcefully at Gore. He reminded the Bishop of the various interpretations that different historical epochs had made of the articles of the creed; from the historical point of view, he argued, "The intention of the Creed is to provide a religious valuation of the fact," not to give a "string of historical statements."[36] To corroborate this interpretation, he pointed out that the Greek statement of the creed collected all that it has to say in "one long breathless sentence, and so concentrating our attention on the Person in whom we express our faith, and the nature of faith as a whole, rather than on each separate statement that we make about Him."[37] Consequently, the function of a creed is

[34] *The Basis of Anglican Fellowship: An Open Letter to the Clergy of the Diocese of Oxford* (London: Mowbray, 1914), esp. pp. 4, 6, 15.

[35] "Bishop Gore and The Church of England," *Outspoken Essays* (London: Longmans, Green, 1919), p. 113.

[36] J. F. Bethune-Baker, *The Miracle of Christianity* (London: Longmans, Green, 1914), p. 11.

[37] *Ibid.*, p. 12 Compare the statement of H. H. Henson, "There is only one miracle that matters to the Christian, and that is the miracle of Jesus. . . . The reason why this miracle is vital to Christianity is the fact that it alone is capable of being accredited directly to every individual Christian." "The Authority of Jesus," *The Creed in the Pulpit*, p. 12, preached on Oct. 29, 1911.

not to provide the Christian community with veridical historical statements, but, rather, it serves as a vehicle for the affirmation of the believer's
and the church's faith in the Person whom they worship. In practical
terms this means that the recital of the creed does not have to intend any
particular mode of understanding the creedal statements, such as a particular view of the Virgin Birth or the resurrection.[38]

Moreover, Bethune-Baker attempted to controvert Gore's use of the
idea of "miracle." Already in *Lux Mundi* Gore had stated his position
in regard to the idea of miracle. For him and some of his supporters in
the Thompson debate, including H. S. Holland, the main disagreement
they had with the book was that it interpreted miracle as an irruption
into the natural order by God and as man's insight into God's intervention
into that order.[39] Certainly, Gore and Holland wanted to defend the
miracles referred to in the creeds (the Virgin Birth and the resurrection)
as happening, but as happening through nature, not in contradiction of
the natural order. Bethune-Baker, however, argued that there is only one
miracle that is essential to Christian faith, and that is the miracle of God's
gift of faith and life to men. The unique event is what happens to man,
not what happened in the natural order, not even to Jesus Christ.

H. M. Gwatkin, Bethune-Baker's colleague on the Divinity faculty at
Cambridge, responded with an even more strongly worded criticism of
Gore. With much dialectical skill, he charged the Bishop with attempting
to make Tractarianism the official doctrine and practice of the church,
and then test all candidates for ordination on this basis—allowing, of
course, he remarked with sarcasm, that those who cannot subscribe to
this interpretation should be permitted to honorably, that is, with the
retention of their integrity, leave its ministry. But, Gwatkin argued, to
accept this approach to creedal orthodoxy would be a complete reversal of
the historic position of the Church of England; and what must be reasserted in contradistinction to the position of Gore is the Reformation

---

[38] A. E. J. Rawlinson used a similar argument when he claimed that the conciliar creeds
were by nature different from the earlier baptismal creeds, "Henceforward they became
symbols of corporate worship, expressions of loyalty to Christ and His Church rather than
of detailed orthodoxy, doxologies rather than declarations of individual doctrine." In
his article "Clerical Veracity," reprinted in *Dogma, Fact and Experience* (London: Macmillan, 1915), p. 203.

[39] *Miracles,* ed. H. S. Holland (London: Longmans, Green, 1911).

tradition of the Anglican communion. As in the case of his colleague, Gwatkin insisted that he could accept the creeds himself, but he wanted to protect against the effort to give the creeds an authority that was independent of the Scriptures and thereby isolate them from critical investigation. The Thirty-nine Articles, he pointed out, assert that the creeds must be "proved by most certain warrants of Holy Scripture." The diastasis was clear; the question of primal authority was brought to the fore, and Gwatkin put his position in a succinct sentence, "The Protestant tries the development by the words of the Lord, the Catholic construes the words of the Lord into agreement with the development." [40] In a clear way, Gwatkin forced the question of the locus of primary authority. This was the issue at stake.

Another strong response came from a man who was personally close to all those involved in the Oxford struggle, Professor William Sanday, Lady Margaret Professor and Canon of Christ Church, Oxford. Sanday was not only a friend of Gore, he was highly respected by the *Lux Mundi* group for his New Testament scholarship and judicious judgment in matters of biblical interpretation. Consequently, it was to the dismay of Gore and Scott Holland, among others, that Sanday not only defended the liberal clergy against charges of insincerity and pleaded for liberty of interpretation, but also felt compelled to align himself with those whose attitude toward miracles had been attacked. Of his declaration, Cyril Emmett commented a few years later, "This avowal was in the true sense epoch-making; it marked a new stage in New Testament criticism in England, precisely as Dr. Gore's contribution to *Lux Mundi* marked a new stage with regard to Old Testament criticism." [41]

Sanday's unhappiness with Gore's position was concentrated on the Bishop's contention that a Christian must accept the authority of the creeds in an unequivocal manner. On the nature of the creeds, Sanday was ambiguous; sometimes he spoke of the creeds as the reflection of the church's belief at a given time, but at other times he maintained that the creeds were to be understood as summaries of Scripture and thus derive their authority in the last resort from Scripture. In regard to this

[40] H. M. Gwatkin, *The Bishop of Oxford's Open Letter, An Open Letter in Reply* (London: Longmans, Green, 1914), p. 8.
[41] *Conscience, Creeds and Criticism,* p. 5.

last point, he stressed the issue that Gore had not wanted to acknowledge with its full weight, "If our conception of the Bible is thus profoundly affected [i.e. by historical criticism] our conception of the Creeds must be affected equally." [42]

The issues involved crystalized in a debate between Sanday and N. P. Williams of Exeter College, Oxford. Williams was a defender of the high church point of view; a perspective from which he argued,

that Christianity is not a mere mode of feeling, but includes as one of its constitutent elements a definite body of ideas; that these ideas have been revealed by God through Jesus Christ . . . that the task of conserving these ideas has been committed to the Christian Church . . . and that it is not competent for the Church to alter, suppress, or mutilate these ideas in their essential nature.[43]

In response, Sanday sharply distinguished their positions, "The real difference between us is a difference in the definition of truth, especially in relation to authority." [44] Even more extreme, Sanday was prepared to redraft the creeds, if that were possible, so that once again they would be accurate summaries of the faith that the church now held. Here, again, his ambiguity about the nature of the creed is evident; for in response to the question, what would be the ground upon which this new creed would be validated? he candidly replied, "For me, the ultimate standard of judgment is what I conceive to be the truth." [45]

In this discussion the two ends of the spectrum were brought into clear view. On the one end, Williams represented a willingness to acquiesce to the authority of the Holy Spirit as expressed in the church's formulation of the creeds; moreover he was ready to argue that these

[42] William Sanday, *Bishop Gore's Challenge to Criticism* (London: Longmans, Green, 1914), p. 9. See Scott Holland's defense of Gore in "Nature and Miracle," *Creeds and Critics* (London: Mowbray, 1918), pp. 127-28. Holland argued that the German critics Sanday called to his support were not reliable guides, the New Testament has an authority the Old Testament does not possess, and that miracle should be understood as the fulfillment of the natural order.

[43] William Sanday and N. P. Williams, *Form and Content in the Christian Tradition* (London: Longmans, Green, 1916), p. 22.

[44] *Ibid.,* p. iv, cf. also pp. 94-95.

[45] *Ibid.,* p. 94.

creeds must be accepted *ex animo* if one is rightly to claim membership in the Christian community or inheritance of its legacy. On the other end, Sanday represented the position of one who would accept the Divine authority for theology only as its influence is effective in the act of interpretation by the trained intellect of the scholar. Man is never merely the passive recipient of God's authoritative acts; the student himself is active in and contributor to any interpretation that he makes of the New Testament and the creeds.

The debate had reached a dangerous point. Too much was at stake for the hierarchy to ignore it any longer. Even though English bishops have been said to take the position that one should let sleeping dogs lie, even when as a matter of fact they are barking so loudly that they are disturbing all the neighbors,[46] they could not shut their ears to the penetrating cries from both sides and especially from Gore and his friends who felt that the very life of the Church was threatened. In Convocation, the bishops of the Church of England reaffirmed two earlier resolutions: the first from May, 1905, in which the Apostles', Nicene, and *Quicunque Vult* (Athanasian) creeds were reaffirmed, and the second from Lambeth in 1908, which stated that "the historical facts stated in the creeds are an essential part of the faith of the Church." April 30, 1914, the convocation stated their position.

These resolutions we desire solemnly to reaffirm, and in accordance therewith we express our deliberate judgment that the denial of any of the historical facts stated in the Creeds goes beyond the limits of legitimate interpreation, and gravely imperils that sincerity of profession which is plainly incumbent on the ministers of Word and Sacrament. At the same time, recognizing that our generation is called to face new problems raised by historical criticism, we are anxious not to lay unnecessary burdens upon conscience, nor unduly to limit freedom of thought and inquiry whether among clergy or among laity. We desire, therefore, to lay stress on the need of considerateness in dealing with that which is tentative and provisional in the thought and work of earnest and reverent students.[47]

[46] Roger Lloyd, *The Church of England, 1900-1965*, p. 100.
[47] G. A. K. Bell, *Randall Davidson: Archbishop of Canterbury (1903-1928)*, (London: Oxford, 1952), p. 683.

The statement intended to be cautious and conciliatory, and it accomplished its purpose. As several exegetes were quick to point out, the statement condemned only denial of the historical facts, not the questioning of them; and such an interpretation seemed to allow for indefinite suspension of judgment. Secondly, even denial only "gravely imperils" one, and therefore no final judgment was passed.[48]

The issue was quieted for a moment, but the peace came only by means of a compromise that left everyone free to his own interpretation and the question of authority unresolved. In principle, one may agree that such a convocation should not try to delineate finally the authoritative interpretation of the faith of the church; but to leave the question open was in itself a significant indication of the condition within the church, and it remained a stimulus for continued discussion of the sources and nature of doctrinal sanctions.

AN OVERVIEW

Ideas are powerful, and though they may work more slowly than their advocates would like, they have their influence. The style of life was changing, there was a transposition of the center of culture and, in a stark manner, the question of authority forced itself upon the national consciousness. From the last decades of the nineteenth century there had been a general reaction against the attempt to impose authority upon society as a whole or upon individual persons in an external, arbitrary fashion, and all the religious thinkers were agreed on this. Charles Gore insisted that the church no longer had any right, and certainly no longer possessed the ability, to enforce her standards upon a democratically informed society that found its strength in the freedom and integrity of each person. Even though the creedal foundations of the church were to be reaffirmed in answer to the contemporary perplexity, Gore argued that the creeds were authoritative only insofar as they were confessed with sincerity and acknowledged to be normative by an act of free decision. There was a certain ambiguity in Gore's treatment of the way in which authority within the church was to be defined, but there was no question

[48] Cf. Cyril Emmett, *Conscience, Creeds and Criticism*, p. 9.

about whether any authority that the church possessed could be made mandatory for the person who was not authentically within the Christian community. The problem of authority for Gore, therefore, was a two-fold one: first, whether or not the person, in the integrity of his personhood, would become a member of the church. If such a commitment were made then he came under the church discipline and committed himself to its regulations in regard to belief and practice. But, secondly, there was also the problem of what constitutes the valid authority within the church. This question worried Gore as much as the first one, and it was over this question that he fought his battles with Thompson, over Kikuyu and with Henson. For Gore, there was an authority that all Christian people ought to acknowledge and to which they should give unalloyed obedience, and this authority was to be found in the conciliar creeds that represented the consensus of the united church. Since the church was also interpreted as a continuation of the incarnation, Gore held that the decisions of the church had the authority of Christ and were as binding on the disciple as the authority of her Lord.

Gore's opponents within his own church also recognized the two sides of the problem; they too maintained that there were two spheres in which life was lived—the secular and the sacred; and they too recognized that the question of authority was different in the two areas. For man in society there was obedience due the civil authorities; but there was, also, the question of the ultimate sanctions by which one would abide and the values that would govern his political actions. For the thoroughly secular man the answer could be given in any number of ways: the sovereign value may be the state, a utilitarian principle, democracy, humanism, socialism, Marxism, conservative or liberal political platforms—their names are legion. But if a man placed his trust in God then this faith both informed his civil actions and brought him into a Christian community. Whatever this community, it too must face the question of its authoritative base, for guidance was needed in order to regulate the worship of God and direct the ethical responsibility of the votaries. It was precisely at this point that the discussion went apace within the Anglican Church. What were to be the constituting principles of its life? Gore answered in terms of the creeds. But others proposed variant answers. For some, such as Sanday, the authority that must be recognized was disciplined, humbly receptive reason. Hence the theological and ethical principles that are contemporarily valid are those which have been worked out in this generation by those who have faithfully studied the sources and interpreted their meaning in the light of present knowledge. No longer could an uncritical repetition of the creeds suffice; the creeds must be made amenable to the historical study of their origins and conform to the Bible as interpreted by scholars. But the base is clear—it is the enlightened reason of man.

For others among the Anglicans, Gore's search for authority in the church had led him to the wrong point in history. There was a strong Protestant element in the church, and for these people the Bible alone was to be acknowledged as the standard for doctrine and practice. The search for an undivided church with its creeds was misplaced. The creeds were subject to correction by the Bible and must be kept constantly under the aegis of this superior source. For some of these persons it was the Bible uncritized that held the supreme position; for others it was an enlightened, critical study of the Bible that was given the preeminence, but for both groups the creeds were too old and not old enough. They represented a pre-Reformation but post-biblical period of the church's life, a period that was not to be emulated.

There was a third group within Anglicanism that was opposed to Gore's approach, and this was represented primarily by the Cambridge professors who entered the fray at the time of the Thompson debate. For Bethune-Baker and Gwatkin the question was one of using both of the traditional authorities—creeds and Scripture—and using the results of the historical study of both to arrive at a position that could be affirmed by intelligent men of the day. This approach intended to be broader than any of the preceeding efforts. They would agree with Sanday, but they would also include the study of the development of the Church of England, observe how it had come to its doctrinal positions in the past, attempt to combine all this into a meaningful affirmation for the present day. At this time, these men represented the most strenuous effort to maintain the *via media*. Comprehensive in outlook, critical in approach, they attempted to retain the past in forms acceptable to the present. Their opposition to Gore was essentially rooted in the fact that he had forsaken the middle way and was pleading for one among the many formative influences in the life of the church.

The Modern Churchmen represented the left wing of the spectrum within the Church of England. Hastings Rashdall, Percy Gardner, and their fellow liberals were less controlled by traditional authority than were the other groups already mentioned. They moved away from creedal, biblical, or historical bases to a philosophical foundation. Influenced by idealistic presuppositions, they interpreted Christian faith in the light of this philosophical position and argued that the definition of the Church's faith and its authority must be derived from a consideration of what is acceptable to modern thought in its distinctive psychological mode as conscious rationality. Consequently, from the vantage point of idealism they reinterpreted the traditional Christian doctrines and contended that these interpretations alone were congenial to and possible for the contemporary believer.

As the second decade witnessed the increasingly severe struggle over the locus of authority in Christian life, there was a growing insistence upon the primacy of religious experience. William Inge had already stressed this theme in his study of mysticism and its application to the present situation. With the publication of *Foundations* the implications of this position were made explicit. This latter series of essays extended the idea of experience to call for mutual reliance upon personal religious experience and the spiritual experience of the church through the ages. Especially with Rawlinson, there was an effort to balance conflicting emphases and draw a composite description of authority that stressed both objective givenness and subjective commitment and obedience.

As this survey indicates, within the fold of the Church of England were to be found the most radically different interpretations of the meaning of faith and the authority for life. Every doctrine was in dispute, every organizing principle questioned by one or another of the combatants. Anglicanism represented a composite position in the sense that she contained within her boundaries people with a variety of views about how Christian faith was to be understood and what were its sanctions. If the social situation of the nation may be described as a conglomeration of ideas, varied commitments, and diverse thrusts, with little assurance about what it was that held the nation together, then the Church of England reflected the general situation. Within her own sphere there was a similar struggle with the same questions. The Church was bound together by her position of establishment and episcopal continuity, and in this was unity; but beyond this common ground everything was imprecise. The years at the turn of the first decade of the twentieth century were years of crisis, years of transition, and years of desperate searching for both the nation and the churches.

VI

DOCTRINES OF THE CHURCH: ANGLICANISM

The cultural transformation that was taking place as Victoria's reign was coming to a close necessitated a new self-understanding on the part of the churches. Increasing urbanization; the acceptance by civil authorities of responsibilities that had once been the province of the church, such as education and social welfare; the erosion of the rigid hierarchy in social status; and popular disinclination to associate with institutional religion were some of the basic factors that made it evident that the churches were living in a new time. The tremor of sociocultural foundations was inevitably felt. Even in the sturdily constructed churches the reassessment of foundations and the question of mission came to the fore.

At any time, self-interpretation is tempted to special pleading, deception, defensive posturing, and aggressive challenge, especially in a context where self-uncertainty is reinforced by external pressure and hostile persons. As we shall see, all these attitudes or actions were present at one time or another in the discussion of the nature of the church and the relation of the churches to the state. Nonetheless, it must also be said that with few exceptions the discussion usually moved on higher ground; and in most of the commentators there was an impressive degree of candor and fairness combined with goodwill and a keen sense of the importance of the issues.

As we describe the discussions within the church about the church it will be helpful to look at two specific issues that were forcing self-reinterpretation upon the churches, namely their role in primary education and the effects of religious establishment by the state. In the last quarter of the nineteenth century the question of the relation of the civil government to the Anglican Church became greatly agitated. For half a century the Nonconformists had been gaining legal, political, and educational rights—rights that gave rise to utilizable civil power. While the real strength of the "Nonconformist conscience" as a political entity was probably overstated by such leaders as Hugh Price Hughes and John Clifford, Nonconformity encompassed approximately one half of the population, and the awareness of this numerical strength gave rise to insistent demands in regard to the educational system.

The nineteenth century had also witnessed significant changes within the Church of England that reflected upon the issue of religious establishment. At the beginning of the century, the churches generally and willingly accepted the privileges and responsibilities that establishment brought. Two movements, however, helped to force change in the churches' self-understanding—namely, the movement toward democracy, which was gathering momentum by the 1840's; and the Tractarian reformation. The democratic spirit in civil government initiated reform in many directions, including church life. The religious counterpart of this movement was the evangelical revival, which had emphasized the unique value of each man, stressed the distinctiveness of spiritual commitment as opposed to conventional observance, and attempted to emphasize the distinct status of the church as a spiritual community. Subsequent to the evangelical movement, and also in the 1840's, the Oxford (Tractarian) Movement came into being in direct antagonism to actions of the civil authority and sought to reaffirm the special rights and authority of the Anglican Church. These two movements combined to raise the issue of the nature of the church in general and of establishment in particular; increasingly, the primary issue was that of renewed churchmanship, but connected with this prior issue was the matter of self-government.[1]

One of the primary responsibilities that the established church had always assumed was the provision of education, and its close connection with the state gave to this ecclesiastical institution special obligations and rights. The Nonconformist Churches, however, also attempted to provide for the educational needs of their constituency, with the consequence that there was much overlapping of territorial claims as well as of denominational interests. Friction was inevitable.

By 1895 the demand for reform of public education, especially the system of secondary education, was general. The background of this demand was to be found in the education act of 1870, which had expressed the intention that the primary schools should remain Christian, but nonsectarian. Some freethinkers objected to this continued intrusion of religion into state education, but by and large the struggle over what was to be taught was fought between the established and the non-established churches.[2]

In addition, there was the further problem of the specifically church schools, both those which were controlled by the Anglicans and those which were controlled by the Nonconformists. The act of 1870 established school boards in geographical areas where the educational needs of the people were not being met by the privately (usually church) controlled schools, although where voluntary schools were in existence the state continued to provide financial support. Since most of the voluntary schools were Anglican foundations, the Nonconformist church-

[1] Cf. *Church Assembly: Church and State, Report of the Archbishops' Commission on the Relations Between Church and State, 1935.* (London: Press and Publications Board of Church Assembly, 1936), pp. 1-40. Also Norman Sykes, *The Church and the Twentieth Century* (London: Macmillan, 1936), pp. 1-50. Sykes argued that while the Tractarians defended the spiritual authority and freedom of the church they did less than might have been hoped for concrete reform. Nonetheless they rendered an important service in recalling the church to her origins and establishing her distinct nature as a Christian community. See pp. 26-28.

[2] Halévy makes the important comment that unlike France where the question of religious instruction was fought between Catholics and Freethinkers, in England it was a struggle between religious bodies. *History of the English People in the Nineteenth Century,* V, 165. This is a fact that reveals the peculiar character of the controversy in England, and it lifts up a significant aspect of the English cultural situation.

men usually supported the state schools and the Anglicans supported their own educational institutions. But conflict was inevitable, and the most intense struggle arose in those areas where the voluntary church schools were sufficient for the number of students and where, therefore, no state schools were established and non-established churchmen were forced to send their children to Anglican institutions. To escape this situation, which they considered a denial of their rights, Nonconformists demanded that school boards be set up universally so that in every area state schools would be provided for the children who wished to attend. At the same time, Anglicans were worried by the circumstance that the state schools were already rapidly increasing, a fact that meant a concomitant decrease in the percentage of children enrolled in their schools. From the Anglican perspective, the establishment of school boards was a one-way street; the boards were proliferating, and the inroads they were making seemed ominous. In addition, the financial burden that was placed upon Anglicans was increasing as they were forced to support both the state schools through local taxes and their own schools. In sum, both sides were dissatisfied, and both were clamoring for change.

In 1902 the demands reached a crescendo. Under the leadership of Arthur Balfour the government made an effort to enact a new law that would modify the 1870 legislation. Two major changes were effected: school boards were abolished, and the authority was shifted to County Councils represented by an education committee; and the distinction between schools maintained out of the tax rates and the voluntary schools was removed. As a result, all the schools were placed under the control of the county education committee, which had the authority to determine the general curriculum and to hire or dismiss teachers.

Whatever the long-run importance of the act—and it was a significant contribution to the reformation of the old system—the immediate response of the Nonconformists was explosive. At once protest groups were organized, and some leaders resisted the implementation of the act by asking their followers to refuse to pay taxes designated for the schools. Among the most radical of these leaders was the Baptist John Clifford, a man of stalwart courage and fiery temper. Clifford and his supporters gained a remarkable degree of success, numbers of protesters had their property impounded, and a small group was actually jailed for their refusal to pay taxes. Robertson Nichol, editor of the *British Weekly,* added to the cacophony with his vehement comments, which were read with relish by many who were infuriated by what they considered a take-over by the Anglican establishment. Some of the leaders of the Nonconformists, however, weighed the disadvantages of the modifications against the enlargement of opportunity for education and were convinced that it was a workable compromise, at least as one step on an extending stairway. Chief among these were Hugh Price Hughes and J. S. Lidgett, the Methodist leaders, and R. F. Horton and A. M. Fairbairn among the Congregationalists.

The struggle as a whole, however, brought little credit to either side, and the bitterness engendered between the established and the nonestablished churches reached an unprecedented height. In retrospect, it is ironical that the century that was to become known for its ecumenical efforts should have opened with such turmoil and invidious accusation. Important issues were at stake, and the matter of education forced reinterpretation in regard to inherited traditions, other churches, and the state; it was a question of the role of the established church in society and the authoritative influence it could exert.

The education controversy alone, of course, did not precipitate this need; although this struggle brought one matter to sharp focus, there were other factors. All the churches had internal conditions that reinforced this necessity for self-reinterpretation. Within Anglicanism the resurgence of Catholic interests as expressed in the Tractarian movement—a movement that was predicated upon a distinctive understanding of the church—was now in its third and fourth generations, and its gains required consolidation in terms of implementation of its doctrines. Among the Free Churches, there had been a revival of interest in ecclesiology under the leadership of R. W. Dale; and even if his interpretation of the nature of the church, which emphasized its sacramental function, was not widely accepted it forced the issue of ecclesiology upon the minds of his fellow Congregationalists. Baptists were discovering that the need for cooperation placed strains upon their congregational polity, and Presbyterians were reevaluating their Reform heritage and their present status. Methodism was the least affected in terms of changing doctrine or theoretical interpretation; their attachment to Wesley's church-manship remained intact, but the lack of interest in doctrinal redefinition was largely mitigated by their practical interests, both evangelistic and social.

At stake was another dimension of the churches' authority. The form-ative and preserving power of the institution of the religious communities also constituted a perplexing and provoking issue. Already we have seen how the reassessment of the primal religious authorities had become a fundamental issue. Now, attached to the question of the grounds of faith was the issue of the churches' authoritative influence in the civil, so-cial, and cultural life of the nation. What was the relation of the ecclesi-astical institution to politicians and political structures? This question both the established and the non-established churches were forced to answer, for both were concerned to be responsible to their environment.

Involved in the effort at self-definition was a consideration of the nature of the church as the Body of Christ, or a corporate, worshiping community. Probably the most significant work to come from the Angli-can tradition in the last decade of the nineteenth century in regard to this issue was Charles Gore's *The Church and the Ministry,* published in 1888. The book had gone through four editions by the end of the century and continued to be prized by a large number within Anglican-ism well into the present century.[3]

To understand Gore it is necessary to note two preceding documents that set the stage for his discussion, for historical study had, for a quarter of a century, been investigating the biblical and historical grounds of the doctrine of the church. The first influential essay was a part of J. B. Lightfoot's commentary on Philippians, which bore the title, "The Christian Ministry." In this extremely acute and carefully researched essay—later published as a monograph—Lightfoot claimed that the original group of apostles had been called to a temporary office, but that as the church grew in numbers it became necessary to provide for "the emergency" that expansion enjoined. Slowly a permanent mini-stry emerged for the purposes of communication, of instruction, pre-serving community order, conducting worship, and dispensing social

---

[3] It was reissued with certain editorial work done by Cuthbert Turner in 1919.

charities; but the priestly functions and privileges were never regarded as transferred or even as being delegated to these officers, they were simply assumed. By the early second century the episcopal status was firmly and widely established, but the bishop was not a direct inheritor of the apostolic office.

Quite otherwise, Lightfoot argued, the episcopate was formed out of the presbyterial order by elevation. The office had arisen initially in Jerusalem with James, but when Jerusalem fell, John and other surviving Apostles fled to Asia Minor. Finding many irregularities, and wishing to order the life of these churches according to the pattern of the mother church these leaders gave permanence to an office that had probably already existed in germ among the younger churches—that is, with its presbyters and their chief presbyter. Moreover, Lightfoot contended with great vigor, the sacerdotal priesthood was not a part of the early church, though he did admit that there was strong enough evidence for the threefold form of the ministry to make "one hold tenaciously" to this ordering.

This essay by Lightfoot shocked many within the Anglican Church and especially those who were in the stream of the Oxford movement. Equally or more shocking, however, were the Bampton Lectures of Edwin Hatch in 1886, *The Organization of the Early Christian Churches.* In these lectures, Hatch stated that he intended to apply to church history the same critical research methods that had been fruitful in other fields of historical study. As a result of his investigations, he concluded that the form of the church organization was taken over from the familiar and commonly accepted civil organizations of the time; thus, the church has no distinctive form and must be understood as having come together in the same manner and as structuring itself on a pattern that was common to most organizations of the Roman Empire.

Hatch went through the list of church offices and rites in a thorough fashion and found their origin in nonecclesiastical institutions. In terms of the unity of the church, Hatch distinguished three periods: first was the unity created by a common relation to a common ideal and a common hope (this was unity established upon Christian experience); second, there was a subsequent unity that was established upon apostolic teaching; finally, there was unity imposed by Empire political pressure and which took the form of church confederation.[4] The climactic assertion of this study was that the Christian church could and must be understood like any other institution, and its development could be traced by the application of the usual canons of historical investigation.

Charles Gore reacted to the general questioning of the church's organizational character and to these particular presentations. As was typical, Gore was perfectly candid about his reason for writing the book. In the preface of the first edition he wrote, "This book claims on behalf of the apostolic succession that it must be reckoned with as a permanent and essential element of Christianity. It is an 'apology' for the principle of apostolic succession."[5] The argument presented was straightforward: the New Testament and the early Fathers support the position that Jesus intended to establish a visible church (although Gore's documentation from the Patristic period was much more extensive than that from the New Testament and was presented first); moreover, this intention of Jesus was realized in the establishment of a visible church among and upon the foundation of the Apostles. The summation of this argument was stated succinctly,

What primarily constitutes the unity of the Church is the life of Christ derived to its members by his Spirit. The Church is one on account of the spiritual presence which makes her the temple of God or the "Christ-bearer." None the less the Church is an external reality, a visible society; for the principle of the Incarnation, which governs the Church, links the inward to the outward, the spiritual to the material—there is "one body" as well as "one spirit." Spiritual gifts are given by sacraments, and sacraments are visible and social ceremonies of incorporation, or benediction or feeding.[6]

But more must be said than that the church is visible and that it is a continuation of the incarnation insofar as grace is given through its social sacraments. The early records also show that Christ, in founding his church, founded the ministry of the church in the persons of his

---

[4] *The Organization of the Early Christian Churches* (London: Rivingtons, 1888), pp. 186-88.

[5] *The Church and the Ministry* (London: Longmans, Green, 1919), p. ix.

[6] *Ibid.*, p. 48.

apostles; and this office was intended to be perpetually transmitted from its first depositaries. The regularly appointed bishops are a part of the *esse* of the church in that they assure its continuity with the church that Jesus established and to which he committed his Spirit.

In opposition to Rome, Gore held the position that the bishops were intended to form a congregation of equals and in conciliar fashion were to determine the dogma as well as govern the practices of the continuing body. The Roman effort to exalt one bishop and to give him supreme authority, even infallibility, is a perversion and, in its own way, schismatic. What must be defended is the primal unity of the church, a unity that is preserved by the continuous episcopacy. Such an episcopal focus has obvious benefits in that it serves as a bond of unity and provides historical continuity; further, it declares man's dependence upon the gifts of Christ by declaring his priority and his gracious presence in the sacraments; finally, it corresponds to the moral needs of the ministers of Christ's church; it insures and assures the validity of their ministry.

Having stated the controlling presuppositions of his presentation in some ninety-five pages, Gore advanced to assess the historical material in order to judge its support of these contentions. A. C. Headlam was later to comment that this presentation "always works from the dogmatic presentation of his thesis back to the Biblical and historical evidence."[7] This is obvious, and this approach decisively shapes the material. Gore began by asserting the supernatural character of Jesus Christ and the consequent supernatural nature of the church and its ministry, which he established. Gore continued by assuming that the continuity of the church is dependent upon the succession of a ministry that is derived from the initial group of apostles. It would be unfair to suggest that Gore was not completely candid about these presuppositions, indeed he was at pains to make it clear that these were his assumptions. Nonetheless, there is some justice in Headlam's claim that in assuming one of many theories of the ministry, "It is not altogether surprising that he is able to find what he desires."[8] But the essential point,

[7] *The Doctrine of the Church and Christian Reunion* (London: John Murray, 1920), p. 4.
[8] *Ibid.*

151

from Gore's perspective, was the fact that he was unable to find a single exception to his presuppositions about Jesus' intention to establish a visible church "to be the organ of His Spirit in the World, the depository of His truth, the covenanted sphere of His redemptive grace and discipline" and that the idea of apostolic succession has a unanimity of agreement "to an extent which hardly admits of being exaggerated." [9] Several important conclusions may be drawn from this study. The first is that, however venerable in other respects, all presbyterian and congregational polities that have dispensed with episcopal succession have violated a fundamental law of the church's life. Although the Church of England does not condemn these bodies she does necessarily refuse to recognize the validity of their ministries. Furthermore, the principle of apostolic succession alone affords a possible basis for church unity. The Lambeth Quadrilateral, which included apostolic succession as a requirement for organic union among the churches, is not only confirmed but reinforced by his historical survey.

In addition to his discussion of the church, Gore also made an important contribution to the discussion of the establishment of the Church of England. This was an issue that flowed directly from his understanding of the church, and it constituted one of the most critical practical problems that the church and the state faced at the turn of the century. Gore was prepared to acknowledge that theoretically Hooker was correct, church and state represent two aspects of the same society. But practically this was an unrealistic position to take. Democracy by its nature implies that the church has no right to attempt to force its will on the majority of people. Gore called therefore, for a new moral formulation and discipline that realistically assessed what could be made effective in civil life; this was the main responsibility of the established church to the state.[10] In spite of his recognition of the need for Anglican independence and self-government, he was not, by the 1890's, ready to advocate disestablishment; there was as yet no necessary conflict if each part recognized the authority that the other possessed and exercised its own authority accordingly. Because of the advantage that he believed accrued to each

---

[9] *The Church and the Ministry*, p. 298.
[10] Gore, *The Mission of the Church* (London: John Murray, 1892), pp. 127 ff.

partner in this relationship, he supported the continuation of establishment.

But events transpired both in the Anglican Church and in the state that forced a reevaluation. Within the church there was a growing lack of discipline, and since the final appeal was to courts constituted by civil government there was little hope of rectifying the situation as long as the Church of England and the state were interlocked. This awareness was forced upon Gore in the rush of events just prior to the First World War. In civil government there was a mixture of indifference and lack of understanding that was fundamentally distressing. By 1914, through the Kikuyu controversy, he momentarily made up his mind and declared, "I think Disestablishment, more than anything else, would throw us upon our principles." [11] Two years later, in a quieter mood, he was to once again say that he was prepared to press for autonomy within the limits of the present establishment, though he did not regard disestablishment with the same horror as most churchmen.[12]

Another member of the *Lux Mundi* group wrote a book on the church in the last decade of the nineteenth century. R. C. Moberly, in *Ministerial Priesthood,* reinforced the positions Gore had taken and added some distinctive notes of his own. He claimed that the only viable ground upon which a doctrine of the church may be built is that of a dogmatic theology, and his book was a theological, not an empirical description of the church. Moberly opened his discussion by questioning several of Lightfoot's assumptions in his essay on the ministry. Lightfoot, he claimed, presupposed that the relation of inward reality to outward form was accidental; he assumed that it cannot be a matter of great importance whether ministerial authority grows out of the life of the church body by evolution or is devolved ministerially through the action only of those who themselves have been similarly accredited as ministers before; he assumed that the church is, in the first instance, a plurality of individual units and by aggregation it becomes an articulated unity. On the constructive side, Moberly's chief effort was to show that the inward and outward are necessary coimplicates; each demands the other. On

[11] *The Basis of Anglican Fellowship,* p. 48.

[12] Cf. James Carpenter, *Gore,* pp. 261-62, for a discussion of Gore's attitude in regard to establishment.

this basis, it may be argued that the unity of the church is the first thing that must be affirmed, for this unity is the expression of the unity of God. The visible body is the spiritual church, and it is so even while it remains imperfect. In this presentation, Moberly was clear that the *esse* or the being of the church is the Spirit of Christ; as a consequence, the ordinances of the ministry and sacraments are not essential to the church's being, although they are essential to the church's life. That is to say, these particular ordinances have been ordained by God and because of this they are essential and, in a secondary sense, even " 'intrinsically' efficacious." [13] God may not be bound to these instruments, but we are, and as members of the church we are responsible for obedience to them.

With Gore and Liddon, Moberly argued that the ministry of the church of Christ is representative, not vicarious; this means that the ministry is a function of the whole body in its priestly character. "Christian ministry," wrote Moberly, "is the instrument which represents the whole Spirit-endowed Body of the Church; and yet withal is itself so Spirit endowed as to have the right and the power to represent instrumentally." [14] But this ministerial status is devolved from the original apostolic authority, and what apostolic succession really means is a belief that each generation genuinely cares that its ministers are ordained by those who themselves received power to ordain.

Gore and Moberly gave clear and impressive expression to one concept of the Christian church, but there were other voices within Anglicanism that were pressing to be heard. In radical contrast to this position were those who expressed more Protestant convictions. In 1899 some members of this group brought out their own manifesto on the *Church and Faith*.[15] The authors of these essays intended to base their interpretation upon "the rock of the Holy Scripture," and emphasize afresh the Reformed and Protestant character of the Church of England. F. W. Farrar rejected the "Roman" (essentially Gore's) concept of priesthood and argued

[13] *Ministerial Priesthood* (London: John Murray, 1897), p. 60.

[14] *Ibid.*, p. 99.

[15] (Edinburgh and London: Blackwood, 1899). Essays by Henry Wace, F. W. Farrar, C. H. H. Wright, R. E. Bartlett, T. W. Drury, Frederick Meyrick, H. C. G. Moule, P. V. Smith, Montague Barlow, Richard Temple, E. H. Blakeney.

that the title, when used at all, always applies to presbyter or curate and has nothing to do with sacrificial priesthood. "In the Church of Christ, then, there were, in the true sense, no 'priests,' but only the one High Priest Jesus Christ; no altar, but, by way of metaphor, His cross; no proper sacrifice but the one offering of Himself, once offered, and once for all." [16] In like manner he repudiated all forms of real presence in the eucharistic elements (Christ is present only spiritually and in the heart of the faithful receiver), and auricular confession. What, then, is the essence of the church? How may the true church be described? What is the relation of the true church to the historic episcopacy?

In a straightforward statement, R. E. Bartlett spoke for the contributors: the essence of the Catholic Church is established by its relation to Jesus Christ, a relation that also involves a certain continuity among its members. Christ called a people into relationship with himself, he did not give instructions or set patterns for the organization of the church. He did not provide for a threefold form of the ministry or establish the church upon the historic episcopacy. The only true test of catholicity is allegiance to Jesus Christ. This implies that the true church is the invisible church, and consequently there is no one form of church government that may claim "divine right." Episcopacy is, nonetheless, a venerable and historic form of government; it does serve to link the present with the past, and where it exists no wise man would insist on its extinction. But if episcopacy denies the democratic nature of the church society or claims exclusive rights for itself as the divinely sanctioned form of church government, then it must be denied. Central also to the argument, as here presented, is the freedom, indeed the necessity, of recognizing the fully Christian character of other Christian groups that do not have any connection with the historic episcopate. Can we, Bartlett asked, deny the title of "church" to those who represent the most intelligent and progressive of Christian communities? The Reformation tradition within the Church of England and the relation of the Church of England to the Reformation bodies must both be reaffirmed.[17]

In 1901, the Bishop of Salisbury, John Wordsworth, published his

---

[16] *Church and Faith*, p. 65.
[17] *Ibid.*, pp. 144, 150-52.

historical study of the church under the title *The Ministry of Grace*. In this book he took a broad church position in which he recognized the value of the historical episcopate, but also its variegated forms in the development of the Christian church. There was, in his writing, no presupposition that a form of government was given to the church, rather he attempted to show that the development of the office of bishop was a "natural" process that went at different paces in different communities; but he also recognized the place that the apostles held in the early church and the continuing need for the preservation of the true faith and unity.[18] The office of the bishop grew out of the life of the church and answered practical needs in the existence of the church. Thus, he argued, the episcopacy constitutes the link between the charismatic ministry of the first age and the local ministry of the second and third centuries; the charisma passed when the Christian body was sufficiently penetrated by the Holy Spirit to choose its own offices and representatives. Hence, once again, the position and the role of the bishop were determined by the body of Christian believers, and the essence of the church was located in the dominating presence of Christ in the Holy Spirit.This was not to claim that the historic episcopate did not have apostolic foundations, but it was to define the apostolic base in terms of functions in the body rather than in terms of divinely given and mediated order or in terms of necessity for the life of the church.

Added to the general discussion of the time was the publication by F. J. A. Hort of *The Christian Ecclesia* in 1897. Through his study Hort was led to the conclusion that in its original sense the term "Apostle" was not intended to describe the habitual relation of the twelve disciples to our Lord during the totality of Jesus' ministry. Strictly speaking it only applied to them in their mission among the villages.[19] As a consequence, he denied that the apostolate was even an office of government constituted by Jesus in the church. "There is indeed, as we have seen, no trace in Scripture of a formal commission of authority for government from Christ Himself. Their commission was to be wit-

[18] John Wordsworth, *The Ministry of Grace* (London: Longmans, Green, 1901), pp. 121-24.

[19] F. J. A. Hort, *The Christian Ecclesia* (London: Macmillan, 1897), p. 26.

nesses of Himself, and to bear that witness by preaching and healing." [20] The conclusion was that the apostles were not in any proper sense officers of the *ecclesia*. Such a word from so distinguished a scholar added to the controversy,[21] and made the Anglican self-understanding all the more uncertain.

The work of Lightfoot and Hort had wide influence. Hastings Rashdall, representing the liberal wing of the Anglican Church, acknowledged special debt to their work. In a series of sermons preached at Lincoln's Inn at the turn of the century, Rashdall defended the necessity of institutional religious life, but he also contended for a spirit of charity and a wide allowance for differences in valid forms of structured life. Working with the presupposition that the whole church membership constitutes the authentic priesthood, he developed the line of thought presented by his mentors. There are legitimate orders for the special job of leading the congregation, but these orders are always to be understood as representative of the whole body and are not fixed by any uniquely valid tradition. The church exists to increase the love of God, who is Father, and to enhance the brotherhood of men, and insofar as it does this by its worship and social involvement it is reaching toward the ideal that God has set for his people. The thesis of Rashdall's book is stated in a direct manner, ". . . the primary and most important business of the Church is not the definition of dogma or the practice of a cult, but the application of the fundamental ideas of Christ, not only to individual conduct, but to the public life of a Christian society." [22] But, because of his conviction that institutional worship and brotherhood enhances personal religious development, Rashdall attempted to keep alive a dual emphasis upon personal maturation and public responsibility.

Equally clear voices were to be heard from the Anglo-Catholic wing of the church. Darwell Stone lucidly expressed the understanding of the church that this group held. The church that Jesus intended, he claimed, was a visible society of baptized people that was sustained by the authority of the apostles and that, in fellowship, joined in hearing

[20] *Ibid.,* p. 84.

[21] See Gore's reply, *The Church and the Ministry,* appendix M, pp. 379-80.

[22] Hastings Rashdall, *Christus in Ecclesia* (Edinburgh: T. and T. Clark, 1904), p. 133.

the word, receiving the sacraments and worshiping God.[23] In his discussion of the unity, holiness, and catholicity of the church, Stone consistently made a distinction between the objective and subjective sides of these attributes. In each case there is the reality of unity, holiness, and catholicity as they are given by God; and there is also the fact that these qualities are only partially realized by the visible church. Nonetheless, the tension between the ideal and the partial realization succors the life of the community. In the discussion of apostolicity this position comes to its clearest expression. Stone first stressed the mission of the church as the community sent by Jesus Christ, but he also argued that the general stream of patristic teaching represented the test of apostolicity as communion with the historic episcopate. Hence, the marks of the true church are precisely those defined by the enlarged form of the Nicene Creed, "One, Holy, Catholic, Apostolic." And all these marks must be present for a true church to exist.

The role of the bishop comes to the fore in the discussion of the teaching office, an office that is necessary for the propagation of Christian truth and the sacramental life of the church, which, he argued with some caution, meant the seven rites to which the word "sacrament" was "most commonly applied in the Middle Ages." Stone supported the doctrine of baptismal regeneration in an absolute manner and held a view of transubstantiation, though he had philosophical reservations about the term.

The Eucharist differs from other sacraments as regards the effect produced in the matter itself. In the case of Baptism the matter, that is, the water, is used as an instrument whereby a result is effected in the person who is baptised; but the water itself remains water only. In the case of the Eucharist the matter, that is, the bread and the wine, not only is used as the instrument whereby the person who receives the Sacrament is benefited, but also becomes the body and blood of our Lord.[24]

Within the general diversity of opinion, mention should also be made of William Temple's essay on the church in *Foundations*. This article

[23] Darwell Stone, *Outlines of Christian Dogma* (London: Longmans, Green, 1900), pp. 107-8; also *The Christian Church* (New York: Edwin S. Gorham, 1906), Chap. I.
[24] *Outlines of Christian Dogma*, pp. 176-77; also pp. 158, 184.

was neither as distinguished nor as immediately significant as his essay on Christology, but it was distinctive in that it attempted to carry the implications of the earlier essay into the elucidation of the meaning of the Christian community. For Temple the church was the body of the resurrection, the society of those who are "risen and ascended with Christ." [25] In the language of his earlier essay, which we shall look at more closely in a later chapter, the church is the organ of the "will" of Christ, and in this sense it is the continuation of his purpose. With this mention of the church as the completion of God's will in Christ for all mankind, Temple in his own way agreed with the general Anglican insistence that the church is a continuation of the incarnation; although he was careful throughout to make a clear distinction between the perfection that belongs to Jesus Christ and the imperfection of the empirical church. Temple spent the greater part of his article exploring the character of the church as expressed through the Eucharist—the supreme symbol of the church's nature—and in its unity. In the end, he claimed, the sacramental life of the church—that is, as it continues the embodiment of the will of Christ—shall reach its consummation when Christ shall bring all things unto himself.

The general character of Temple's presentation represents a mediating position in the present controversies, but whether such mediation was possible on the grounds he suggested was the important question. Rawlinson's appendix, "The Christian Ministry," in the same volume also attempts this mediatorial role. It is impossible, he claimed, to trace historically the explicit development of apostolic succession, although one can establish the threefold ministry at least in the second century. Nonetheless, on theological rather than historical grounds he felt there was predominant value in retaining the historic episcopate. The continuing authority of the episcopacy, he maintained, embodies the principle of continuity with the past, the idea of authority is enlarged beyond that of one local church, the office rather than the man is magnified, and it provides for the mediation of the "Catholic" type of piety.[26] But he also warned that misuse or abuse of the office must be defended against

[25] *Foundations*, pp. 339-40.
[26] *Ibid.*, p. 394.

so that no improper exercise of authority or magical view of orders is allowed.

Both of these expositions attempt to establish a middle way in the sense that they want to retain a primary place for the sacramental and ministerial character of the church, but the vital issue remained: Where is the primary authority for Christian faith and life to be found? Is it located in the visible Christian community? Is it to be located in religious experience that is sometimes mediated by the church and may be reinforced by participation in the life of the church? On this issue both Temple and Rawlinson basically agree that the church is a crucially important support to religious experience, but they do not affirm the absolute place which the church has in the establishing and sanctioning of Christian life. Because of their emphases upon the primacy of religious experience with its self-authenticating character, the church becomes an important but extrinsic means to founding and strengthening the spiritual life. Consequently, whatever they say in the way of insisting upon the significance of the church, it does not have the same functional position in their thought, nor does it have the same intrinsic importance as the church had for Gore, Moberly, or Stone. This discussion does, however, help to make clear once again the manner in which the Doctrine of the church was ingredient to seeking viable foundations —the name of their volume was not without point—for a Christian way of life.

RECAPITULATION

The discussion of the doctrine of the church once again lifts up the great theological variety that characterized the Church of England. The social and cultural transformation precipitated heated self-interpretation, and perhaps the external pressures made the internal discussion all the more intense and sharply focused. Several major issues help to delineate the alternatives that were supported. Fundamental to the entire discussion was the issue of authority. The search was for viable foundations in the Christian community, foundations that would serve as a sure anchor in the convulsive wave that was sweeping away inherited sanctions. For some, such as Gore and Stone, the doctrine of apostolic succession and the consequent validity of ministerial orders served to provide this support. For a more liberal interpreter like Rashdall, the individual conscience and reason were the seat of final authority, and the church was useful as an institution insofar as it enhanced and supported the Christian person. For conservative interpreters among the evangelicals the biblical authority remained absolute, and the institutional life of the redeemed community must always be referred to this presumably clear norm.

Historical investigation combined with the changing social ethos to force such discussion upon the Christian community. As a result of the studies of the late nineteenth century, two cardinal issues were singled out: the question of the role of the episcopacy, and the emphasis upon the visible church. The significance of the episcopacy was universally acknowledged, and within the Church of England there was no disposition to deny this inheritance. There was wide divergence, however, in regard to the source of an episcopal form of government. For some, eg., Gore, Moberly, and Stone, it was written into the fabric of the church in such a manner that it belonged to the very essence of the church. For many others it was a utilitarian development that, though it was not intrinsic to the life of the church as such, had proved to be a successful polity and should be retained as contributing to the well-being of institutional Christian life. This position was held by the Cambridge scholars Hort and Lightfoot, the evangelicals, and broad churchmen such as Wordsworth and Rashdall. In the split over the issue of apostolic succession distinct differences in the understanding of its own nature cut deeply through the Anglican Church.

Connected with the question of episcopacy were the diverse interpretations of the church as visible or invisible and how this related to its most authentic expression. The continuity of the *esse* of the church with its visible form was stressed by those who tended to "Catholic" rather than "Protestant" interpretations of the Body of Christ; also, among the former, the church as the continuing incarnation was emphasized. If Jesus instituted the church and gave it an organizational form then the true church is to be found where these forms are historically actualized. If, however, organization is taken to be secondary to a redeeming relationship with Christ, a missionary task, or both; and if it is believed that Jesus did not intend any single form of polity; and if it is acknowledged that the visible church contains both wheat and tares, then the emphasis is placed upon the invisible church.

The invisible church, as it was usually interpreted, is composed of those whom God alone knows to be within his redeemed fellowship. Men cannot know who all these members are, nor does participation in the life and ritual of an institutional structure insure participation in the true church of God. Penultimate value must be assigned to the visible church. Open to the variant situations to which it must witness, the visible community must always point beyond itself to the purposes (divergent as these were with the different interpreters) for which it exists.

The question of the purpose or purposes for which the church exists brings us to the crux of the discussion of the nature of the church. Underlying the variant interpretations of the commission and character of the Body of Christ was the question of the place and validity of the sacraments. Those who represented a more "Catholic" or high church position were fundamentally convinced that the gospel was continued and preached through the sacramental life of the church, and a valid sacramental exercise was the church's most significant task. While the sacraments were not unimportant for the other interpreters, they were of extrinsic value or subserved other aspects of the church's existence. Thus the question of whether the ministry of the church was sacerdotal was a critical question for Gore and Moberly as well as for those who disagreed with them, such as Lightfoot or Rashdall. If the sacraments were at the center of the institution's existence and if they were correctly administered, then the Spirit of Christ was present, and the true church was drawn around the sacrament. There may be among the worshipers wheat and tares, but the church is visibly present in the sacrament, and it continues to live in those who have authority to perform the sacramental rites. For those who did not so singularly stress the sacraments the reality of the church's life was to be found in the faith and life of its continuing membership, in both their personal commitment and life of service.

Throughout the era, the discussion of the nature of the church was never completely separated from the question of an established national church. The older interpretations of Hooker, which stressed the inherent interinvolvement of the church and state, were almost universally rejected. The freedom and independence of the church were recognized as a necessity, but the mutual responsibility of religious and civil powers continued to be emphasized. The national church was important for utilitarian purposes, but only if both the religious community and the civil government were well-served was the interconnection of significant value and worth preserving. What the specific value was would be cause for continuing debate.

In concentrating upon the doctrine of the church within the Anglican communion we have inadequately stressed the growing awareness of the need to carry on discussion of this theological issue with the Nonconformists, and to this development we shall turn in the next chapter. Although some would disagree on exact details of the arrangement, Hastings Rashdall expressed a concern of great numbers when he wrote just prior to the coronation of Edward VII,

On the Coronation Day the Church of England will stand forth conspicuously before all men as the representative of our national Christianity. That is her true position. She claims to be not the only branch, but the most ancient, the most comprehensive, the typical and representative branch of that Church of Christ which consists essentially of all Christ's followers in this land. Would not her position be all the stronger if a future coronation should see the representatives of the leading Nonconformist bodies assisting officially in the ceremony, and joining in communion with the Sovereign and the bishops? If such a ceremony were possible, if such an honorary and historic primacy among sister Churches should come to represent the habitual relation between the Church of England and the Churches in England, the Church of England would have become at one and the same time doubly national and doubly catholic.[27]

With such hope, some in the Church of England entered the new and troubled century.

[27] *Christus in Ecclesia*, p. 314.

VII

DOCTRINES OF THE CHURCH: NONCONFORMITY

Dissent was born as a new type of churchmanship; consequently the doctrine of the church was a central issue for the Free Churches in England. Originally, the Free Churches had attempted to express two principles in their ecclesiology—first, the membership of the visible church should approximate as closely as possible that of the invisible church; and, second, polity should embody the intention of Jesus Christ as this was revealed in the Scriptures. By the last half of the nineteenth century confidence in these principles was beginning to dissolve. The erosion of confidence was due to the interaction of several factors: the biblical warrant was made ambiguous by critical research, depreciation of liturgical forms raised a concomitant question about the nature and significance of the sacraments, and the effort to enhance the role of the laity tended to undercut the unique role of the ministry. At the same time, the role of Nonconformity in the national life with its gain in social and political power effected a redirection of attention from the interior life of the church to involvement in its sociopolitical environment.

We have already mentioned the revolt against dogmatic theology that characterized the Free Churches at the turn of the century. This revolt, as John Webster Grant indicates, was not merely an opposition to creeds as such, but on a wider front, it was a revolt against the idea that a church is defined by common beliefs.[1] The results of this depreciation of doctrine had important implications for the churches' self-understanding. Uncertainty about the doctrinal base of the polity of the Free Churches led to pragmatic and expedient justifications of their structure. No longer was there a general confidence that their polity represented anything more than a peculiar historical development and, having lost the assurance of a biblically based ecclesiology, interest was turned to the practical responsibilities of the Christian community. Furthermore, the interpretation of the sacraments increasingly represented a retreat from traditional Calvinism and R. W. Dale could claim that even by the 1870's Congregationalists had become "For the most part Zwinglians of the purest type."[2] This tendency to move away from their distinctive sources continued among the Congregationalists through the turn of the century, and the development of the New Theology emphasized the difficulty of discussing the church in terms of its peculiar life or divine purpose. On the whole, the church was described in terms of its practical functions and its contribution to man's spiritual and social self-fulfillment. Hence, the Christian community was increasingly interpreted as a useful instrument for the establishment of a new social order, or, in R. J. Campbell's conception, as a means of bringing in the kingdom of God. But even among those who did not follow the trail of the New Theologians, the belief that the church was of intrinsic value had fallen by the wayside, and there was no widespread mourning its loss. In general, it may be claimed that the adherents of the social gospel, whether or not they were also exponents of the New Theology, evidenced little interest in questions about the theological foundations of the church or of churchmanship.

---

[1] John Webster Grant, *Free Churchmanship in England, 1870-1914*, p. 117. This is the best single source for a study of this theme in this era.

[2] Quoted in *ibid.*, p. 76.

Among the Baptists, the most pressing issue was that of centralization. Local churches found increased need for one another for benevolent activity and for practical implementation of common tasks. The growth of denominational bureaucracy seemed inevitable, and, to an increasing number, it appeared a good thing. From the time of J. H. Shakespeare's election as Secretary of the Baptist Union in 1898, this movement took on greater strength, and the dynamic personality of this leader was to carry the Baptists into interdenominational as well as intradenominational participation.

Methodists also were involved in self-reassessment. Entering the last quarter of the nineteenth century, an impetus was given to Methodist ecclesiology by the Fernley Lecture of Benjamin Gregory in 1873.[3] In these lectures, the church was defined primarily in terms of its mission; the task of the Christian community, Gregory claimed, is to convey the redeeming power of Jesus Christ to the world. No standard pattern was given by Christ for the church, but he did assign a unique place to the apostles as the symbol of unity—not so much as the foundation of the Christian community as the coping stone of its earliest structures. Throughout his discussion, Gregory distinguished between the visible and the invisible church; the invisible church is the true fellowship of the saints, and the visible church was to represent that fellowship as closely as possible. The visible church is the community of the redeemed, of those who had a genuine experience of redemption by Christ, and the historical continuity of the visible church is predicated upon the continuation of the fellowship of believers from generation to generation. Holiness is the key mark of the true Christian community, and holiness is to be found in the life of the members. Not that church members are perfect, but the most important aspect of the church's historical existence is found in their spiritual maturation. The Body of Christ represents a reality given by God; but it also stands as an ideal, as a goal to be achieved, a character of holiness to be won. Gregory concluded his book with a vision and a hope that there would be a wide, voluntary

---

[3] *The Holy Catholic Church, the Communion of Saints* (London: Wesleyan Book Room, 1885). Cf. Reginald Kissock, *Church or No Church: The Development of the Concept of Church in British Methodism* (London: Epworth, 1964), pp. 89-90.

federation of churches, varying in polity and ritual, but sharing a common faith in fundamental doctrines and in their service to the world.

All these churches, the Free Churches and the Methodists, began to sense a common alliance. In part, this commonality was a result of their shared opposition to the established Church of England. Since mid-nineteenth century there had been a strenuous campaign to undercut religious establishment, and by the final decades of that century there was growing confidence, at least among the more optimistic, that establishment could be terminated by the close of the century. The desire for the state to be neutral in its treatment of the churches was strong; the slogan,"A free church in a free state," became a rallying cry not only in dissenting church conventions but also in political rallies. The argument for disestablishment was double-pronged. On the one hand, there was the contention that there should not be any preferential treatment given to any one church at the expense of others; while, on the other hand, there was the argument that the established Church was in bondage to the state and needed freedom for its own spiritual well-being (needless to say, not all Anglicans appreciated this help from the non-established churches, but, as we shall see, there were some who agreed in principle with this second argument). The most positive aspect that came out of the changed conditions was that the Methodists and Free Churches looked again at their own characters and recognized points of common self-understanding.

Early in 1890 Hugh Price Hughes requested J. Guinness Rogers, a Congregationalist, to write an article for his magazine *The Methodist Times,* and in this article Rogers broached the idea of occasionally holding Free Church congresses. At the same time, Henry Lunn, a Methodist, was engaged in organizing informal meetings of church leaders, and he called a more official meeting for Manchester in January, 1892. These ideas struck fire, and an exploratory meeting was held. On a motion by Alexander Mclaren, a Baptist minister, the group voted to convene a Free Church Congress in Manchester for November, 1892. Over 350 delegates from all the leading Free Churches, were present for this first meeting; and with enthusiasm delegates proceeded to organize the National Council of Evangelical Free Churches. The general acceptance and the impact of the council was remarkable. Denominations that had been separated and that had insisted upon their distinctiveness suddenly found it possible to accept one another in such a fellowship, and by 1899 they had produced a Catechism that manifested a basic theological agreement. In spite of this doctrinal consensus, the Free Church Council was more concerned with practical matters than with doctrine, and their newfound strength prepared them to flex their political muscles. There were, of course, those who looked with uncertainty or suspicion upon the achieved cooperation, notably R. W. Dale, but the yeast of fellowship was spreading, and some even hoped for organic forms of union.

The men who led this movement for union were a distinguished group. Hugh Price Hughes was the greatest figure in Methodism in the last decade of the nineteenth century. Although he was liberal, he never appeared on Liberal Party platforms as he hoped to keep the church politically active but uncommitted to a single party. J. Guinness Rogers and Alexander Mackennal were Congregational ministers who, as leaders of their denomination, were sensitive to the Congregational tradition in churchmanship but who saw in the Council the basis for new hope. John Clifford, an aggressive, beloved Baptist, though more radical than many of his fellow Baptist ministers, was ardent in his affection for his church, as well as the unity of the churches. F. B. Meyer, another eminent Baptist, also participated in this movement. None of these men were seeking unity as a way of denying their own peculiar past. For the leadership, at least, the effort at fraternity was a natural and valid response to the challenges of society and the developing spirit within the churches.

In addition to the meetings between the various churches, there were also signs that the individual denominations were becoming aware of their international fellowship. In July 1891, the First International Congregational Council met in London; and later, in the year 1905, the first Baptist World Congress met in London under the leadership of J. H. Shakespeare. Methodists were also moving together; several years of preparation issued in the formation of the United Methodist Free Church in 1905 from the union of the Bible Christians and the Methodist New Connection. In addition, the remaining and larger bodies of Methodists— the Wesleyan, Primitive, and United Methodists—were beginning to explore the possibility of uniting, an exploration that came to fruition in 1932.

In retrospect it is possible to trace the diverse lines along which these hopes for union were to develop. The Congregationalists and the Presbyterians grew in appreciation of common roots and mission; Baptists tended to remain separate although they participated in a number of common tasks; Methodists were redirected toward union with the Church of England. But whatever the later developments, the interest in union at the turn of the century was significant; the Nonconformist churches were adapting themselves to a new England. The older modes of individualistic pietism and evangelization were passing, and a new sense of being bound together in faith and mission was enveloping the church life.

The question of polity was an indispensable element in this fresh apprehension of joint life, and it required careful reconsideration, although the awareness of the stringency of this requirement was not generally clear. Among the Baptists, the received traditions were reaffirmed. In spite of the practical and administrative alterations, there was a tendency to keep their separate character as individual churches. Charles Williams stated the general Baptist position in 1903.

Baptists apply to a church their first principles—viz. that no individual man or community of men can rightly claim authority to prescribe what believers shall do or leave undone in the service of God. . . . They attempt to form their churches in accordance with the instructions which are given in the New Testament and after the model of the churches originated and founded by the Apostles.[4]

In addition, he claimed, the Baptists do not regard either baptism or the Lord's Supper as sacraments in the "ecclesiastical" sense of the word; that is, they are neither the cause nor the medium of grace. Baptism is to be limited to believers, and each local congregation is *per se* the church of Jesus Christ. Thus, it is within the local community that the Lord's Supper is held, for it is the special meeting of believers with one another and with Jesus Christ.

[4] *The Principles and Practices of the Baptists* (London: Kingsgate Press, 1903), p. 28.

In a similar manner, the Methodists perpetuated their own traditions. Their inherited theology was not seriously questioned, but their primary interest was centered in a pragmatic approach to institutional life and social involvement. The Methodist churches had not separated from Anglicanism over the issue of a distinctive type of churchmanship or even on directly theological grounds. Methodism had come to life as an evangelical revival within Anglicanism; it separated because of practical exigencies, and it continued to interpret its life in terms of practical considerations. Thus, J. S. Lidgett always maintained that the catholicity of the church was not defined by doctrine or by authority to administer the means of grace; the true ministry of the church is that of proclamation; the task of evangelization was central. [5]

Among the Congregationalists and Presbyterians, however, there were at least some leaders who felt the need for fresh effort to understand the nature of the church. The two theologians who led the way in the assessment of this issue were P. T. Forsyth for the Congregationalists and John Oman for the Presbyterians.

Forsyth was a dogmatic theologian, that is, he was a theologian who was interested in the confessional and systematic aspects of theology; further, he was completely convinced that any valid ordering of church worship or ministry had to be rooted in its "dogmatic" foundation, a foundation that he referred to as "Jesus is Lord and God." [6] Upon this base, there is to be developed the "doctrinal" interpretation. Doctrine represents the church's explication of its dogma; it is dogma expanded as ecclesiastical consensus matures. Finally, there is the more adventurous "theology" that freely investigates, speculates, and helps winnow the pure grain of doctrine. The church always stands in need of all three dimensions of activity—the reaffirmation of its dogma, respect for its doctrine, and vigor in its exploratory theology.

The immediate cause of Forsyth's deep concern over the dogmatic foundation of the church was the radical challenge that the decline of churchmanship in general and the use of the New Theology in

---

[5] *Apostolic Ministry*, 113-14.

[6] *Theology in Church and State* (London: Hodder & Stoughton, 1915), pp. 3 ff. Cf. also *Faith, Freedom and the Future* (London: Independent Press, second impression 1955), p. 285 for a discussion of the role of the church.

particular had precipitated. The entire conception of God, he claimed, was in danger of being shifted from that of divine majesty to the single significance of being a servant to man. But the God who exists for man's benefit in the end becomes depressingly boring, and such a conception undercuts both the life and mission of the church. Thus the recovery of an adequate view of God as revealed in Jesus Christ, i.e., the re-finding of the church's dogma, was the prime essential of the time. Only the church that is self-understanding is, in the last analysis, of any service to men; and only the church that is doctrinally understanding can adequately offer its worship to its sovereign Lord.

Forsyth's chief contribution to ecclesiology is to be found in his book *The Church and the Sacraments.* In describing his position, Forsyth wrote, "The view here taken is neither memorial and Zwinglian nor is it High Catholic. It is sacramental but not sacramentarian, effective but not sacrificial. . . . The audience is Free Church, but the treatment means to be Great Church."[7] In his effort to present his theological interpretation of the church, Forsyth began at his usual point: the church is founded by the gospel, "The Church is where that gospel is."[8] That is to say, the gospel that proclaims the redemptive activity of God in the death of Jesus Christ is the foundation stone of the church. The church is created by the gospel; it is the reality of the cross that calls the community into being and preserves it in being. The church and the gospel are inseparable; for the Body of Christ has its existence in the life-giving power of the One whose coming is gospel. Thus, the gospel is the basis of the church without which it cannot exist and without which it has no purpose in the world.

In distinction from the usual Anglican positions of the time, Forsyth clearly set his own direction, ". . . the Church has a more direct connection with Redemption than with Incarnation. . . . The Church is not the continuation of Christ, but His creation and His response."[9] The church is the redeemed society; it is the community that has been created by the redeeming activity of Jesus Christ, and it is the community that exists to proclaim—through the means of grace and through

---

[7] *The Church and the Sacraments,* p. xv.
[8] *Ibid.,* p. 134.
[9] *Ibid.,* p. 83.

its service to the world—the continuing power of that redemption. On this interpretation, the church is, so to speak, the atonement becoming actual among men in the constitution of a new humanity.

If the gospel is the originating power of the church, what is its organizational form? In answer to this question Forsyth was clear that every form of the church must subserve its mission as the bearer of the gospel. "The true Church is where the Gospel creates its own institutions, prescribed by the situation, and flexible to it for God's purpose; and where the existence of a professional ministry witnesses that a Gospel for life must issue in a life for the Gospel." [10] In explicating the character of the organized Christian community, as seen from this perspective, several features are emphasized. First, the church rests upon an objective fact—the fact of God's grace. The fellowship of the church is the fruit of this grace, for Christian love for one another is predicated upon and is a response to God's love for man. Secondly, the church is a divine creation and not a voluntary association. With this insistence, Forsyth turned his back on all "social contract" theories of the church, theories that were prominent among Free Churchmen. The regeneration wrought by Jesus Christ convokes a gathering of a people. In direct repudiation of Hatch's theory that the church was like other secular institutions that are created to perform certain specifiable acts or to attain specific goals that men might establish, Forsyth insists that the church has a uniqueness; it is formed by God; it is the community that has been regenerated by grace and that is given its tasks by that grace. The church is the gathering of those who have been called by God and who have accepted the redemption and discipleship that he has proffered. This means that *"the same act which sets us in Christ sets us also in the society of Christ."* [11] To be in Christ is to be in the church, and any act that is made to join the people of Christ—e.g., an act of confession—is only making explicit what is already implicit, namely, incorporation into Christ. Finally, the church has its unity in Christ; that is, his redemptive act creates the Body of Christ. The church has unity in the fundamental sense that it has one Redeemer, it has a common source of its life, and a common providence for its

[10] *Ibid.*, p. 49.
[11] *Ibid.*, p. 61. Cf. p. 65 for the reference to Hatch.

preservation. Because of the inviolate primacy of Jesus Christ in the church, he reigns as absolute monarch. To describe the gathered community in democratic terms is to detract from the true nature and existence of the church's constitution. The first word about the people of God, therefore, is that they belong to Christ in an absolute manner; the church exists under the sovereign righteousness of its Redeemer and Founder.

The continuation of the church is guaranteed by its apostolic nature. Once again Forsyth exhibits his distinctive perception, as he argued that the real successor of the apostolic authority is to be found not in the continuing hierarchy but in the canonical scripture. Consequently, the actual church always has two dimensions to its life: it is a local congregation, and it is a part of the one church, drawn to unity by its Lord. What this means is that the one church has many manifestations. "The Church in the town, or in the house of So-and-so, means the total Church as emerging there, looking out there, taking effect there. The Church in the great sense is not composite, but organic. Its life is given to its members, not compiled from them. The Churches, no less than their souls, are members of one another."[12] The true Body of Christ appears locally, temporally, incompletely. Where there are people gathered together by Christ, there is the church. Thus the church is not a means to the kingdom, it is the kingdom in the making, it is the kingdom coming-to-be in a particular place and time.

The role of the ministry in this body is essential. "The Church is made by its gospel, and the gospel is the special trust of the ministry in the Church, as it is of the Church within the world."[13] In appointing its ministers, the community simply confirms and conforms to the already present call of God. The church has selective power, but it does not have creative power in regard to its ministry. Nonetheless, the ministry is crucial. Its significance is to be found in its proclamation, in its recital of the redeeming event of Jesus' death. In this sense, the ministry is sacramental for the total Body in that the ministry has been entrusted with the vital core of the church's existence; and, in

[12] *Ibid.,* pp. 66-67.
[13] *Ibid.,* p. 130.

the final analysis, the servants of the Word proclaim the distinctive gospel that creates and sustains the redeemed community.

A major concern of Forsyth was the ecumenical character of the church. Convinced of the importance of acknowledged unity in Christ, he became an exponent of union. The type of union he envisioned was that of "the United States of the Church," that is, a federal inclusiveness of the Body of Christ. Sectarianism was deplored, for it failed to recognize the common rootage of all churches, and it frustrated the mission of the church. At the same time, absorption or organic unity was not a part of his hope; the united church was to be a federated community. So strong was his conviction of this need, he wrote, "The Kingdom of God can only come by the Church of God, and only by a united, free and independent Church." [14] The ideal for which he contended was a "Christocracy" that was superior to both autocracy or democracy. The structure of the church should be fashioned in such a way as to make the Lordship of Jesus Christ absolutely clear and to bring all other structures and functions under the guidance of his redemptive purpose.

Finally, Forsyth made a strenuous effort to resuscitate the importance of the preached word and the sacraments, which he preferred to call the means of grace. The proclaimed word and the two sacraments are the two primary expressions of the gospel in the worship of the church. All three of these means of grace need to be reset within the corporate life of the Christian community, for they are the acts of Christ present through the Holy Spirit. They are not individual acts, and they are not simply symbols unrelated to the real presence of Christ. These sacramental events convey the gospel message of redemption—the gospel that created and sustains the church and to which she witnesses by the continuation of her sacramental worship. As against many of the prevalent Nonconformist attitudes, Forsyth attempted to reassert the real presence of Christ in the sacraments and the continuing importance of sacramental administration to the proclamation of the gospel.

Quite apart from the question of the intrinsic worth of the interpretation of the church that was propounded by Forsyth, it is difficult

[14] *Ibid.,* p. 120.

to assess its influence upon Congregational thought in general. R. W. Dale had in the last half of the nineteenth century endeavored to reclaim a sacramental emphasis and had attempted to renew interest in a strong doctrine of the church as a sacramental institution. After the turn of the century W. E. Orchard, of King's Road Chapel in London, had moved in the direction of high churchmanship but finally converted to Roman Catholicism.[15] Others followed Forsyth's lead more closely, but the majority resisted any movement toward sacramental renewal or doctrinal churchmanship. Consequently, the movement toward high churchmanship—even in the sense of Forsyth's position—did not win a majority of the church.

Among the Presbyterians, the leader in the effort to reinvestigate the nature of the church was John Oman. F. R. Tennant once remarked that Oman's creativity and originality were evidenced by the fact that he did not owe so much to any one as to himself—a tribute not lightly given. Oman wrote three books that dealt with the church, and for a man who was not unusually prolific, the proportion indicates the importance that he attached to the subject. In the preface to the first of these books, *Vision and Authority,* he stated the reason for his interest: namely, the present divisions in the English churches (this was written during the struggle over the education act and disestablishment). "Nothing short of a return to first principles . . . affords hope of a solution which shall neither fail in charity nor in earnestness."[16] As a response to this situation, Oman presented an interpretation of the church that, he was convinced, would most directly meet the valid demands of the time and of the Christian message. Building upon his conception of authority, which he understood as the appeal of truth to man's capacity for spiritual insight, he defined the church as the community of those people who have acknowledged Jesus as the truth. According to Oman God always begins his activity with individuals, and so the church also has its beginning where individuals name the name of Jesus with the insight that Peter possessed. Yet the church also implies a corporate group, a company of people. So it is that the Body of Christ is truly

---

[15] Cf. his autobiography, *From Faith to Faith* (London: Putnam, 1933).
[16] *Vision and Authority,* p. 132.

constituted as two or more believers come together in common worship of God and have love among themselves. Essentially, no more than two are needed to constitute an authentic Christian community, and any increase must be understood as simply an expansion of this primary fellowship. Against the charge that this means an individualistic Christianity where corporate life is not adequately realized, Oman made two replies. First, even though the supreme religious subject is the individual, it is not the individual as a discrete unit; rather, it is the individual in his "place," it is the individual accepting his position in the universe as God's creature, in human relationships as a free man in a kingdom of free men, and in worship as participant in a long tradition of men who have shared his faith.[17] Second, to worship Christ in the company of one's fellows is to be made a part of a new social order. The old order was heteronomous, it represented an attempt to bring cohesion by the use of arbitrary, external sanctions. But the new order of Christian community is the shared experience of freedom. And such freedom, which comes from the worship of God, is acknowledged by this newly created community, so that the integrity of each is valued and the responsibility of each is nurtured. "The obedience of the free among the free" becomes the watchword of the true fellowship.[18]

Oman played down the place of institutional forms and external modes of discipline. The continuity of the Christian fellowship is rooted in the succession not of office but of insight, not of historical continuity but of spiritual affinity, which comes with the sense of a shared goal. With slightly muted disdain he denounced the pretentions to apostolic succession, and grounded his understanding of continuity in unity that is found in fellowship.[19]

One reason for sitting extremely light to church orders and rituals was to be found in Oman's distrust of all human authority; but a second reason was based upon his conviction that the church is not an end in itself, rather it serves the kingdom of God. That is to say, the people of God are called to serve all humanity, not to enlarge their

[17] *Ibid.*, pp. 81-82.
[18] *Ibid.*, p. 167. Also *The Church and the Divine Order* (London: Hodder & Stoughton, 1911), p. 50.
[19] *Vision and Authority*, pp. 124-27, 130.

own importance; the church has been called to give herself in the service of freedom, not to become a heteronomous authority. The rule of the Christian community should read,

Organize a church by insight and love and not by power under any disguise. This alone may be all comprehensive. . . . They are true Catholics who worship God by the spirit of God, and need no aid of sacerdotal ally . . . and have no confidence in mere largeness and visibility of organization or earthly rank of church dignitary or earthly splendour in priest or temple.[20]

What are the organizing authority and the regulative principles of the gathered fellowships? Oman began with a clear separation between the effort of secular societies to organize on the principle of each man ruling his neighbor (to do right is clearly as much advantage to oneself as to one's neighbor, a fact that reinforces the role of constraint in society) and the principle of a Christian society that is built on the plan of each man ruling himself. Insight and discipline are needed if external authorities are to be allowed to wither away, but this is just what Christian faith and life presuppose. Hence the Christian community always lives between the two dangers of antinomianism and the imposition of external authority, but acknowledged and shared vision of God brings both freedom and community. To be Christian is to live as a person under God and this in the recognized community of fellow worshipers.

There are two visible signs that set the local fellowship apart: the creed and its organization. In regard to the creed, Oman was careful not to attempt a catechetical statement; rather, his emphasis was upon the personal influence of Jesus Christ. The word "personal" in this description has a double meaning. In the first place, it is personal in that grace is manifest in this person; grace is not a power, it is a person, it is Jesus Christ. But, secondly, man's experience of God in the person of Jesus is responded to in such a way that it is an immediate, personal experience of the believer. Revelation is found in the interaction between persons, and the integrity of each is the cardinal reality that must be safeguarded. If this understanding of revelation be accepted, then it

[20] *Ibid.*, pp. 156-57.

follows that the great creedal affirmations find their certainty not where the system is most completely articulated, but when the experience of the faithful is most assured. "Men are not all able to give a name to their thoughts about this Man, but if faith in Him always means power in conflict and peace in trial, they must in their heart of hearts give Him the name that is above every name."[21] Thus no church can retain any article in her creed that she is not able to demonstrate in her life. A viable "creed" is not to be understood as formulated doctrine but as shared vision, as common acknowledgment of the Lordship of Jesus, as experienced fellowship with God and fellow believers, and as a directive to Christian service.

But the actual, concrete church must have some policy, some guidelines for her communal life and work, for the church must not only attract but must also marshal resources of men and their means. Whatever the institution undertakes, however, she must exercise her authority in conformity with the method of Christ, that is, she must utilize her authority in such a way as clearly acknowledges the integrity of those with whom she is dealing. Theoretically, there is no one valid form of the community. All types of organization may be inspired by the same spirit, yet some forms serve that spirit better than others. Consequently, the continuing effort of every church must be to organize itself in such a way as to enhance the fellowship of love and to encourage individual freedom and responsibility.

In relation to this theological context, it is not surprising that Oman explicitly rejected Gore's interpretation of the origin and nature of the church. Jesus, Oman claimed, did not found a society, provide officers with external authority, or make a sharp distinction between clergy and laity. Many things count against Gore's claim, including some New Testament evidence—especially Jesus' concern for the nation as a whole and his apocalyptic expectation. The apostles were such only in regard to a special mission of healing and teaching upon which they were sent (here he followed the study of F. J. Hort); their true designation was that of disciples. Also the Last Supper referred only to Jesus' imminent suffering and the kingdom of God; it was a rite that, rather than

[21] *Ibid.*, p. 229.

turning some of his followers into sacrificing priests, sealed his disciples into a fellowship in which the cross becomes the unifying symbol of life and service. There is no ecclesiastical program or hierarchy; the church is a society based on love, equality, and common service. The movement from the centrality of the prophetic to the centrality of the office of the bishop (this was Hatch's thesis) was the greatest loss to the church.[22]

As would be expected from the movement of this presentation, Oman was hostile to the entire idea of a state church. The principle reason he gave for this opposition was that it was built upon an inadequate understanding of both Christian faith and Christian community. Richard Hooker was the chief offender in establishing the theological foundations for such an idea, but his entire conception was built upon the false notions that the confession of Jesus as Lord is an outward confession, that faith is the acceptance of certain articles of belief, and that baptism as a rite admits one into a visible society. On this foundation, Hooker easily built a theory that related the visible church with the nation.[23] Against this, Oman maintained that the church must have its own life in order to acknowledge God's rule of freedom through faith, and in order to share this realized freedom with others by its prophetic witness.

We have looked at Forsyth and Oman at some length, but this was necessary, for in these men we have two of the most distinctive and thoroughly explicated doctrines of the church to be found within the Free Churches. In the contrast between their positions was to be found the options that were most obviously open to serious theological reflection among the Nonconformists.

In the dissenting churches, as in Anglicanism, a struggle with the question of authority led to a reassessment of the nature of the church. The organizational life of the Christian community and the influence of the denominational bodies upon civic and cultural life, as well as upon their own votaries, were all open to investigation and reevaluation.

It was typical of Nonconformist thought in spite of Forsyth, that the emphasis was upon the invisible church; God has called and knows who are true participants in the life of Christ. The visible church has

---

[22] *The Church and the Divine Order*, pp. 23-24, 46-52, 105.
[23] *Ibid.*, p. 260.

no single valid form, nor is it to be accorded a status that makes it more than an extrinsic value to the realization of God's will in the world. Consequently neither a continuous form of community life nor a special status to an unbroken leadership was considered essential. The viability of the church's form is reckoned only in terms of stewardship in regard to its mission.

But variant interpretations of mission issued in divergent conceptions of the most authentic style of church life. For Forsyth and Lidgett, who stressed the doctrine of atonement, the essential life of the church was to be found in its proclamation—by word, sacrament, fellowship, and service—of this redemptive event. For Oman, who stressed the orders of God that enhanced moral selfhood, the church must be so structured and must so assert its authority as to lead to full moral maturation. In both cases theological presuppositions determined the understanding of church organization.

Among the more significant factors of Nonconformist churchmanship were the growing interest in ecumenical life and the awareness of the influence of the dissenting churches upon society. Church unity was the child of internal developments and external pressures. Internally, the different denominations were becoming increasingly aware of the values they shared in common with others of their denomination around the world and with others of Free Church or Protestant persuasion. Externally, there was increasing recognition that union was efficient and provided new strength. In a social environment that increasingly challenged Christian commitment, unity was not a luxury. In a context that called for a strong Christian mission, union was a necessity. A troubled history of growing separation and recurrent splintering was firmly braked as a new vision of a possible oneness of Christ's people was more generally shared. For these reasons, the twentieth century was to be the ecumenical century.

Social and political influence by the dissenting churches was acknowledged to be a necessity by their adherents. Already, some argued that signs of their power were to be found in amended educational laws, legislation for better working conditions, shifts in social status and economic policy. Nevertheless, within the Nonconformist churches the relation between their own churches and the state was not a settled issue.

Was their role a prophetic one? Was there to be an identification of Christianity with socialism? What were the differences between the religious and civic communities? If Nonconformity did not have to struggle with the question of its own establishment—however it might debate the case of the Church of England—it did have a similar problem in regard to the mutual conditioning of church and society.

With both of these questions of ecumenism and social responsibility, the Nonconformists were led to a renewed effort at self-interpretation. In this they were not distinctive, for with both issues they shared problems that were common to the life of every Christian community in the era.

By the turn of the century there were also signs of mutual awareness and creative interchange between Anglicans and non-established churchmen. One of the most illuminating documents of the era for capturing the main themes and the flavor of the discussion that developed was to be found in a report by William Sanday on a conference held at Oxford, December 13-14, 1899. [24] Among the members present at the conference were Father Puller of the Society of St. John the Evangelist, Cowley, St. John; C. G. Lang, high churchman and future Archbishop of Canterbury; Moberly, Gore, and Holland from the *Lux Mundi* group; Archdeacon Wilson of Rochdale and E. R. Barnard of Salisbury, broad churchmen; a Reverend Mr. Davison from the Wesleyans; Fairbairn, Arnold Thomas, and Forsyth, who were Congregationalists; the Reverend Mr. Salmon of Aberdeen from the Church of Scotland; as well as Arthur Headlam, an independent-minded Anglican theologian; and Sanday, the moderator. The purpose of the conference was to explore points of agreement or at least mutual understanding, a possibility that seemed bright as the spirit of the participants was cordial. The resulting document is an excellent rendition of the tone and content of the discussion.

In the course of the interchange the variety of positions was clearly stated. Archdeacon Wilson set the tone for the broad churchmen.

We assume that the fact of our Lord's conferring on His Apostles, and on the whole Church, the gift of the Holy Spirit, and promising His own perpetual

[24] *Different Conceptions of Priesthood and Sacrifice* (London: Longmans, Green, 1900).

181

presence wherever men gather in His Name, as it assures the Church of a perpetual advance into the clearer interpetation of His Mind and Will, so also it gives to every generation the indefeasible right of self-government and adjustment to needs; and bids us look for the absolute and ideal truth respecting the function of a ministry in each age, not as something to be extracted solely from the thoughts of the past, but as something to be won by patient truth seeking, and by lives led by the spirit of Christ.[25]

The most sustained struggle, however, was between the high churchmen and the broad churchmen who sided with the nonconformists, and issues were engaged at several crucial points. First, there was the question of the uniqueness and finality of the propitiatory work of Jesus Christ, a question that bothered the evangelicals because of the eucharistic interpretation of the high churchmen. After some probing and questioning Gore and Holland made very clear statements that they held the atoning work of the cross to be unique; though for Gore the concept of "sacrifice" was more inclusive and could be applied to the sacrament of the Lord's Supper, "propitiation" was limited to the work of Jesus on the cross, once for all. Father Puller and Lang preferred to speak of an eternal atonement, and Moberly remained rather ambiguous as to his own stance in this regard.

Moberly, by his statement, raised the second major issue: what is the relation of Christ to the church? Repeating a sentence he had used in his earlier work on the church, *Ministerial Priesthood,* he held that, "What Christ is, the Church is; because the Church is the body, whose breath is the spirit of Christ; because the Church is Christ." [26] Gore reiterated his agreement by asserting that the very essence of Christianity is the realization of Christ in the visible body of the church. Fairbairn questioned Moberly about the continuity of the Spirit and the church. Moberly replied in a statement that exposed the cardinal issue.

I do not think it would be right to say *simpliciter* . . . that where the Spirit of Christ is, there is the Church. In other words, I believe that, while the whole meaning of the Church is Spirit, there is, nonetheless, such a thing as a *true* and *proper* outward organization of the Church; and that in the orderly

[25] *Ibid.,* p. 52.
[26] *Ibid.,* p. 143.

continuity of that organization is the due historical expression of the Spirit on earth.[27]

This was the most difficult hurdle to agreement—two forms of church government, each of which was taken by its proponents to be valid, but one, at least, claimed to be the only "true" and "proper" outward organization. Forsyth, at the very end of the meeting asked Gore what difference it would make to the definition and organization of the church if it were found that the New Testament church was congregational in its form of organization? Gore replied, "It would make the vastest difference. I think that all New Testament considerations lead not to the congregational but to the other view." [28]

Here was the dividing point, but there was also at least one important agreement, namely the almost universal interest in the continuity of the church and concurrence that the priestly function belongs to the Body of Christ—that is, the priesthood of the whole body was affirmed. The broad churchmen seemed less interested in this theme than were either the *Lux Mundi* members or the Nonconformists. But Gore, Moberly, Fairbairn, and Forsyth all made this a point of their agreement.

Sanday, in his editorial comments, emphasized that the most fundamental division was over the question of psychology, and this as expressed by Canon Bernard and Moberly. Bernard argued that no view of "mystical union" ought to be taken that evacuates the meaning of a personal, independent existence of each soul.[29] The fundamental question is that of the relation of Christ to the individual. Moberly, in contrast, stated, "Whether we think of the individual personality of a Christian, or of the Christian corporate body as a whole, I think we are wrong when we essay to find what either is by itself. . . . Either individual personality or the corporate Church, is what it is by virtue of an identity of spirit more than of body—with Christ." [30] Forsyth complained of this "Ecclesiastical pantheism," but in these definitions resided the heart of the

---

[27] *Ibid.,* p. 168. Moberly went on to say that he reserved any judgment about those who were not members of this visible body, but he did hold their ministry to be irregular.

[28] *Ibid.,* p. 171.

[29] *Ibid.,* p. 143.

[30] *Ibid.*

discussion of the nature of the church, and it was also to carry over into the understanding of the person of Jesus Christ.

Interest in church cooperation, and possibly union, continued with quickening tempo especially after the turn of the century. But if the general pace was faster it was also sporadic, for impedimenta arose as self-understanding required pauses for introspection, as conflicts and tensions developed both within Anglicanism—such as the Thompson affair, *Foundations* and Kikuyu—and Nonconformity—such as the New Theology movement, and as intradenominational union was considered and sometimes effected. But the ecumenical spirit was blowing where it would, and its most concrete expression was the interdenominational conference at Edinburgh in 1910. The effort of this meeting was to find ways in which the various churches could join together in their missionary concern and activity. Hopes were high that this would lead the churches into closer unity through mutual understanding and the sharing of common tasks. In one important sense the hopes were realized, and Edinburgh came to represent a major milestone on the way to a strong ecumenical movement and the World Council of Churches. Once again, the movement was not straightforward, progress was juxtaposed with wariness, dubiety, and some opposition. But, even at the time of its meeting, the Edinburgh Conference was viewed by many as an adumbration of a new era in the life of the Christian churches. In florid language W. H. T. Gairdner described the opening session of this conference.

So the delegates pass up the slope on this evening of the 14th of June 1910, towards their council-hall on that historic ridge. There, on its sky-line, dark against the late, mellow radiance of the neverending northern summer day, are the corona of the old Cathedral, the spire and twin towers of the two Assembly-Halls . . . Edinburgh! city of memories, of symbolic pictures from the past! . . . Is "Edinburgh" to be also, one wonders, a city of hopes, the symbol and indicator of something that is yet to be? [31]

Perhaps it was. Certainly for many churchmen it was a significant climax to much work and hope and, possibly, it was also a sign of things to come.

[31] *Edinburgh 1910* (Edinburgh: Oliphant, Anderson and Ferrier, 1910), pp. 33-34.

VIII

CHRISTOLOGY: LOGOS AND KENOSIS

Christology was the culminating issue in the religious thought of prewar England. That the doctrine had this position was not because of the distinctive contribution of English theology either in terms of uniqueness of theory or impressiveness of accomplishment. Indeed, a discussion of this christological development may properly begin with at least mild disclaimers about its importance in any purely theoretical sense;[1] but the discussion does have significance and, in its own way, uniqueness, for it is in Christology that the disparate issues of the era were drawn together.

[1] H. R. Mackintosh has commented with candor, "Apart from the Unitarian positions defended with so much dignity and impressiveness through a long series of years by the late Dr. Martineau, we do not find in the theology of English-speaking races much that need be chronicled [from nineteenth century thought], whether in the way of external criticism or interior expansion of traditional Christian doctrine." *Doctrine of the Person of Jesus Christ* (Edinburgh: T. and T. Clark, 1912), p. 275. Cf. also William Sanday, *Christologies Ancient and Modern* (Oxford: Clarendon Press, 1910), p. 59.

In retrospect, it must be remembered that the close of the nineteenth century was not the first period of English post-Reformation church life when there was an erosion of creedal foundations. In the second quarter of this same century the Oxford Movement had arisen as an effort to secure and reinvigorate creedal Christianity after more than fifty years of neglect. Explicitly, the culmination of this movement, in regard to Christology, found expression in H. P. Liddon's Bampton Lectures of 1866, lectures that were a powerful effort to reaffirm the full authority of the Nicean formulation in which Jesus of Nazareth was declared to be God incarnate. Both facets of the formulation were stressed. Liddon clearly affirmed the humanity of Jesus, for this too was in the creed; but he was convinced that the most serious doctrinal threat was presently coming from those who would deny or compromise Jesus' divine nature. His thesis was stated with directness: "Our Lord Jesus Christ, being truly and perfectly Man, is also, according to His Higher Pre-existent Nature Very and Eternal God; since it was the Second Person of the Ever Blessed Trinity, Who, at the Incarnation, robed Himself with a Human Body and a Human Soul." [2] Liddon defended this traditional statement in its full extent; thus, although he insisted that Jesus Christ, as man, participated in the full range of human existence, he placed his main stress upon the fact that this man was also God, and, as God, Jesus possessed all the divine attributes—omnipotence, omniscience, and omnipresence, as well as holiness, love, and justice.

These lectures were a forthright, undiluted statement of traditional orthodoxy. But the dominant spirit of the time was increasingly unprepared to accept a reiteration of a past decision, and especially a past decision that seemed so distant from current, perplexing issues. Thus, within a generation of the time of Liddon's lectures several new emphases in christological interpretation appeared, emphases that represented efforts to meet some of the interrogations that were being forced upon theology. Once again, the question of authority loomed large, and christological discussion constituted a reinvestigating and reaffirming of this unique ground of Christian faith. The three themes

[2] *The Divinity of Our Lord and Saviour Jesus Christ* (London: Longmans, Green, 1869), p. 34.

that came to clearest focus in this struggle for fresh understanding were those of immanence, *kenosis,* and the Jesus of history. We shall look at the first two of these issues in this chapter.

IMMANENCE AND LOGOS CHRISTOLOGY

The idea of the immanence of God was reinforced, as we have seen, by idealistic philosophy and the influence of evolutionary theory. The combined strength of these intellectual movements forced theology to reinterpret the activity of God in such a manner that his modes of working were continuous with both evolutionary interpretation of the processes of nature and the idealistic emphasis upon the conformity of these ideas. By means of the process of natural development, it was possible to present the theme of God's continuous creation, which worked through the natural world, reached its most distinctive expression in self-conscious human beings, and, among men, found its consummation in the person of Jesus Christ. By combining idealism and evolutionary theory a fundamental continuity from nature to man to God was maintained.[3]

So appealing was this mode of interpretation that theology at the turn of the century was increasingly attracted to these philosophical bases. In consequence, Christology, as representative of God's creating and incarnate presence in man's history, became the focal point of theological interest; but to understand this concern it is necessary to recognize the changes that were taking place in the interpretation of the person of Jesus Christ. Edward Caird succinctly indicated the basic transposition when he remarked that all of the metaphysical questions that were formally discussed in terms of the relation between the divine and the human nature of Christ were now being discussed in terms of the relation of humanity in general to God. The doctrine of the incarnation was

---

[3] J. R. Illingworth gave most direct expression to this combination when he wrote in his *Lux Mundi* essay, "Evolution is in the air. It is the category of the age; . . . It is the object of the following pages to consider what popular misconceptions of the central doctrine of religion, the Incarnation, have been remedied; what more or less forgotten aspects of it have been restored to their due place; what new lights have been thrown upon the fulness of its meaning, in the course of our discussion of the various views of evolution." "The Incarnation and Development," *Lux Mundi,* pp. 181-82.

being set into the wider context of the doctrine of creation. "There is," Leonard Hodgson wrote, "a parallel between this episode in the history of British theology and the Logos-doctrine of the Patristic age." [4] The analogy was not without point, for Jesus Christ in his twofold nature as Creator and Incarnate Lord became the central emphasis in the theology of the period, and it was no accident that such an interpretation arose when idealism was the reigning philosophical persuasion.

Emphasis upon the *logos* doctrine made God's immanence in the world a primary theological postulate. Jesus Christ was to be understood first as Creator, the second Person of the Trinity, the Creative Word or Reason (a concept that was always congenial to idealism). Understanding or rational comprehension was the desired goal, with soteriological concerns taking a second place in theological interest. It was within the context of the universal presence of God's *logos* that the particular presence of the *logos*-as-Jesus was understood; the *logos*-structure of the cosmos was given in creation, and this constitutive reality as grasped by rational man has priority over its concrete exemplification in history. Hence, the concrete event is made intelligible by its correspondence to the general philosophical description of reality. Such a *logos* theme provided theologians with a basis upon which they could accept both the doctrine of evolution and the conformity between the mind of man and ultimate reality, and with many nuances they developed their interpretations. This placing of *logos* Christology as the foundation stone of theology led to the incarnation—rather than the atonement—being given the cardinal place in the interpretation of the person and work of Jesus Christ. The drama of man's salvation was not simply an intrusive event on the stage of the natural world, God's activity was understood to be ingredient to and inwardly transformative of the entire order of reality. In the incarnation, as this was widely explicated, there was provided the key for understanding the continuity of God and nature, of nature and man, of man and Jesus Christ and of Jesus Christ and God. Hence, the *logos* theme made it possible to draw all reality into relation with Divine Being.

[4] *Doctrine of the Trinity* (London: Nisbet, 1943), p. 125. Caird's comment was quoted by Hastings Rashdall in *Philosophy and Religion* (London: Duckworth, 1909), p. 180.

For the Anglicans *Lux Mundi* gave a strong impetus toward this type of interpretation, but the earlier influence of Brooke Foss Westcott must not be passed by too quickly. By his concentration upon the *logos* theme in the fourth Gospel and through his writing on the incarnation he prepared the way for this emphasis in *Lux Mundi* and ensuing Anglican theology. In a sermon on "The Incarnation and Creation" Westcott stated his thesis clearly.

The forces of Nature, so to speak, are revealed to us in the Bible as gathered together and crowned in man, and the diversities of men as gathered together and crowned in the Son of Man; and so we are encouraged to look forward to the end, to a unity of which every imaginary unity on earth is a phantom or a symbol, when the will of the Father shall be accomplished and He shall *sum up all things in Christ*—all things not simply all persons—both *the things in the heavens and the things upon the earth.*[5]

The immanent *logos* has created and sustains the entire natural order, and, because of this, man, as preeminent *logos*-bearer, is given a responsible stewardship for that order. This conviction led Westcott into affirmation of social righteousness and involved him in concrete social activity, such as his espousal of Christian socialism and his work in the Christian Social Union.

Lux Mundi inherited and forwarded all these interests. Then in 1891 Charles Gore, in his Bampton Lectures, *The Incarnation of the Son of God,* brought to focus the themes that would dominate Anglican theology for two generations—namely, the incarnation as *logos,* the kenotic understanding of the *logos* become flesh, and the authority of the creeds.[6] The basic presupposition that underlay these lectures was the unity of nature and grace. Through Jesus Christ, as preexistent *logos,* the triune God created the cosmos, and all order, power, and beauty in nature are to be ascribed to him. In Jesus Christ, as Incarnate Lord, nature has received its crown, for Jesus brought the creative intention of the Godhead to its mature fruition. Hence, Gore claimed, the cosmos in its totality is to be understood as having its origin in God's creative Word,

---

[5] *Christus Consummator* (London: Macmillan, 1886), p. 103.
[6] Cf. *The Incarnation of the Son of God* (London: John Murray, 1891). Also A. M. Ramsey, *From Gore to Temple* (London: Longmans, 1960), pp. 16-18.

for the *logos* is present in all created reality as its constituting principle; moreover, this same Word became flesh, and the created order was brought to its inherently possible consummation. Gore refused to allow the doctrine of Jesus Christ to come into conflict with or be interpreted as inconsistent with the natural order, since nature is the *logos'* own creation. Indeed, he claimed, a Christ who was discontinuous or contradictory to nature would have lacked significance, especially rational significance, for God's creatures.

At the same time, a counterbalancing doctrine was also brought into play, for Gore drew a distinction between the completion of nature as this was anticipated by the natural expectation of men and that which was accomplished by the incarnation. Even though Gore did not stress the doctrines of the fall or of redemption as much as some of his evangelical contemporaries, especially among the Nonconformists, he was aware that natural man is afflicted with blindness, a blindness that results in a perversion of human expectation and hope. The natural man had sight, but sight dimmed by the veils of sin. Sin was an impediment and as such qualified the emphasis upon rationality; but, in his book, stress was placed upon the continuity, fulfillment, and enlightenment that were achieved by the incarnation of Jesus Christ, who as *logos*-incarnate connects the beginning to the end, the *arche* to the *telos* of creation.

In this early period after the publication of *Lux Mundi,* perhaps the clearest and certainly one of the most influential statements among the Anglicans of the relation of immanence and Christology was that of J. R. Illingworth in his book, *Personality Human and Divine.* Illingworth was a member of the *Lux Mundi* group, a faithful parish priest, and a careful stylistic craftsman. He brought to his writings a quality of quiet reflection and strong feeling. Methodologically, Illingworth proceeded from an investigation of human personality to statements about divine personality. Beginning with an analysis of the development of human self-consciousness, an analysis carried on completely in normative, philosophical terms, he expounded his position that human personhood possesses qualities of unity, uniqueness, and freedom. Man could now, according to idealistic psychology, be seen as a spiritual being—that is, as a member of a spiritual order that transcends the controlling limitations of sensible experience and that is the only region in which self-consciousness and freedom have place.[7]

Given these unique qualities of human personality it was possible, Illingworth contended, to construct a natural theology. If theology follows this line of argument, the highest category that can be applied to God is that of "person," for God possesses "in transcendent perfection, the same attributes which are imperfectly possessed by men."[8] The proper study of man is at least the beginning of the proper study of God.

The incarnation remained central throughout his discussion. For since the incarnation could presuppose man's natural conviction that God was personal, it must be understood as fulfilling his "natural anticipation."[9] Thus, although men could know in a general way and actualize in an imperfect manner the qualities appropriate to their nature as persons, the true significance of selfhood was to be found in the life of Jesus Christ as portrayed in the gospels; in consequence, the gospel depiction of Jesus sets the norm of human self-realization. What Jesus reveals, in short, is that love is the highest value in the attainment of personal maturity. Jesus' uniqueness, unity, and freedom, as well as his relation to other men, were brought to fulfillment by the permeation of love in his life. He became the exemplar of personhood in its full development. As a result, the task of Christian theology is that of interpreting the meaning of the incarnation so as to explore and illuminate characteristics of true human nature.[10]

Once more, as in the case of Gore, the emphasis was placed upon the incarnation as the central theme of the gospel; the atonement took a secondary position, and the reconciling work of Christ, it was implied, was that of enlightener rather than one who creates men anew. In Gore, and even more in Illingworth, the continuity between God and man, as found in the idea of immanence, tended to dominate the interpretation of the relation of God and man, in regard to both the fall and the restoration. The ideas of personality and development were keynotes of the period. But the doctrine of atonement was not com-

[7] *Personality Human and Divine,* pp. 2, 45.
[8] *Ibid.,* p. 74.
[9] *Ibid.,* p. 192, also p. 203.
[10] *Ibid.,* pp. 12-13, 200.

pletely neglected, and another member of the *Lux Mundi* group brought it clearly into prominence.

In 1901 R. C. Moberly published *Atonement and Personality,* a theological book that quickly became widely respected. The public acceptance of the book indicated the sensitivity to the times that the author possessed, a sensitivity that was located primarily, as the title indicated, in the relating of the doctrine of atonement to prevailing conceptions of human personality. The preface clearly stated the theme: no explanation of redemption can be adequate that is not, at every point, related to personality, and no explanation of personality is adequate that is not stated in terms of the atonement.[11]

In the central chapter of his book, Moberly explicated his contention by defining personality in keeping with Illingworth's description and emphasizing the integrity or inviolate character of human personhood as this is expressed in free will, reason, and love, each of which categories are realizable in their fullest sense only in relation to the atonement effected by Jesus Christ. But such an assertion must be set in its proper context; that is, all these qualities of true personality are inherent in each person, so that every man, by the immanent presence of the Holy Spirit, possesses the potentiality that may be actualized as fully matured selfhood. But in every man these qualities are imperfectly realized, and personal development is retarded. Only the atoning work of Jesus Christ, as this is mediated by his Spirit, is able to release man from the bondage of a will bound by lower self-interest and imperfect love and brings selfhood to its truest realization.[12]

Moberly summed up his point, and revealed the foundations of his position when he wrote,

Whilst, then, it may be true that philosophical thought is more or less explicitly teaching us that created personality is not and cannot be, a really distinct or self-subsistent centre of being; that all existence must be, in its ultimate reality, not multiplicity but unity; that the particular can only reach its own proper self-realization in the way of relation, as part of the universal

[11] R. C. Moberly, *Atonement and Personality* (London: John Murray, 1901), p. xiii.
[12] *Ibid.,* pp. 216-17.

and absolute: it is plain that at least to Christian theology the corresponding language is not strange, but inveterately familiar and congenial.[13]

Moberly's utilization of the immanental theme did not imply a smooth, easy transition from the condition of bondage to sin to the condition of being a free man in Christ. There is a change, a portentous change, which is effected by the atonement, for genuine transformation of persons is brought about by God's indwelling Spirit, which is the inward presence of the Incarnate Lord. By the Spirit, men are incorporated into Christ and thus are able to become, to the degree their limitations allow, like him. The atonement is the ground upon which the possibility of this incorporation is built, the actualized spiritual personhood is the fruit of this participation.

The important word in Moberly's analysis is "participation." His position is predicated upon a mystical union that is a full, reciprocal relation, between penal and moral theories and between subjective and objective theories of the atonement. He attempted to balance diverse elements to do justice to the richness of the union that God realized in Jesus Christ. It is of primary significance that for Moberly this union came not with creation but with the incarnation, although the doctrine of redemption is in continual interplay with the doctrine of creation. The historical event of Jesus Christ has a creative role as an exemplification of the providential process of God's creation, but, as with Moberly's *Lux Mundi* friends, the idealistic view of history remains regnant.

The year after *Atonement and Personality* appeared, W. R. Inge published one of the most direct explications of *logos* Christology to be found in the era in a chapter entitled "The Person of Christ" in *Contentio Veritatis*. Characteristically, he stressed that the *logos* was creator of the world and was in the world from the beginning. The development of this principle was an integral part of human history, but it was primarily entrusted to the moral sense of the Hebrew nation, the intellectual capacity of the Greeks, and the political ability of the Romans. In the appearance of Jesus Christ at the "fulness of time" all the anticipations from this past were brought to completion, and the purpose of creation was realized. The incarnation—which is the taking of manhood

---

[13] *Ibid.*, p. 254.

into God, not the conversion of the Godhood into flesh—is the supreme object and accomplishment of creation. Inge declared,

Taking as our guide the unique historical Incarnation in the past, we may say that the complete revelation to man of God's purposes concerning man, and the complete subordination of the human will to the Divine Will, so that it may act unswervingly in carrying out those purposes, are what constitutes union between the human and Divine natures, and that the realization of this union in mankind, as it was once realized in Christ is the far-off Divine event towards which the whole creation moves.[14]

Godhood and manhood are to be understood in the closest relation, they can not be mutually exclusive. To say this is not to identify the development of the human race with God, "but the cosmic process, of which the Word of God is the creating instrument, the Immanent Life, and the End is, as I have said, a real 'moment' or 'phase' . . . of God's life, and the laws which govern it are the laws in which His will always and everywhere manifests itself, in so far as it can be manifested under the imperfect forms of time and space."[15] Thus, union with God is the consummation of human life. This was the implanted principle of creation, it was the realized actuality of the incarnation, and its actualization is the anticipated hope of all creation. Only the principle of the *logos* makes possible this interpretation, an interpretation that is in keeping with the severest demands of the mind and heart.

Throughout his discussion, Inge made it clear that the incarnation as a historical event is a symbol and not the cause of man's redemption. His discussion of the importance of historical occurrence was conditioned by two factors: first, knowledge of God comes through immediate religious experience, not through conviction about past historical happenings; second, most real being, or eternal reality, is absolutely primary, and empirical reality only reflects, as a shadow, the meaning and significance of that realm. On this basis, Inge argued that when theologians put historical propositions into their creeds, they do so because they are convinced of important truths in the spiritual order that are in some way

[14] *Contentio Veritatis*, p. 64.
[15] *Ibid.*, p. 82.

dependent upon or even inseparable from certain historical events. "Whether these physical manifestations were *necessary* it is impossible for us to know; but at most they can only be *efficacia signa,* not the efficient *causes,* of our redemption. It cost more than this to redeem our souls." [16]

In Inge's statement we find the major themes of *logos* Christology presented in a forthright manner—the ubiquity of God's indwelling Spirit, the universal revelation of God in his creation, incarnation as the fulfillment of the past and the adumbration of the future. Here was Platonic Christianity in attractive, modern dress. Among the Anglicans we have mentioned, Inge was the one most influenced by idealistic modes of thought that subsumed concrete history to eternal ideas; and the movement, especially in his case, toward a *logos* Christology was a movement toward ultimate being and away from transitory historical events. Although the same tendency was incipiently present in Gore and Illingworth and, with ambiguity, in Moberly, as we shall see, those theologians, such as Forsyth, who stressed the atonement and the cross as a singular, once-for-all event (excluding those who emphasized the eternal atonement) were stressing the integrity and distinctiveness of concrete historical events. In so doing they questioned the continuity of God and nature, the idealistic faith in reason, and *logos* Christology. The different views of history resulted in different christological and soteriological formulations.

Among the Nonconformist theologians and especially among the Congregationalists, the last decade of the nineteenth century witnessed a concomitant stress upon the idea of immanence. We have already indicated how this theme came to its most unqualified expression in the New Theology of R. J. Campbell in 1907. In his affirmation of "monistic idealism" with its emphasis upon the unity of God and man, Campbell caught a prevalent trend of thought, but to illustrate the various ways in which theologians were subscribing to the idea of immanence we can take two less well known Congregationalist theologians, Joseph Warschauer and K. C. Anderson. [17]

---

[16] *Ibid.,* p. 95, cf. also pp. 85-86, 90-92.
[17] Warschauer's most important works were *Jesus: Seven Questions* (London: James Clarke, 1908); *Problems of Immanentalism* (James Clarke, 1909); and *The New Evangel* (James Clark, 1907). Anderson's most important books were *The Larger Faith* (London: A. & C. Black, 1903), and *The New Theology* (London: 1907).

These two men are of special interest from the standpoint of our study because of the differences in the way they treated the idea of immanence. Joseph Warschauer stood within the evangelical tradition, although he possessed a liberal spirit and was congenial to new learning. Such a man represented a large number of Nonconformists who wanted to perpetuate the good that had been inherited from the past but who were not afraid of a changing present. The past was not to be disregarded for the sake of the present, nor the future denied for the *status quo;* consequently, he represented a conservative though receptive response to the theme of immanence. What the idea of God's indwelling had to teach was important, but it was not the only truth. It is interesting that the title he originally thought of for his *Problems of Immanence* was "The Truth of Transcendence," and throughout this book he was concerned to show that the idea of immanence, which has a rightful place as the starting point of theological work, requires the completion that is afforded by transcendence. Thus, although the presence of God is to be found both in physical nature in general and in human nature in particular, it is completed in Jesus Christ, who transcends man as completely as man transcends the animal creation.[18] In other words, while it may be claimed that man is inalienably akin to God, he is also "everlastingly other than God"; and upon this likeness-in-difference between God and man Warschauer built his interpretation. Because of the likeness, there is continuity upon which any doctrine of the nature of Jesus Christ or the redemption of man must be built. Because of the difference, Jesus Christ functions as the unique individual who can renew man and bring man back into that relationship for which he was created. Throughout Warschauer's discussion the focus is always upon the person and work of Jesus Christ in whom are correlated the themes of immanence and transcendence.

Jesus, who entered this world in the normal way, who passed through a normal childhood and youth; who was a stranger to no human emotion, who worked for his livelihood, shared men's joys and griefs, knew hunger and thirst and weariness, who agonized in Gethsemane, and tasted what it is for a man to die—He is indeed the Son of Man; but none the less, nay all

[18] *Problems of Immanence,* p. 40; cf. also pp. 14-21.

the more is He, through whose moral vesture the Spirit shone with undimmed splendour, the Son of God, the Light of the world, the Way, the Truth and the Life . . . it is He, and none besides, who has for us the value of God. The knowledge of the Father is through Him: only the Son has it; only the Son has it to give.[19]

In this passage, Warschauer made central the continuity of grace and nature in the complete humanness of Jesus' maturation; yet he also emphasized Jesus' transcendence over other men as seen in his unique possession by the Holy Spirit and his unique role as the mediator of the revelation of God to men.

With the second Congregational minister, K. C. Anderson, we move in a more radical direction. The tension between immanence and transcendence was released with the result that immanental modes of thought became completely dominant. Anderson was a liberal who had the courage to follow his convictions to their logical conclusion, and he was a pathfinder whose interest in the future kept him from looking back. Throughout his book, *The Larger Faith,* he celebrated the new spirit that the century was breathing, a spirit that had its roots in romanticism and idealistic philosophy, and that was presently affecting social theory, government, literature, art, and religion; a spirit that he characterized as the acknowledgment of the presence of God in nature and humanity.[20] Anderson affirmed his primary indebtedness to Friedrich Schleiermacher, but in his own words he provided a classic expression of the liberal, immanental thought of the period.

We need no longer speak of the methods of the Divine approach to man. God is not outside man, living in another realm that He needs to approach him. Revelation is not a special message in the Bible, but the unveiling of the Divine in human experience, the development of the consciousness of God in the soul of man, the unfolding of the universal mind and will in human history, the disclosure of an immanent purpose in the ordinary course of things. . . . Creation itself is a redemptive process. Redemption is the completion of that process of evolution which has been in the thought of God from

---

[19] *Jesus: Seven Questions,* pp. 106-7.
[20] *The Larger Faith,* p. 19; cf. also pp. v-vi.

the beginning—the perfect and final emancipation of man from the animal, and his realization of himself as a spiritual being.[21]

For Anderson, this declaration of the emancipation of theology signalized the most creative possibility since the time of the early church. From Augustine onwards, he claimed, Western Christendom (as it developed through the Middle Ages and the Reformation) had stressed the bifurcation, the terrible chasm, between God and man. Now, however, there was a possibility that theology might return to the more congenial emphases of the Patristic writers (a tradition that he believed had been kept alive in the Eastern churches) and establish itself upon the fundamental continuity that exists between God and man. With a cry of emancipation, Anderson hailed the emergence of Western theology from its abortive pilgrimage through a long, dark tunnel into the light of God's radiant, omnipresent Spirit.

Anderson's book appeared three years prior to the time when R. J. Campbell brought these same issues before a wider public, and the fundamental assumptions of Campbell's theology and his elucidation of the content of theology are kin both in tone and substance to this statement. But what is of more general importance is that for a rather large number of Nonconformist theologians the idea of the immanence of God constituted the foundation upon which a viable interpretation of the religious life must be based. Unrestrained by the creeds and freed from explicit biblical authority by higher criticism, the Free Churches produced a small group of theologians who pushed their presuppositions as far as they would go. In terms of Christology, Anderson was explicit in stating that if one accepted these liberal assumptions then Jesus became the supreme but not the unique instance of God's indwelling.[22] There were, of course, also opponents, strong opponents, from among the Congregationalists, such as P. T. Forsyth,[23] but we shall turn to Forsyth's part in the discussion later.

[21] *Ibid.*, pp. 89-90.

[22] *Ibid.*, p. 40.

[23] Forsyth wrote, "At the present hour it is not the idea of evolution or the biologists or the anthropologists that need give us much concern. . . . Our real concern begins when the evolutionary principle is carried into the history or religion; when it is made to organize the new knowledge . . . [so that] no religion is final." *The Person and Place of Jesus Christ* (London: Independent Press, 1909), p. 42.

In the case of both the Anglicans and the Congregationalists the idea of immanence possessed persuasive power and fundamentally informed the christological discussion. In the other Nonconformist bodies, such as the Methodists, the Presbyterians, and the Baptists, these tendencies were not as marked, but it is also true that these groups did not produce the body of theological literature at the turn of the century as the Anglicans and Congregationalists.

The most important matter in regard to the influence of immanence, however, was not to be found in the number of persons affected; rather it was to be located in the reasons why it had its effect and the type of hope it offered for a viable statement of christological themes in the changed sociocultural context. Some commentators have professed to find in this emphasis a reaction to the Deism of the eighteenth century with its transcendent, isolated God; but the more immediate influences of Spencer, Darwin, and Hegel, as well as the social transformation of the era, constituted the most vivid backdrop against which this emphasis must be understood.

Concern to meet the intellectual disposition of the era, to conform to the spirit of the time led to certain rather exclusive emphases. The pervasiveness of the idea of immanence tended to overshadow the fallen condition of man, the continuity of God and man veiled the discontinuities that classical theology had also stressed. The doctrine of creation took precedence over the doctrine of the atonement. The incarnation was viewed as the continuation, if not also the consummation, of the processes inaugurated in the creation, and therefore the *ab extra* character of God and the uniqueness of Jesus were both compromised. The seriousness of this compromise was a topic of fundamental importance, for the question of any Christology, from a biblical point of view, is whether the early kerygma knows anything of an incarnational Christology such as is represented here and whether the development of the *logos* theme in the hands of its interpreters was sufficiently Johannine. Forsyth raised the basic question from an evangelical point of view: is Christianity final? Or does the development of immanental potentiality in evolutionary terms always point to some new revelation? Is the ultimate court of appeal Jesus Christ or a philosophical understanding of nature and developmental processes?

We have mentioned the way in which idealistic and evolutionary themes combined to give a peculiar character to this conception of Christology, namely the interpretation of the evolutionary process in such a manner that personality (human self-conscious rationality) stood at its apex, and at the pinnacle of human self-realization stood the unique person of Jesus Christ. But, in addition, other points should be made. In one sense, the emphasis upon the incarnation and the value of personality was calculated as a critique of the implication of biological evolution that would reduce man to the status of an animal whose emergence did not guarantee a unique place in the created order. Hence, the emphasis upon the affinity of man and God provided a way for eulogizing man, for heightening his importance, and for evaluating him as standing beyond the natural world. Although this interpretation was to become choice game for later commentators who criticized the easy, if not naive, view of the continuity between man and God, the important contribution of these thinkers must not be overlooked, namely their denial both of a materialistic interpretation of the universe and of a reductionistic naturalism corroborated by evolutionary ideology. Against both of these tendencies they affirmed the dignity of man.

Furthermore, this high estimate of man must not be divorced from the political and social interests that were manifested by many of these same theologians, for although there was no universal identification of the theological conviction about the dignity of man with the affirmation of a perfectable society, there was, both for Christians and for the wider community, a corroborative interaction between the two areas. Theologians generally protested against a social expression of the struggle for survival that biological evolution might be taken to support, a position that would have obvious affinity with a *laissez faire* social philosophy. At the same time, the theological doctrine of the incarnation—with its consequent belief in the dignity of man, in human freedom for self-determination, and especially in the moral claims that attended the recognition of the inviolate integrity of the natural world and every man—provided both impetus and substance to a liberal, progressive social philosophy and practice. Among the idealist philosophers we have already seen this social concern, and, now, among the theologians who were influenced by this philosophical position there was an interpretation of the evolutionary process in such a manner that it was value-oriented and value-achieving. These values, it was claimed, were supplied by the doctrine of the *logos* and the incarnation, and its implications for understanding human nature and society were of cardinal importance.

It is impossible in such an amalgam as I am describing to speak in terms of cause and effect. Neither the current science nor philosophy produced, in a straightforward manner, the particular brand of theology that emerged. Nor can it be claimed that theology alone created a new social strategy, even on the part of the religious community. But what may be claimed is that there was a symbiosis of religion and culture, each mutually conditioning the other. From the perspective of theology, it is evident that in the doctrine of the incarnation a large number of thinkers were convinced that they had found a base into which other ingredients could be mixed and made more intelligible. Christ the creator, Christ the indwelling sustainer, Christ the consummator—these were the themes; the incarnate *logos* was alpha and omega, the first and the last, the beginning and the end. And within this providential ordering of God was contained the whole of the created world and the One who at every moment and at the decisive moment was present to his world.

It is important to connect this with our discussion of the search for authority and to note that in the revival of *logos* Christology we have a new attempt to establish the authority of Jesus Christ and the viability of Christian commitment. The sovereignty of Jesus Christ is implanted in the very nature of created reality. According to this argument, the world is constituted by God's creative Word and is sustained by his continuing presence. Upon this foundation is established man's own existence and his understanding of his environment. To be related to Jesus Christ is to be related in a total manner to the providential processes that constitute the cosmic order. As is evident from this account, the authority of *logos* Christology was intrinsically related to the authority of idealistic philosophy, and this type of christological construction must be understood as a utilization of a prevailing philosophical position for expression of and endorsement of a stance of faith. In a time of turmoil when so many structures seemed in danger of falling, the reaffirmation of the rootage of Christian life in an ultimate reality that was realizing its purposes even in the fitfulness of human history provided assurance of ultimate sanctions.

THE SELF-EMPTYING OF GOD

Logos Christology, pervasive as it was, was only one part of the complex reassessment that characterized the turn of the century. A second major theme that was developed, especially during the first decade of the twentieth century, was that of *kenosis* or the self-emptying of God that took place in the incarnation. The idea of *kenosis* was not new to theology, at least not to German theology where it had been discussed for over half a century; but it was new to British thought in the last quarter of the nineteenth century, and not simply as a direct inheritance from the Germans.[24]

The idea of *kenosis* was both extremely rich and quite complex. It is a difficult idea to define in general, for each new expression of it qualifies any general definition. Consequently, rather than proffering a definition or an explanation at the beginning we shall investigate the way in which this theme took shape in the hands of several significant interpreters.

In his *Lux Mundi* essay, Charles Gore concluded his discussion of "The Holy Spirit and Inspiration" by insisting that a distinction must be drawn between what Jesus revealed and his human life as the revealer. "The Incarnation," he wrote, "was a self-emptying [*kenosis*] of God [in order] to reveal Himself under the conditions of human nature and from the human point of view. . . . Thus he *used* human nature, its relation to God, its conditions of experience, its growth in knowledge, its limitation of knowledge."[25] Immediately this interpre-

---

[24] To whom the origination of this idea in England is to be ascribed is not altogether certain. In 1887 A. J. Mason of Pembroke College, Cambridge mentioned it in his book *The Faith of the Gospel,* and T. K. Cheyne claimed origination of the idea (a claim that he made is his Bampton Lectures of 1899). But it was certainly Charles Gore who raised the issue in such a way as to give it prominence in English thought. See James Carpenter, *Gore,* p. 160, and William Sanday, *Christologies Ancient and Modern,* pp. 74-75.

[25] *Lux Mundi,* p. 360. A. M. Ramsey is surely wrong when he claims that *kenosis* appeared in *Lux Mundi* incidentally (cf. *Gore to Temple,* p. 30). On the contrary, this

tation was brought prominently before the attention of the theological community. H. P. Liddon, from whose Bampton Lectures I have quoted and in which he affirmed the full divinity of Jesus Christ in traditional creedal terms, raised a distressed voice—Gore had forsaken the strong bastions of the faith and had opened the doors to the attacking modernists. The phrase that struck Liddon most sharply was Gore's admission that Jesus possessed only limited knowledge, even though Gore had insisted in a footnote that "this limitation of knowledge must not be confused with fallibility or liability to human delusion, because it was doubtless guarded by the Divine purpose which led Jesus Christ to take it on himself." [26] This question of the limitation of Jesus' knowledge, which would deny him the attribute of omniscience, was the point on which the first round of an ensuing struggle was to be fought.[27]

The most evident explanation as to why Gore felt it necessary to utilize a *kenosis* theory seems to be that the critical evaluation of the Old Testament made it impossible for Jesus to be correct in several of his historical references to the Old Testament materials. From this, Gore went on to list other assumptions, particularly about the natural world and historical events, which Jesus shared with his contemporaries. Since scientific and historical knowledge had progressed, and men now knew that these assumptions or conclusions were wrong, omniscience could no longer be attributed to Jesus. Certainly for Gore, who had stressed the *logos* doctrine, there was no chasm between God as creator and Jesus Christ as man within the context of the natural order. Continuity was basic, and any limitation only indicated a different mode of expression, not a contradictory or contravening factor. Thus, having admitted the limited nature of Jesus' knowledge, Gore claimed that this did not

---

assertion was the inevitable climax of the argument; especially after Gore had explicitly stated on p. 336 that the whole Trinity is present in every function of the Father, Son, and Holy Ghost he had to state how this was so in the case of the Son.

[26] *Lux Mundi,* p. 360.

[27] Opposition to this position was fierce, and in 1903 a group of Anglican leaders explicitly repudiated this notion in the following declaration, "Since the human mind of our Lord was inseparably united to the eternal word, and was perfectly illuminated by the Holy Spirit in the discharge of his office as teacher, he could not be deceived, nor be the source of deception, nor intend to teach, even incidentally, for fact what was not fact." This was signed by G. Body, H. R. Bramley, W. Bright, T. T. Carter, W. M. G. Ducat, C. W. Furse, D. Grieg, C. D. Hammond, W. H. Hutchins, J. O. Johnson, E. C. Lowe, P. G. Medd. Quoted in Ramsey, *Gore to Temple,* p. 8.

impede his ability to reveal fully and truly the nature and intention of God. The kenotic doctrine had one chief virtue as far as Gore was concerned—"we seem to be moving within the lines of dogma and doing justice to all the intimations of Scripture." [28]

Kenosis Christology meant for Gore that the incarnation involved an act of self-sacrifice by Almighty God; yet, at the same time, the work of the Eternal Son was in no way interrupted by the incarnation. These were the two strands of a single cord that Gore wanted to keep bound together. What was primarily at stake was the acute christological question of how one is to interpret the paradoxical situation in which, on the one hand, Jesus manifested fallible knowledge and, on the other hand, he was reported as saying, "I and my Father are one." This problem, with which every Christology must deal and provide some answer if it is to be viable, came to the fore in the kenotic controversy, and the significance of the kenotic interpretation was that it faced this problem in a candid manner. In the case of Charles Gore, there can be no doubt but that he genuinely wanted to do justice to both creeds and Scripture, to both the divinity and the humanity of Jesus; and yet there can be no doubt but that if the conciliar definitions are taken strictly, Jesus Christ is understood to be possessed of all the divine attributes, though the scriptural records, if interpreted from the standpoint of modern, scientific thought indicate that Jesus was not all-knowing. A compromise was requisite, and the solution Gore preferred was that of interpreting Jesus' incarnate existence as one in which he had voluntarily abandoned his omniscience in order to become fully man. The voluntary character of the decision retained the idea of a sovereign decision; God was self-limited. The insistence that Jesus was fully man, he felt, was essential to a viable Christology. First, it was essential because of his continual insistence upon an *analogia entis* (a fundamental, ontological continuity) between God and man. If Jesus Christ is not fully man, then there is a break that cannot be overcome, and the continuity between creation and incarnation would be false and the unitary work of the one God would be disrupted. Second, the humanity of Jesus was essential because of the participation of Jesus

---

[28] *The Incarnation of the Son of God,* p. 163.

in the full range of human experience, and, for this reason, Gore criticized the tendency in Catholic thought that sometimes tended to remove Jesus from the arena of the vicissitudes of life.

The kenotic theory, then, in Gore's mind and in the thought of many of his successors, was calculated to accomplish several distinct but important functions. It was an effort to secure two poles: Jesus Christ as the second Person of the Trinity, as this was anchored in the divine center of the consciousness of Jesus; and Jesus Christ as man, as this was anchored in the rest of his experience. In addition to its importance for interpreting the person of Jesus Christ, Gore maintained that this doctrine protected God's unchanging redemptive purposes for man that were woven into the fabric of the cosmos; and it revealed the costliness of God's redeeming act. In short, God's full redeeming purpose was presented through a channel appropriate to our human condition. At this point Gore was caught in a dilemma that all theologians meet— namely, God is present in Jesus Christ in such a manner that he is revealed to men in this particular event, yet he is revealed in such a way that most men do not recognize this revelation. In other words, God is both revealed and hidden in Jesus Christ; God is present, but only to the eyes of faith; the historical Jesus reveals God, but in an indirect fashion. To try to meet this problem, Gore used the language of abandonment, a metaphor that had many problems but that attempted to indicate that God is present in Jesus Christ, yet present in a restricted (a self-imposed restrictive) manner. Insofar as he is present, he is revealed; insofar as his attributes are restricted, he is hidden.

J. M. Creed applied Emil Brunner's general criticism of kenotic Christology to the British theologians and said that they went astray in part through their preoccupation with the psychological approach to the person of the incarnate Lord[29] This criticism has more force in relation to later expressions of the theory than it does to Gore; yet even here there is a correctness to the judgment.[30]

It may be true that Gore was not himself primarily concerned with

[29] *The Divinity of Jesus Christ* (London: Fontana, 1964, first published in 1938), p. 85.

[30] A. M. Ramsey and James Carpenter both challenge this criticism in regard to Gore, but, as we shall argue, there is a merit in pointing to this fact. Cf. Ramsey, *Gore to Temple*, p. 5; Carpenter, *Gore*, pp. 176-77.

psychology, but it was also true that he presupposed the psychological interpretation of his time, an interpretation that placed great stress upon man as a self-conscious, self-determining moral agent. Further, it is understandable that the description of Jesus was made upon the basis of these assumptions. Creed did not explore the connection at this point with requisite extensiveness, but he was correct in pointing to the fact that psychology did play an important part in the kenotic view of Jesus Christ.

Rather than argue that the kenoticists, especially Gore, went astray because of the prevailing psychological interpretation it is wiser simply to note how this perspective influenced their explanations and how it complicated their problems. Thus, in the discussion of the divinity and humanity of Jesus Christ everything was understood as being filtered through Jesus' conscious awareness, and since for idealism the real and the rational were continuous, if not identical, the limitation of Jesus' conscious knowledge of the real world indicated a disastrous failure of his omniscience and consequently undercut his authority. In his Bampton Lectures, Gore had already affirmed the continuity of nature and grace; reality was known through inspired, rational understanding. Hence at the crucial point where grace was most prominently manifested in a personal life, any discontinuity seemed to contradict perfect grace and perfect reason. Because of the interpretation of personhood in terms of self-determining, conscious personality, Gore was no longer able to fall back upon some of the traditional interpretations that had used the concept of impersonal manhood; the attributes of personality were now limited to individuals and were no longer ascribable to nature *qua* nature, nor to any amorphous realm of the impersonal. As a consequence, Gore's interpretation was fundamentally conditioned by the psychology of the time. Nevertheless, it must also be said that Gore came to the problem of omniscience in Jesus from a consideration of the accounts in the gospels, and the perplexities that he found here were only reinforced by the psychological assumptions.[31]

---

[31] John S. Lawton, *Conflict in Christology: A Study of British and American Christology from 1889-1914* (London: S.P.C.K., 1947), pp. 262-63, forcefully raised the question of the influence of the psychological dimension of the theological discussion; and in this he followed the lead of H. M. Relton, *A Study in Christology* (London: S.P.C.K., 1922).

In our discussion of the kenotic theory and in our effort to trace some of its ramifications we have, perhaps, concentrated unduly upon the writings of Charles Gore. He did have the distinction of being the most influential exponent of this theme in Anglican theology at the close of the nineteenth century, but one other of the *Lux Mundi* contributors deserves mention at this point, namely Henry Scott Holland. Holland was a close friend of Gore and himself attained the distinguished position of Regius Professor of Divinity at Oxford. He was preeminently a preacher, and his theology was primarily contained in his sermons; but it was penetrating and comprehensive theology and is worth remembering for its intrinsic value.[32]

Holland was a Balliol man, a student of T. H. Green, and a leader among the *Lux Mundi* friends. D. M. MacKinnon claims that Holland's Christology was a type of kenotic doctrine, but it did not represent an effort to explicate the relation between the Divine and the human in Jesus with philosophical or metaphysical exactness. Rather, he was interested in the idea insofar as it aided the proclamation of the gospel that in the life, crucifixion, and resurrection of Jesus Christ God was revealed; but he also acknowledged that this revelation was in the form of a Divine incognito. The suffering Christ as the revealer of the power of God was movingly proclaimed in his sermons. God's strength was manifest in weakness, the incarnation is the victory of Jesus Christ's moral will, which set strict limits upon his use of the Divine attributes.[33] Holland related the death to the exaltation, the suffering to the glory of Christ. In this emphasis there is a new dimension added to the kenotic discussion. The question of the person of Christ is riveted to the cross and plunged into the earth; it is the revelation of God's indwelling, but now the presence of God is made evident in his crucifixion, in his identification with man at the point of deepest suffering. Such revelation does not identify God with the world and certainly not with the

---

[32] A significant study of Holland and one of the few attempts to assess his work is to be found in two articles by D. M. MacKinnon, "Christian Optimism: Scott Holland and Contemporary Needs," *Theology*, Nov., 1952, pp. 407-12 and *Theology*, Dec., 1952, pp. 448-53. Cf. also H. S. Holland, *Logic and Life* (New York: Scribner's, 1882); *Henry Scott Holland: A Section from His Writings*, ed. B. M. G. Reardon (London: S.P.C.K., 1962).

[33] *Miracles*, pp. 69 ff.

beauty and order of the world. On the contrary, God is manifest as present at the nadir of human experience—he makes his presence known at the most crucial juncture. Through his acceptance of death Jesus also proclaimed God's resurrecting power and his glory. Thus, the *kenosis* is a self-emptying that is the obverse side of his triumph. "The Cross has only power to save as the Cross of the Risen Lord." [34]

Concomitantly, there were others who were exploring the kenotic idea, and chief among the earlier of the Nonconformists to adopt this point of view was A. M. Fairbairn. In *Christ and Modern Theology,* Fairbairn claimed that the conditions under which Christ lived his life were the same as those of all nonmiraculous humanity, but through this ordinary humanity God had revealed his redemptive purpose for mankind. "There was a normal manhood," he wrote, "but a supernatural function." [35] The miracle of Christ's revelation, then, was not to be located in the conditions of his human existence, not even in the uniqueness of his nature as God and man; rather the distinctiveness of Jesus is to be found in his redeeming work. Here the evangelical emphasis upon the redemption effected by Jesus Christ came to the fore. Because the primary concentration was not upon the incarnation and therefore not upon the nature of Jesus Christ, Fairbairn felt free to move directly to the question of Jesus' redemptive activity. He was not delayed by long discussions of the nature of the one who is incarnate; the question of Jesus' authority did not reside, in this interpretation, in his incarnate nature so much as in his atoning work, and once the primacy was given to Jesus' activity the problem of the two natures was relegated to a subordinate position. Fairbairn claimed that it was impossible to separate Christ's person and office—there is continuity throughout, but the switch in emphasis was crucial; and its importance resided in the fact that Fairbairn interpreted the person of Christ in terms of his work and found continuity because he extended the accomplishment of Jesus in his work to cover the question of his person. What is that work? It is that of the founder of the kingdom of God, the One who rectifies the relationship between man and God and between man and

[34] *Ibid.,* p. 121; cf. also p. 134.
[35] *Christ in Modern Theology,* p. 354.

man.[36] But Fairbairn also went further in his discussion of the kenotic theme and claimed that the external or physical attributes of God, such as omnipotence, omniscience, and omnipresence, were in the incarnation separated from the internal or moral attributes of truth and love. The external attributes were sacrificed, but the internal attributes were not; also the external attributes were under the command of the internal attributes—love directs omnipotence.[37] Everything was subsumed under the gracious activity of Jesus—activity that was comprehensive to the point that Fairbairn did not explore in a thorough manner the doctrine of the person of Jesus.

After the turn of the century, this idea of *kenosis* won an increasingly prominent place in English theology, though many different variations were played upon the theme. To indicate how the issue was developed it will be helpful to look at the two people who carried this theme through with the most rigor, Frank Weston and P. T. Forsyth. Again, it is important to note that Weston was a high Anglican and Forsyth a Congregationalist; for the theme was pervasive, and theologians from the Established and Free Churches went in large numbers to this possibility for christological interpretation.

Frank Weston, the Bishop of Zanzibar, is perhaps best remembered for his active prosecution in the Kikuyu affair, an affair that called forth his most stentorious side. He fought hard for the necessity of an apostolic ministry and church discipline and won the malediction of many of the more moderate as well as liberal churchmen. In his earlier book on Christology, however, we have a remarkable achievement in sustained attention to the issue of *kenosis* and its implications. As he introduced *The One Christ,* he flew his colors in unmistakable style.

Let us give up our claim to independence of judgment. For there is no such thing as an unbiased student of Christology. The Lord Christ lives and reigns, and each man who gazes upon Him that he may investigate His history is driven to adopt a definite attitude towards Him. . . . And on that attitude

---

[36] *Ibid.,* p. 355. Throughout this discussion the influence of Albrecht Ritschl is obvious, in the concentration upon the work of Jesus Christ, in the lack of concern to explicate the doctrine of the person of Jesus Christ; and in the emphasis upon the kingdom of God Fairbairn reflects this indebtedness.

[37] *Ibid.,* pp. 476-77.

we depend as we pass to judge the Creeds and Scriptures. To maintain the contrary is to deceive oneself.[38]

This study was an attempt of a man who was committed whole-heartedly to the creedal formulation of the divinity of Jesus Christ but who was also convinced that the creed required fresh interpretation. With a keen sensitivity to nuances, Weston argued that the ego of this unique man, Jesus Christ, was the permanent, divine subject for his human experience. In approaching this issue he admitted the limitation of Jesus' knowledge, but he did not want to adopt the language of depotentiation that Gore had used; rather, he insisted that all the attributes of God essentially belong also to Jesus, and in some way this must be explained. God is fully present in Christ, and this cornerstone of faith must not be surrendered. The Son of God in becoming incarnate *added* to himself a human nature, but the second Person of the Trinity remained the subject or the ego of this human personality. At the same time, this divine ego was self-restrained, so that the human person of Jesus must be understood in a special way. Passively, his ego was limited so that he received only those experiences which were mediated to him through his human body and mind. Consequently, Jesus' knowledge was limited to what these experiences would yield. Moreover, in regard to his maturation, his personality developed as would that of any other man, and his interactions with other men and his relationship with God were conditioned by the capacities of his human nature. Actively, this meant that Jesus could will and do and therefore reveal whatever, but only whatever, could be expressed by and through his human personality. In sum, the self-restraint of the Son is directly proportionate to the measure of the development of this particular human person. To state the relation of Jesus to God in this manner may be seen as setting a new and subtly different sequence: divine humiliation is located in the *logos* who becomes man, rather than in the man Jesus who is humiliated in the experience of the cross. Though for Weston the humiliation of the *logos*-man is comprehensive and can include both acts, the incarnation is given primacy over the crucifixion.

[38] *The One Christ* (London: Longmans, Green, 1914), p. xxvii.

Looked at from above, in terms of the *logos*, Jesus' consciousness as man bore the marks of self-sacrificing love and of immense self-restraint. But looked at from below, Jesus' human consciousness is that of the perfect Son of God, who at every moment observed and realized the true humanity and the true God-relationship that his nature allowed. Weston concluded,

For myself, the daylight shines most fully at the point in which I am able to assign to the universal sphere of Logos-activity all the self-limitation that was necessary for the mediation of Christ's consciousness by His manhood. The child Jesus was able to be a perfect child, not because He as Incarnate restrained divine powers lest they should overpower His boy-nature, but because as Incarnate He is at every moment observant of and obedient to the law of self-restraint which He as unlimited Logos wills should be imposed upon Himself. . . . The Logos as able to limit Himself and conscious of that ability is to be regarded as in the sphere of the universal and eternal relationships; the special, incarnate relationships are to be conceived as those of the Logos self-limited, who knows Himself only as Logos limited in manhood.[39]

The *logos* actively and continuously knows himself to be limited and consciously wills to live under this restriction. This emphasis upon Christ's self-consciousness was symptomatic of a change that had come over the christological interests of the period. For Gore, attention had been focused upon the limited historical or scientific knowledge that Jesus possessed. Now, a decade later, the emphasis was placed upon the personality of Christ, and the question had become, in what sense could the Jesus of history have been conscious of himself as the universal *logos*?[40] The answer that Weston gave focused upon Jesus' will: the eternal *logos* wills to be incarnate, and the human Jesus accepts the limitations that this imposes. It is the volitional act that sets the possibility for understanding how the eternal *logos* can restrict himself to human form. This switch of emphasis to the will or volition becomes an important theme in later developments, especially in the thought of William

[39] *Ibid.*, p. 159.

[40] Cf. John Lawton, *Conflict in Christology*, p. 278. Lawton has recognized more clearly than any other interpreter the change that was taking place in this regard and its significance for christological interpretation.

Temple. The volitional struggle, however, once again tends to be in the context of the advent of the *logos* as flesh, and the inner violence of Jesus' struggle in facing the cross—"Not my will but Thine be done" —is in some danger of being lost.

Perhaps the most significant aspect of Weston's statement was his ability to delineate carefully the strands of kenotic discussion and thereby go beyond the less precisely stated positions of Gore and Fairbairn. In addition he affirmed the relation of the humanity and divinity in Jesus Christ, so that the divine *logos* retained an inviolate personalness. There were reciprocity, interpenetration, and mutuality, and all with a deep respect for the integrity of the eternal *logos* and the finite Jesus. The psychological dynamics of the person of Jesus were central to this theory and constituted one of the areas that most needed further exploration. While no clear line may be drawn between the influence of God on the self-will of Jesus, separation and integration must both be stressed. Weston attempted to keep this balance, but it was precarious and remained in danger of distortion.

The second major explication of the *kenosis* theme was developed by P. T. Forsyth. One of the prime accomplishments of Forsyth was the care with which he investigated this problem of the person of Jesus Christ, even though he, more than any other theologian of his time, consciously placed his primary emphasis upon the role of Jesus as redeemer. The order must be carefully set: Christology is the corollary of soteriology. Nonetheless, no doctrine has been as much affected by the influences of the time, he claimed, as that of the person of Christ. In this impingement, however, he saw hope: "With the modern growth of psychology, and the modern revolution of metaphysics, such formulae were bound to dissolve. . . . But the metaphysic of history, the modern primacy of personality, and the new stress upon experience, coupled with a critical historicism equally modern, have opened a better way." [41]

Forsyth's main contention was expressed in his phrase, "Christology must be moralized," a theme that he mentioned time and again and by which he meant that any viable doctrine of Jesus Christ must respect the integrity of the moral personhood of the human Jesus and every

[41] *The Person and Place of Jesus Christ*, p. 217.

other man, as well as the moral character of God. The discussion of Christology must be set within the context of God's redemption, which creates man in a new fashion as a moral person (as a new man in Jesus Christ) by moral means (with respect for the integrity of man's personhood). His attack on traditional christological formulations was centered upon their tendency to be too impersonal and "physical," i.e., concerned with the exact natural components of Jesus' nature. Further, traditional theories often attempted to explain the two natures of Jesus Christ as the result of God's immediate, powerful uniting of two incompatible natures into one person, rather than understanding this as a union achieved through the integrity of Jesus' personhood.

If this basic starting point is acknowledged, then, Forsyth claimed, we have the possibility of understanding the divine character of Jesus. For example, the attribute of omnipotence when applied to Jesus does not refer to sheer power; rather it is power used under moral conditions for moral purposes. In this light the cross may be seen as the final affirmation or expression of God's omnipotent holiness subduing all natural powers and forces. God's sovereignty was appropriately expressed through weakness.[42]

As regards the *kenosis* theme, Forsyth argued that the best way to describe Jesus Christ was as one who "potentially" possessed the attributes of God. But this potentiality was actualized only insofar as respect for the human nature of Jesus would allow. Self-reduction or self-retraction by God was expressed through Jesus' human limitations. Divine attributes, therefore, have their definitive definition in the life, death, and resurrection of Jesus Christ. Summing up his position, he said,

Let us cease speaking of a nature as if it were an entity; of two natures as two independent entities; and let us think and speak of two modes of being, like quantitative and qualitative, or physical and moral. Instead of speaking of certain attributes as renounced may we not speak of a new mode of their being? The Son, by an act of love's omnipotence, set aside the style of God, and took the style of a servant, the mental manner of a man, and the mode of moral action that marks human nature. . . .

What we have in Christ, therefore, is more than the co-existence of two

[42] *Ibid.,* pp. 222-23, 227-28.

natures, or even their interpenetration. We have within this single increate person the mutual involution of the two personal acts or movements supreme in spiritual being, the one distinctive of man, the other distinctive of God; the one actually productive from the side of Eternal God, the other actively receptive from the side of growing man; the one being the pointing, in a corporeal person, of God's long action in entering history, the other the pointing of man's moral growth in the growing appropriation by Jesus of his divine content as he becomes a fuller organ for God's full action on man. The two supreme movements of spiritual being, redemption and religion, are revealed as being so personal that they can take harmonious, complete, and final effect within one historic person, increate but corporeal.[43]

Throughout his discussion Forsyth attempted to hold to two fundamental principles: on the one hand there was God's absoluteness and freedom, and on the other hand there was the significance of human life. In terms of the concrete, historical existence of Jesus Christ he found the kenotic doctrine to be the most satisfactory way of maintaining both of these themes. But he also went beyond much of the kenotic discussion by closing his study with a strong affirmation of the *plerosis* or the Divine self-fulfillment in Christ. In the end, the God who humbled himself and became a man shall exalt this man, Jesus Christ, and manifest his full glory as the second Person of the Holy Trinity. Humility is brought to triumph, the Lowly One has been proclaimed Lord of all creation.[44]

Whether any of these *kenosis* theories was theologically adequate was soon to become a matter of much debate. The strength of these theories was that they did preserve the conviction that Jesus lived a truly human life. Whether there were sufficient scriptural warrants for basing a *kenosis* interpretation upon Philippians 2 was doubtful, but the theological attractiveness was obvious. Yet, in all the developed positions there remained an ambivalence between the recognition that God's revelation in Jesus Christ involves a hiddenness, and an effort to explain the reasons for and the mode of that hiddenness—thereby, to a degree, making God's presence manifest. In this sense kenotic theories, in a subtle manner, refused to allow the full mystery of God's presence in

[43] *Ibid.*, pp. 307, 343-44.
[44] *Ibid.*, pp. 323 ff.

this historical person. On the reverse side, it may be claimed that neither the divinity nor the humanity of Jesus was made distinctly comprehensible—so neither the mystery nor the explanation have their full weight. In an effort to protect the humanity of Jesus, there is the possibility that his person is split into two different states of being, one concealed and one revealed, and thereby disallowing the full unity of one person in two natures.

All these tendencies are only tendencies, not fully developed positions; but if the kenotic themes are extended in their natural logic these possibilities do constitute serious problems. The basic question of this position now comes to the fore: is God fully present in Jesus Christ? All those who espoused kenotic theories wanted to maintain that God's presence is at least authentically manifested in Jesus Christ, but authenticity they did not equate with fullness. Insofar as perfectly obedient humanity can reflect God's love and grace, Jesus is the final revelation, but the psychological dynamics of the man Jesus and a reinterpretation of the manifestation of the attributes of God were used to qualify christological understanding.

Once again, it is worthwhile to recall our claim that in the statements on Christology we have the focusing of the multiple issues that faced theologians in the peculiar cultural setting of the prewar era. In the discussion of the immanence of God we found the emphasis upon *logos* Christology bringing together idealistic philosophy, evolutionary theory, and social concerns. Philosophical and theological foundations were established by which Christian faith was rooted in the nature of reality itself, and upon this foundation the authority of Jesus Christ and of Christian commitment was reaffirmed. In the *kenosis* discussion we find several pressing issues being combined and recast, for kenotic Christology was a sustained attempt to adapt ancient formulations of faith to present sensibilities and modes of thought. Scriptural criticism and the study of personality forced reconsideration of the creedal definitions of Jesus Christ. What is more significant is the basis upon which this reconsideration rested, namely, a tenacious hold upon the humanity of Jesus Christ, a grasp that emphasized the serious interest of these theologians in relating Jesus to the natural world, to human society, and to the individual's self-understanding and possibility for mature personhood.

Kenotic Christology had a profound devotional significance insofar as it emphasized the cost of God's gracious concern for man; it made an appeal to reason insofar as it attempted to clarify the relation of the eternal *logos* to the historical person of Jesus; and it had a soteriological significance insofar as it identified Jesus with the condition of men, yet in such a manner as to offer redemption. But the impact of this discussion came to its clearest focus when it attempted to affirm the authority of Jesus Christ as Lord. The kenoticists were struggling to maintain the Divine sovereignty of Jesus Christ even as this was expressed through the limitation of his humanity. The Lordship of God is expressed through Jesus Christ as he creates faith and is appropriated by that faith in the life of the believer. Thus, authority expressed itself through a personal interplay that opened man to the ultimate source of life, to self-understanding, and to moral responsibility. Jesus Christ, whom the Scripture and creeds presented as Lord, remained Lord, and in the disconcerting rapids of social and cultural change he was claimed as an anchor and a guiding star.

IX

CHRISTOLOGY: BORROWINGS
AND NEW DIRECTIONS

The interpretation of Christology in England was not limited to the two issues of *logos* and *kenosis*. Other important themes were developed, there was some borrowing from foreign sources, and new avenues were being explored. By the last decade of the nineteenth century the question of the Jesus of history and historical investigation of the gospel accounts were coming to central importance. In this search for the person of Jesus, psychology was utilized in a new manner, and a fresh assessment of Jesus' nature was a part of the theological ferment.

English theology in the nineteenth century was committed to the historical accuracy of the Gospels, and so little was this seriously questioned that there was much use of the gospel materials to construct biographical accounts. Works such as John Seeley's *Ecce Homo* in the sixties had helped to stress the importance of seeing Jesus through historical eyes, and as the nineteenth century progressed a renewed conviction about the historicity and the completeness of the account in the Gospels was evident. A. M. Fairbairn expressed this confidence when he stated that, as a result of research, "we stand . . . face to face with Him in a sense and to a degree unknown in the Church since the Apostolic age."[1] Hastings Rashdall spoke of Seeley's book as being a "fifth gospel" for many in his generation, and William Sanday as late as 1910 intended to write "what is commonly called a Life of Christ" as the culmination of his own biblical studies.[2] On the whole, this interest remained a firm possession of English theologians, although in some quarters questions were raised about the biblical records and their historical accuracy. Percy Gardner, an Oxford don and Modern Churchman illustrated this position of dubiety.

When doctrine is based on historical record, and when for proof of it we are referred to writings of doubtful authorship, coming down to us out of the mist of ages, and bearing obvious signs of human weakness and ignorance, we cannot help shrinking in doubt and terror. Is it on such evidence as this that we are to risk the well-being of our souls? . . . It seems impossible. . . . For this reason there seems to me grave objections to the view of the historical origins of Christianity often taken by English churchmen.[3]

We have already seen that among the idealists there was a serious question in regard to the ultimate importance of history or its status in reality, but even if it were admitted to have only symbolic value it was worth investigating for that value. Nonetheless, what is of much importance is the fact that the general historical trustworthiness of the gospel accounts—whatever the metaphysical status of history itself—was not seriously questioned; the conviction that the gospels were historically reliable remained unshaken. Hence, at the turn of the century the historical Jesus was important for the majority of conservative and liberal theologians.

[1] *Christ in Modern Theology*, p. 295, see also p. 17.

[2] *Christologies Ancient and Modern*, p. v. Interesting in this connection was the work during the teens of this present century when T. R. Glover explicitly acknowledged that the Gospels were not primarily biographies and consist only of collections and reminiscences, memories and fragments, and then went on to write what amounted to detailed biographical accounts of the life of Jesus. See esp. *The Jesus of History* (London: S. C. M., 1917), pp. 13 and 222. It was as though he was completing the work of the Gospel writers.

[3] Percy Gardner, *A Historic View of the New Testament* (London: A. & C. Black, 1901), pp. 22-23.

Among the Nonconformists this emphasis reinforced an interest in Ritschlian types of theology, particularly its christological themes.[4] Anglican theologians were somewhat slower to turn in this particular direction. With general correctness a writer in the *Church Quarterly Review* could breath a sigh of relief as late as 1905—"Ritschlianism, although it has found many Nonconformist sympathizers, has not yet made any considerable impression in the Church of England."[5] But within less than a generation this could no longer be justly claimed, and soon Ritschlian themes combined with indigenous sensitivity to the moral quality of Jesus and created a strong stream, through the modernists, within Anglicanism.

The influence of Ritschl on christological discussion in England was channeled principally through the work of his disciples, for Ritschl had so stated his position that two divergent interpretations were fruitfully developed. On the one hand, there was the stream developed by Harnack, which stressed the importance of Jesus' teaching, especially about the Fatherhood of God, the brotherhood of man, and the kingdom of God; and although it was argued that Jesus himself preeminently embodied these teachings the main drive of the argument was toward a concentration upon his teaching. For Harnack, Jesus was the origin but not the essence of Christianity.[6] On the other hand, Wilhelm Herrmann em-

---

[4] As early as 1898 John Scott Lidgett had a section on Ritschl in his book *The Spiritual Principle of the Atonement,* and although he was critical of Ritschl's position, he concluded by saying, "But, notwithstanding, it behoves us to appreciate his witness to the fact that in dealing with man, his sin, and his redemption, we are lifted to higher ground than that of supposed divine politics . . . [and we shall be led] to seek a theory of the atonement in terms of ethical relations, and to inquire whether it is not intended to serve the ethical self-realization of the sinners for whom it is offered." pp. 217-18. We have mentioned Fairbairn's indebtedness and it is worth recalling that Forsyth had studied with Ritschl at Göttingen and acknowledged his debt to Herrmann in an early article in *Faith and Criticism.*

[5] *Church Quarterly Review,* Oct., 1905, p. 31. In 1908 Ernest A. Edghill won the Norrisian Prize at Cambridge for his monograph *Faith and Fact: A Study of Ritschlianism* (London: Macmillan, 1909), in which he investigated the thought of the major German Ritschlian theologians, only to challenge their claims. In 1909 J. K. Mozley published his book *Ritschlianism: An Essay* (London: Nisbet, 1909). This was a careful, mature theological work. Mozley focused his primary interrogation upon Ritschlian Christology. Although he argued that it was inadequate as usually stated by Ritschlians, he defended their attempt to develop a Christology without using the idea of substance (see esp. p. 260). In all it was a fair, though critical study.

[6] The publication of Harnack's *What Is Christianity?* in English translation in 1901 helped to publicize his position.

phasized the centrality of Jesus for faith in an exclusive manner—so exclusive, in fact, that faith could only come to know God as he was revealed in the consciousness of Jesus. Here there was an existentially involved analysis, history as objective description gave way to partici-pation, to shared-life with Christ.

In addition to the direct theological influence of the contemporary German theologians there was, once again, the compounding or rein-forcing factor of the psychological theory that was dominant at the time. The investigation of the human self-consciousness increased the interest in the various aspects of religious experience, and the Ritschlian theologians who stressed Jesus' religious self-consciousness met a pre-pared interest among many English theologians. We shall look first at the Nonconformist reaction to this influence.

We saw in the discussion of Christology that Fairbairn had been influenced by the Ritschlians, but the most distinctive statement of this type of theology was presented by Alfred E. Garvie, a Congregationalist theologian. Garvie never lost his basic evangelical commitment and was interested in Ritschlian ideas as these helped him elucidate the meaning of Christian faith. His first approach to the subject was an extended study of the movement—a study that won him a doctorate from Glasgow —in which he sympathetically expounded the themes found in the whole spectrum of the Ritschlian school. He later claimed in his autobiography that he had never intended to identify his own position with that of the movement; and this may be taken seriously, for he always remained critical of some of the cardinal tenets of Ritschlian theology. In an im-portant statement he set forth his agreement and disagreement with Herrmann and thereby indicated the position that he worked out in his later books, especially in his *Studies in the Inner Life of Jesus,* the very title of which reflected Herrmann's influence.

With the preeminence in the Christian revelation which is accorded by Herr-mann . . . to Christ, no Christian can have any desire to quarrel. . . . But even if we start, as he does, from the inner life of Jesus, His perfection and His grace, as the centre of God's revelation, and valuing that as highly as he does, we should be less exclusive in our appreciation and reverence than he seems to be. In the first place, the life of Christ is an organic unity, and therefore no feature of, no factor in it, can be insignificant and valueless. The evangelical testimony should therefore command a greater reverence, and allow a narrower liberty than Herrmann admits. In the second place, the preparation for Christ in the Old Testament, especially in the faith and hope of the godly, and the activity of Christ by His spirit in the typical religious experiences which are presented to us in the New Testament stand in more vital relationship to Christ Himself than he is ready to admit.[7]

The two objections here mentioned are typical of Garvie's concern: any interpretation of the person of Jesus—"the inner life of Jesus"—must be as comprehensive as the New Testament portrait of Jesus; consequently, the scriptural records are to be taken as a more assured foundation for faith and theology than the Ritschlians admit. And these principles he attempted to explicate in his own studies.

In his major work, which attempted to carry out his theological program, he began by stating that it is "the mind, heart and will of Jesus as revealed in His words and works"[8] that a student must seek to understand. He assumed that the Synoptic Gospels present a reliable, objective account of the life of Jesus (and also that Pauline and Johannine accounts were subjective evaluations of the person of Jesus). In this book, without much ado, he accepted the *kenosis* theme but in spite of any limitation that must, as a consequence, be acknowledged he insisted that the moral and spiritual perfection of Jesus possessed a profound, converting appeal. As between the moral and spiritual qualities of Jesus the latter are of greater value for, in the perfection that Jesus revealed through his spiritual freedom, he made evident his own sense of sonship and communicated this realization to all his disciples.[9] In the first instance, then, Garvie agreed with the Ritschlian emphasis that the controlling consideration in defining the truth about the person of Christ was his worth as experienced in his work as redeemer; as a result, it was futile to strive for an objectivity of doctrine that was distinct from the subjectivity of experience. But he went beyond what he understood to be characteristic of the Ritschlians at a crucial

[7] *The Ritschlian Theology* (Edinburgh: T. and T. Clark, 1899), p. 214.

[8] *Studies in the Inner Life of Jesus*, p. vi. In this book Garvie acknowledged his great debt to Kaftan as well as Herrmann.

[9] *Ibid.*, pp. 69, 269, 277, 284, 301.

point, for he immediately argued that the work revealed the person, Jesus is what he reveals himself to be in his work. And what did Jesus reveal? In addition to the perfect moral character and the absolute religious consciouness Jesus performed a universal and permanent mediatorial function of bringing God to men in grace and men to God in faith.[10]

Garvie wanted to root this discussion in a metaphysical base, and both his desire and his effort revealed his absorption of the ethos of the age. He claimed that God is the absolute metaphysical reality, that personality is the highest metaphysical term, and that the consummation of reality is the personal union of man with God—that is, a *telos* progressively realized in ethical maturation. He summed up his position,

We must first of all consider the relation of God to the world, which is the scene of the Incarnation; that relation for the thinking of today is expressed in the category of *immanence;* we must next ask ourselves how we can describe the process of this Divine activity in and through the world, and at once the term *evolution* suggests itself as the answer; and lastly we must seek to get an adequate category for the highest stage of that evolution, in which we may assume there is disclosed to us the ultimate cause, the final purpose, and the essential nature of that process, and who can doubt that *personality* is the clue which we seek? [11]

The words that Garvie italicized in this quotation are important, for they are the three most crucial words in the theological discussion of the era, and here he attempted to bring all three ideas together. Again, it is significant that Christology is the culmination of his presentation, for Jesus Christ is the true goal of the entire process, and in the manifestation of this personality man recognizes his own affinity and community with God.

Another Nonconformist theologian, this time a Presbyterian, John Oman, also reflected strong Ritschlian themes. But, once more, one

---

[10] "What Jesus *was* in Himself constituted what He *did* for mankind. The Person conceived not *statically* as product of the eternal act but *dynamically* as process of a temporal development is identical with the work. Jesus is for us what He is in Himself." *Ibid.,* p. 474; cf. also 472-73, 484.

[11] *Ibid.,* p. 521.

must be careful not to categorize him too quickly. Philosophically, Oman was out of sympathy with Hegelian forms of idealism and defended a more realistic epistemology.[12] Insofar as Ritschl himself represented a return to Kant's epistemology there was an affinity, for Oman's theory of knowledge was a variety of Kantianism. At the point of Christology, especially in his earlier book *Vision and Authority,* another conformity of perspective was noticeable. Oman emphasized man's native spiritual endowment, which gave him the ability to discern (have a vision of) ultimate value, but he also stressed that there is a necessary interdependence of this potentiality and the objective event(s) that calls it to actualization. There is a coinherence between that which is given and the appreciation of the given; man's capacity for valuation is interdependent with God's gracious offering of that which possesses ultimate value. As was shown in the earlier discussion of Oman's book *Grace and Personality,* he was more dependent upon the prevailing psychology than upon the mainstream of idealistic philosophy; man as a free creature whose integrity is at every point respected by God was the main thesis of his theology, and nowhere did it find clearer expression than in his early discussion of Christology.

For Oman, grace was not an abstract power or an impersonal force. Grace is a person, grace is Jesus Christ. Hence, whenever we speak of God's grace we are speaking of Jesus Christ, who approaches man as man—that is, in a form that is appropriate to man's personhood. Persistently he reiterated his theme: God's encounter with man is in a mode that respects man's freedom; consequently the incarnation says something important about man as well as about God. Christ confronts man as man; he lived a humanly understandable life: "The chief parable was His own life, for His highest appeal to what is spiritual in man was not what He said, but what He was." [13] By "what He was" Oman was not thinking in terms of creedal affirmations, he was not interested in becoming involved in any effort to describe the person of Jesus Christ in terms of two-natures or of substance philosophy; Jesus was known in his immediate confrontation of men, and to no man, not even the

---

[12] Cf. Thomas A. Langford, "The Theological Methodology of John Oman and H. H. Farmer," *Religious Studies,* April, 1966, pp. 229-40.

[13] *Vision and Authority,* p. 104.

apostles, must be surrendered the right of measuring the revelation of God by our own need.

In company with others among the contemporary Nonconformists, Oman centered the revelation that is expressed in Jesus in the cross, and the reason for this is in keeping with Forsyth's desire to "moralize" Christology. The crucifixion is the culmination of God's self-unveiling, for here divine method is most clearly manifest. God's strength is revealed in weakness, his compulsion does not violate man's freedom. By self-sacrificing love and patient tolerance God elicits man's response of trust. What is obvious in this discussion is that the work of Jesus not only is the beginning point for Christology, it is the whole of Christology. Oman does not proceed to interpret the nature of Jesus, he attempted no formulation of the person of the Redeemer. Jesus has the value of God, of this he is clear, but, as in the case of Ritschl, he felt no need to advance any metaphysical description. Christian knowledge does not consist in abstract truths about God, he claimed; it is neither metaphysical nor mystical but prophetic. It is prophetic in that it is knowledge that comes by direct engagement, by the experience of salvation, by hearing the voice of God. In his most concise description of Jesus we have these themes given prominence.

In the life and death of Jesus of Nazareth man has won at once a nearer and loftier conception of God. On this revelation of the Father alone may he now rest his hopes and his affections. Others have taught us of God. But have left Him a vast, inconceiveable abstraction. . . . But when Jesus manifests the Father . . . by a life among common men wherein His holiness surmounts every form of the temptation to consider self, the proof of the Divineness of the revelation lies very near, and the God we discover by it is not afar off. . . . It is a manifestation of the Father to be best probed in the life of duty and temptation, one that will be best known to the soul that has most earnestly put it to the test of his daily struggle and his daily aspiration.

Men are not all able to give a name to their thoughts about this Man, but if faith in Him always means power in conflict and peace in trial, they must in their heart of hearts give Him the name that is above every name.[14]

[14] *Ibid.*, pp. 228-29, cf. also, *The Church and the Divine Order*, pp. 320-21.

224

With Oman, the Ritschlian emphasis upon Jesus possessing the value of God for man and a reluctance to attempt to describe Jesus in metaphysical terms both came to the fore. Traditional christological analyses and dogmas were set aside in favor of an emphasis upon the meaning of Jesus for faith.

Other Nonconformists reacted differently to the Ritschlian theses, and in this connection it is necessary to indicate the relation of P. T. Forsyth to this theological stream. John H. Rodgers has claimed that "one could, with reasonable accuracy, describe Forsyth's whole theological pilgrimage as an inner critique of Ritschlian theology." He further comments "the critique was so radical and basic as to create a position which can only in the most qualified manner be referred to as Ritschlian." [15] The two principal themes that Forsyth inherited from the Ritschlian theologians were the primacy of experience in Christian life and theology, and the givenness of a moral conscience that must be satisfied by any doctrine of the atonement and any satisfactory development of christological themes. Forsyth, however, differed profoundly from the Ritschlians in his stress upon the metaphysical import of theological statements, such as the need to discuss the nature of Jesus Christ in metaphysical terms. He retained his commitment to dogmatic theological construction, and he stressed the miracle of man's redemption by Jesus Christ. In contrast to Oman, it should be made clear that while Forsyth also spoke of moralizing Christian doctrine and stressed the role of conscience, he referred his discussion exclusively to the cross-redemption and not to the natural order or the common fabric of human existence. There is a sense in which the conscience of man remained for Forsyth, as for Oman, the criterion by which doctrine was to be judged; but in Forsyth's case the native conscience of man was brought to self-understanding only by God's presentation of himself as demanding, sovereign holiness and as redeeming sovereign love. In confrontation with the cross, man comes to recognize the meaning of absolute moral demand, human sinfulness, and divine redemption. For Oman this moral recognition was derived from an awareness of the significance of one's

---

[15] John H. Rodgers, *The Theology of P. T. Forsyth* (London: Independent Press, 1965), p. 3, cf. also pp. 4 and 277, n. 5. Rodgers himself does not extensively develop this theme.

total context and one's place within that context and was not in any
primary sense uniquely connected with the event of Jesus Christ. The
focus upon the work of Christ for Forsyth and the concentration upon
the structures of human existence in general constituted the point of
most radical distinction between these two theologians.

From the more liberal position within Nonconformity there was also
criticism of Ritschlian influence. K. C. Anderson in *The Larger Faith*
claimed, "It is an open secret that some of the leaders of the Churches
of Great Britain who in their youth broke with the traditional theology
have been saved to Evangelicalism, if not to orthodoxy, through the
medium of Ritschlian theology." [16] Anderson criticized Ritschl's position,
and especially Garvie's use of Ritschl, because it seemed to imply that
present spiritual experience is, in some manner, evidence for the truth
of past historical facts. But this is impossible, he claimed, for one
cannot posit the Deity of Jesus Christ upon a personal experience of
his moral worth. The whole of Ritschlian theology breaks down at this
point, for it cannot by some *tour de force* of experience bridge the gulf
between a present fact of inner experience and a past fact of outward
history. The only alternative is to separate the Christ of faith from the
Jesus of history and talk about the belief in the first or the historical
existence of the second. "The understanding of this distinction is the
key to the whole theological situation of the present day." [17]

To trace the continued development of and the aroused reaction to
Ritschlian theology leads directly to a debate we have already mentioned.
In January 1909 the Reverend R. Roberts wrote an article for the Hibbert Journal entitled "Jesus or Christ? An Appeal for Consistency." The
title itself suggested Harnack's distinction between the Jesus of history
and the Christ of faith, and this was what lay behind the question posed
by the article. In the ensuing discussion the question that was paramount
was clearly stated by Father George Tyrrell, "Does the predicate 'Christ'
as interpreted by the creeds, agree with the subject 'Jesus,' as determined
by criticism?" [18] Professors Weinel and Schmiedel, two contributors
from the continent, took the position of Harnack, although Schmiedel

[16] *The Larger Faith*, p. 45.
[17] *Ibid.*, p. 58.
[18] *Hibbert Journal: Supplement 1909: Jesus or Christ*, p. 9.

was more rigorous and severe in his negations. Both refused to commit themselves to any dogmatic confession of Jesus as the Christ, though Weinel did insist that in the last analysis Christian faith cannot separate the person of Jesus from the fulfillment of the moral religion of Judaism, and, because of that inheritance, Jesus was the initiator of the Christian religion, which is a religion of moral redemption. The English contributors were more conservative in their response. Even Professor Percy Gardner argued that "the Church is the Church of Jesus-Christ . . . it is built upon a hyphen." [19] Scott Holland predicated his discussion upon the confidence that the two ideas or conceptions—Jesus and Christ —were not in hopeless collision, as Roberts argued; rather the Gospel writers "passed smoothly from one conception to another. They looked for the Christ in Jesus, and found what they looked for." [20] Others echoed the same conviction, particularly E. S. Talbot and Alfred Garvie.

The *Supplement* articles were primarily significant not because they answered the question posed but because they forced the issue upon the English religious community. To put this another way, there was a keen sensitivity to the possibility that there might be a disjunction between the religion of Jesus and the religion about Jesus; the uniqueness of Jesus had become a problem and no longer remained a firm assurance for many. Perhaps the most important contribution from a long-range perspective was that of Scott Holland who argued that this interrogation must be met by a clear statement that the heart of the New Testament revelation was not to be found in a simple study of the activity and teaching of Jesus; rather the resurrection was the crucial event, and insofar as this is taken seriously it may be claimed that Christianity found its originating impulse outside the limits of the gospel story. Christianity began as Christology, and one is not able— by critical study or any other means—to return to a Jesus of history who is uninterpreted by the eyes of faith. Further, Holland argued that the factual account of the life of Jesus was still relevant, for "in Christian faith we are not dealing with 'symbols' of an idea, which can be dropped when once the idea is apprehended. . . . The love of God is only

[19] *Ibid.*, p. 50.
[20] *Ibid.*, p. 128.

to be known and felt in the sacrifices that it has actually once for all made." [21]

This debate exposed the question, and now several distinct responses were made within Anglicanism that reflected the Ritschlian influence, especially as this augmented tendencies present in idealistic estimates of human maturation. Two of the most significant were the positions of J. F. Bethune-Baker and Hastings Rashdall. Bethune-Baker argued that we find in Jesus a newness and originality of thought that sets him apart from the rest of mankind; indeed, it may even be claimed that Jesus was the "first man to know God as He really is." Other men had seen and understood God in part, but the name of Jesus stands uniquely attached to the comprehensive discovery of God. Nonetheless, Bethune-Baker claimed that he did not for a moment suppose that Jesus ever thought of himself as God; on the contrary what Jesus did exhibit was the fact that the being of God and the being of man are indissolubly interrelated. Therefore, in Jesus we see God; God has the qualities that Jesus revealed. "God stands to me for the highest values in life, and because I believe those values were actualized in the person and life of Jesus, I must use the title 'God' of Him." [22] While it would be a mistake to attempt neatly to align Bethune-Baker with any single previous theological position, there were decided Ritschlian and idealistic tendencies in his thought.

Bethune-Baker was an eclectic thinker; he was a catholic-modernist in the sense that he had a strong sense of the church and a deep appreciation of its sacramental life. He was also profoundly influenced by the recent emphases upon evolution and immanence. But in his Christology he continually expressed interest in the moral quality of Jesus. As the result of these influences, he insisted that the incarnation must be set within the context of God; all of creation has its origin in the will and love of God, and in Jesus Christ the Creator most perfectly exemplifies himself. Thus in the man Jesus we have God most fully revealed to and in men; in him the fullest expression of Divine Personality was manifested. Because of this unique position which

[21] *Ibid.*, pp. 121-22. Cf. also Holland's review of Kirsopp Lake's *The Stewardship of Faith* (1915) reprinted in *Creeds and Critics* (London: Mowbray, 1918), pp. 22-23, also 130.

[22] *The Modern Churchman*, Sept., 1921, p. 299.

Jesus possesses, it is legitimate to worship him as the God-man.[23]

In Hastings Rashdall we find also a combination of these two divergent lines. Earlier, Rashdall had stated that he had been impressed with Herrmann's interpretation of the meaning of Jesus, but he had also expressed dissatisfaction with the philosophical base for Herrmann's theology. In an explicit manner Rashdall indicated what he took to be the essence of his christological formulation: (1) Jesus did not claim divinity for himself; (2) Jesus was in the fullest sense a man—he had a human body, soul, intellect, and will; (3) Jesus' human soul did not preexist, but the divine *logos* did; (4) the divinity of Jesus does not *necessarily* imply the Virgin Birth or any miracle; and (5) the divinity of Jesus does not imply omniscience. So far Rashdall had stated his position in propositional fashion. Next, he offered a rational justification for this position. Rashdall was a careful philosopher and student of history; he understood where he was diverging from and where he was perpetuating the classical and recent theological emphases, but fundamentally he was convinced of the congruence or conformity between man and God—a conformity that was most adequately expressed in man's moral conscience. If, he argued, we acknowledge that God is revealed in man's moral conscience, then it becomes possible to accept the doctrine that in a single human life God is more completely revealed than in any other life. To express this in a slightly different manner, if we believe that God is revealed and incarnated in every human soul to some extent, and if we further believe that in the great ethical heroes of mankind God is even more fully revealed, then it is not unreasonable to believe that in one single man this revelation reached its most adequate expression. If this is so, then we are justified in speaking of that revelation as supreme and unique. Thus, he concluded, "in the life and character, the teaching and Personality of Jesus Christ the world has received its highest revelation of God, a revelation, however, which is still being continued and further developed by the work of

---

[23] For a discussion of Bethune-Baker see, W. Norman Pittenger, "The Christian Apologetic of James Franklin Bethune-Baker," *Anglican Theological Journal,* Oct., 1955. This is an important statement even though Pittenger overstresses Bethune-Baker's Catholic Modernism at the expense of the Ritschlian influence. See especially Bethune-Baker, *The Miracle of Christianity.*

God's spirit in other human minds, and particularly in the society of Christ's followers." [24] The indebtedness to Harnack is evident, even as there is also a utilization of idealistic notions of human self-fulfillment.

In this discussion of Ritschlian influences and the question of the Jesus of history, as in the immanental and kenotic theories, we find a number of streams converging. Historical, critical study of the Bible emphasized the importance of the gospel portraits, portraits that stressed the humanity of Jesus. For a number of the more liberal theologians this picture of Jesus was the only adequate foundation for theological statement. The historical and philosophical interpretations that dominated the minds of twentieth-century man seemed to demand adjustment of Christian theology in this direction; and whatever judgment later generations have made of this stream, it must be acknowledged that it was a courageous search for truth and a creative interpretation of God's relation to man. Yet, although agreed at the point that they must return to the historical Jesus, they disagreed as to how the historical Jesus functioned as the revealer of God. For the more cautious, such as Garvie, Jesus revealed God through the perfection of his moral and spiritual life, and, although the subjective response is emphasized, the objective truth that God was in Christ was given a primary position. For Bethune-Baker and Rashdall the relation between Jesus and God became less unique, but both of these men wanted to retain the value of Jesus as the originator of the Christian faith and his supremacy as enlightener of man's understanding of God.

On the whole, Ritschlian influence upon English theology was important in that it helped to shift the emphasis from the person to the work of Jesus Christ. The questioning of Greek substance philosophy and the pressure of critical studies of the Scripture forced interpreters away from attempts to explicate the nature of Jesus to reflection upon his activity in the life of men. This movement represented an effort to retain the centrality of Jesus Christ for Christian faith. Christian experience, as the experience of Jesus and the new valuation of life that he brings, was becoming dominant. To know Christ was to know his benefits, and this was theologically significant even if one must

[24] *The Modern Churchman*, Sept., 1921, p. 256. Cf. also *The Idea of the Atonement in Christian Theology* (London: Macmillan, 1919), pp. 447-48.

remain silent or speak secondarily about his nature. Jesus revealed what human life could mean, and in this revelation he made evident what God intended for every man; Jesus also revealed what the stance of man in relation to God should be and struck the path for men to follow; finally, Jesus revealed the nature of God as gracious love and hereby set the context for man's understanding of God, of himself, and of his fellowman. Whether God is of the same nature as the values man finds in Jesus is the question most types of Ritschlian interpretation left unanswered. Whether an interpretation of Jesus Christ exhausts the interpretation of God also remained problematic, but for the moment Ritschlian concentration upon Jesus Christ provided a new impetus for theological activity.

In all these cases we have the liberal response to the question of authority, of scriptural interpretation and the nature of faith. From the evangelical tradition Garvie continued to attempt to work within the scriptural context. Bethune-Baker and Rashdall found human reason, albeit reason that was congruent with its Divine Creator, to be the final arbiter. But it is a severe injustice to both not to recognize that their theologies are sustained efforts to explicate Christian theology on the basis of the primacy of the Holy Spirit. Neither man described his work in this manner in so many words; nonetheless it is obvious that throughout their discussion the idea of immanence is cognate with God's indwelling Spirit, a Spirit that prepares for and brings to its fulfillment the presence of God in Christ. And again, in spite of their inability to take into account certain aspects of traditional creedal theology, they were clear about their own ultimate evaluation of Jesus Christ, and they attempted to make this understandable to their age.

Whatever the particular response of any given theologian, Ritschlian modes of thought had become widely pervasive in christological interpretation. "We may . . . take the Ritschlian step as characterizing the present stage of inquiry," wrote William Sanday. "Even where the Ritschlian and Pragmatic theories are not held, there is a widespread tendency to look for moral and religious values rather than for metaphysical definition." [25] According to Sanday's discrimination there are

[25] *Christologies Ancient and Modern*, p. 96.

two dominant types of christological interpretation that may be built upon this platform; one he called "full Christianity" and the other "reduced Christianity." By reduced Christianity he meant primarily German liberal interpretations. This interpretation of the person of Christ, he claimed, is constructed for defense and, therefore, is as safely fortified as possible. Christology is reduced to its barest essentials, and only its strongest features are retained. In contrast to this are the full or maximum christological expositions, which affirm all that the creeds have said about Christ. This view represents a complete revolt against the attempts of twentieth-century science and historiography to circumscribe what has traditionally and may still be claimed in regard to Jesus Christ. This latter movement was more typical of English scholarship, and with this response Sanday aligned himself.

Sanday developed his own position by suggesting a "tentative" modern Christology, and he set his effort upon the dual foundation stones of mysticism and modern psychology. From mysticism, that is, from the work of R. C. Moberly—who in *Atonement and Personality* insisted upon the participation of man in the life of God—W. R. Inge, and Baron von Hügel, Sanday drew his primary inspiration. Man must be understood in terms of his inherent relationship with God. But how may this relationship be described? From William James and F. W. B. Myers he took the notion of the subconscious. Unlike earlier interpretation, such as that of James Ward, Sanday was explicit in stating that the subconscious is an active power that combines, modifies, and presents fresh impulses and ideas to the conscious psyche. This treasure-house is the seat of the divine—as well as the diabolical—in man. From James' *Varieties of Religious Experience* Sanday took the hypothesis that whatever it may be on its farther side, the reality with which we feel ourselves connected in religious experience is on its hither side the subconscious ground of our conscious life. This was expanded to mean that the divine indwelling in man is to be found in the subliminal dimension of consciousness.[26]

When these presuppositions were applied to Jesus Christ, we have a way, Sanday claimed, of retaining the creedal description of his single

[26] For his discussion of mysticism and psychology see *Ibid.*, pp. 137-59.

human personality while also referring to him correctly as being Divine. Jesus' human consciousness was entirely human. Whatever there was of divinity in him—that is, in his subsconsciousness—had to pass through the restrictive and restraining medium of his conscious mind. In a clear statement Sanday described the person of Jesus.

We may venture then to picture to ourselves the working of our Lord's consciousness in some such way as this. His life on earth presented all the outward appearance of the life of any other contemporary Galilean. His bodily organism discharged the same ordinary functions and ministered to the life of the soul in the same ordinary ways. . . . Impressions received through the senses and emotions awakened by them were recollected and stored up for use by the same wonderful processes by which any one of us becomes the living receptacle of personal experiences. His mind played over all these accumulated memories, sifting, digesting, analysing, extracting, combining and recombining. Out of such constituent elements, physical, rational, moral and spiritual, character was formed in Him as in any one of ourselves, though with unwonted care and attention.[27]

It is impossible to place Sanday's discussion in any school. It was unique and uniquely placed within its environment. As a creative effort to use the resources of his age this work was significant, and his attempt to defend "full Christianity" reflected a persistent English effort throughout the era.

A CONVERGENCE OF THEMES

We conclude this chapter with a consideration of the contribution of William Temple to the symposium *Foundations*. The first of his essays was entitled "The Divinity of Jesus Christ," and it is upon this article that we shall concentrate our attention. The reason for closing with this particular discussion is not the result of an evaluation that this is the most important contribution on the subject that had been made up to this time in twentieth-century England—although it might be possible to make this disputable claim, especially if we limit it to

[27] *Ibid.,* p. 179.

233

Anglican theology—nor do I place this discussion at the close simply because its historical position was toward the close of the prewar era. Rather, the most justifiable reason for turning now to this theologian and his christological statement is that in this essay we find an eclectic spirit, albeit a critical eclecticism, which is aware of and reacts to many of the themes that have already appeared in the previous discussion.

In company with his fellow contributors to *Foundations,* Temple predicated his position upon the base of religious experience, for it is in men's actual experience of Christ that they are led to believe in him as Lord and to interpret their world in the light of this belief. But upon what grounds do men acknowledge Jesus as Divine? This is the fundamental problem and the question that Temple was convinced must be set straight. The interrogation is wrongly put if it is framed, Is Jesus Divine? For to ask the question in this manner is to assume that men already know what divinity is, and that against this clear background they can come to a conclusion about the identity of Jesus. But, Temple claimed, this is just what we cannot do. In spite of the fact that men do have some knowledge of the Divine through natural revelation this knowledge remains faulty at the point of giving adequate content to the character of the Divine, and the question of the character of the Divine is the most crucial question from the standpoint of religious faith. The wisest way of putting the interrogation, then, is not, Is Jesus Divine? but, What is God like?

To approach an answer to this question we must begin where the disciples began—with the experience of Jesus as he encountered them. And to follow this path the best guide is the Gospel of John. Men, both ancient and modern, Temple contended, begin with a belief in a supreme power that underlies all reality and gives to reality a purposeful meaning. In the ancient world this reality was called the *logos,* in the modern world it might be called Natural Law; but in both cases the question still remained: what is the character of this ultimate principle? Historically, from the Christian perspective, the question can be answered in terms of the experience that the disciples had of Jesus. In this Man, they were convinced, the *logos* was revealed, in him the Supreme Power expressed its most central characteristics. Further, to say that the *logos* became flesh in Jesus of Nazareth makes rational sense:

it makes sense of suffering and pain, it makes sense of sin, it makes sense of love. "The instinct that has led men to worship Christ as God is not illusory; this faith makes sense, and it alone makes sense of our experience." [28]

This, then, is the first step—to insist that it is in the experience of men as they encounter and are encountered by Jesus Christ that they come to know the character of the Power that underlies their lives and all reality. But now we must move to the second stage—how has this man Jesus been described? In dealing with this problem Temple quickly reviewed several alternatives that have been suggested in the Christian theological tradition. It is not necessary to recapitulate this description, but the conclusions that he reached are important. First—and this must be noted because many commentators on Temple's thought have not adequately recognized this dimension—the experience of men with Christ has given the central place to the redemptive work that he preformed. "Redemption is a matter of primary religious importance, whereas the explanation of the world's origin is at least secondary." [29] However, in spite of the recognition of this fact by some of the early Fathers, and especially Athanasius, Greek theology as a whole was a failure, "Chalcedon" was "a confession of the bankruptcy of Greek Patristic Theology," [30] and this failure was due primarily to their metaphysical assumptions that moved upon a materialistic interpretation of substance. It is only with Pelagius and Augustine that Western theology takes on its distinctive hue and concentrates upon the will and therefore upon the distinctiveness of the human person. The emphasis upon the integrity of the individual person was, according to Temple, the breakthrough that enabled theology to deal more adequately with the person of Jesus in his relation both to God and to other men.

Upon the insight that the will is the person, Temple undertook his restatement of the person of Jesus Christ. It must be reiterated that the question with which we are concerned is, What is the character of the world-principle that underlies and gives cohesion to the totality of reality? Again, the Gospel of John provides us with the proper starting

[28] *Foundations,* p. 223.
[29] *Ibid.,* p. 228.
[30] *Ibid.,* p. 230.

point—namely, that in the life, death, and resurrection of Jesus the eternal glory of God is revealed. If by the term "will" we understand "the entire active person" [31] then it is possible to say that Christ and the Father are one in the sense that Jesus is the singular man whose will is united with God's. To say that the wills of Jesus and God are one is to speak in the fullest possible sense of the coinherence of each in the other. It is not to claim something that is only peripheral or less than essential. On the contrary, the unity of wills means that Christ is God; the entire content of Christ's being—his thought, feeling, and purpose—is also that of God. "Thus, in the language of logicians, formally (as pure subjects) God and Christ are distinct; materially (that is in the content of the two consciousnesses) God and Christ are One and the Same." [32]

But some further distinctions must be made. If Christ and God are one is it possible to say that the full being of God is revealed in Jesus Christ? Are there not qualities or attributes, such as omniscience, that Jesus does not reveal, and if so are we to posit some sort of kenotic doctrine? To these questions Temple replied by refusing to fall back upon a kenotic interpretation; in contrast, he maintained that while we cannot say that Jesus Christ is the Absolute God in terms of the fulness of his being, nevertheless, "in all which directly concerns the spiritual relation of Man to God, Christ is identically one with the Father in the content of His Being . . . in content of heart and will Christ is identically one with God." [33] In spite of his protestations, this was a type of kenotic emphasis; for those who held the kenotic theory, especially Weston and Forsyth, said the same thing in regard to the spiritual or redemptive relation which Christ exhibited. And, as Temple admitted, since the Father is greater than the Son, it must be said that something less than the whole Godhead was revealed in Jesus Christ. But the Christian affirmation remains that in Christ the man of faith sees the Father; insofar as the revelation of God can be made in the mode of a human life it is revealed in Jesus Christ. Thus, the confession

[31] *Ibid.*, p. 248. Cf. also Temple, *The Nature of Personality* (London: Macmillan, 1911), p. 22.

[32] *Foundations*, p. 249.

[33] *Ibid.*, p. 250.

of faith says that God is like Christ; the *logos* has been personified.

It is also claimed by the Christian that in Jesus Christ we find what it means to be human. Now it is possible to see, by contrast, what humanity is in its fallenness as well as what human nature might be when there is an affinity of will with the Divine. Because men are sinful there must be a revelation for human life; because humanity is not totally alien to God there can be a revelation in human life. The entire discussion hinged on the transformation of the metaphysical base that Temple effected. To meet the difficulties that the classical definitions of the person of Jesus Christ presented and that recent discussions that worked within the classical framework had perpetuated, Temple attempted to redirect the discussion by a *tour de force*. Even *kenosis* is an unacceptable alternative because it is an attempt to patch up a defunct metaphysic. As a way out, Temple turned to a definition of substance that equated substance with will, and upon the basis of "will" he attempted his restatement. In this new presentation he argued that by interpreting will as the total active personality we can give a viable explanation of the unity that existed between God and Christ and between Christ and men. Christ and the Father are distinct insofar as each is a distinct person or will, but Christ and the Father are one insofar as there is a coalescence of their wills.

Temple was primarily indebted to the psychological understanding of man that was expressed in Illingworth. And this was especially significant because he explicitly stated that his approach was based upon psychology. This meant that for Temple, as for Illingworth, the person is understood as a continuous, self-determined, active personality in which conscious psychic life is given the preeminent and all-inclusive place, though Temple was distinct in that, as a voluntarist, he gave will (rather than intellect) an absolute priority. Once again, there was no interest in the subconscious dimension of personality or its influence upon the conscious state. The only place he mentioned the subconscious aspect was in a footnote in his book, *The Nature of Personality,* in which he rejected Sanday's attempt to restate the Divinity of Jesus in terms of the subconscious (even though the book is dedicated to Sanday).[34]

---

[34] *The Nature of Personality*, p. 116.

Consequently, both in the discussion of the meaning of personality as revealed in Jesus Christ and in the consequent interpretation of personality as embodied in human existence, he remained within the context of conscious mental activity. Charles Gore had stressed the need to turn more directly to an analysis of religious experience, and P. T. Forsyth had emphasized the role of will in the elucidation of the relation of Jesus to God; but Temple took both of these themes and in his own style carried them forward and presented a distinctive approach to christological interpretation.

It is not clear that Temple was as free from the kenotic Christologies as he claimed, and some of the problems that they faced were also difficulties for him. Given his psychological understanding, did his position allow full weight to the human development of Jesus? That is, since he stressed self-conscious volition, was he able to deal adequately with the stage of pre-self awareness in childhood as this pertains to Jesus? Further, the dynamics of the relation between two wills (God's and Jesus') are replete with difficulties as long as one stresses conscious, knowing, volitional action. Temple moved from a discussion of metaphysical explorations of the nature of Jesus in terms of Greek substance philosophy, but insofar as he emphasized the will as the defining principle of personhood one was left again with a need for elucidation of the dynamics of or acknowledgment of the mystery of how two wills could become one.

With Temple we come to the close of the christological discussion of the era. Among the theologians we have considered, we find the prevalent concerns of the time once again being expressed: what is the primal sanction for Christian faith; how may this faith be assimulated with contemporary intellectual sensibilities; what does Christology contribute to our understanding of God, man, and society? These questions were consistently addressed by the Christian thinkers of the era, and in the elucidation of the meaning of Jesus Christ were to be found their proffered answers. Jesus Christ is the source of Christian experience —whether one focuses primarily upon him or is led to God by him— and if one takes his own perspective upon life from the vantage point of that experience he has a strong, yet adaptable position. The Ritschlian emphasis upon the work of Jesus Christ rather than his nature facilitated the shift of focus to his influence upon the life of men. But in England the shift was never complete, and throughout the era there was continual wrestling with the question of Jesus' nature. What was required was an employment of contemporary modes of thought to explicate the meaning of Jesus Christ both for personal experience and for an interpretation of the world.

Even as this is said, however, it must be acknowledged that in reaching this point we still have no easily definable trail to follow, no clear pathways that direct to the future; and any value that is derived from the study of the period is not to be located primarily in conclusions that were reached. It was, we should remind ourselves, an era of explorers.

X

. . . AND THEN THE WAR

The change and conflict that had characterized British life for the first decade of the twentieth century was brought to its climax by the throes of war. The social conflicts, the parliamentary crisis, and the economic struggles were interrupted by the challenge of Germany. The impossible had happened, the war that could not take place was taking place, and for the first time since 1815 Great Britain was involved in a major European conflict.

Herbert Read commented about the First World War, which has always remained "The Great War" in English minds: "It must be remembered that in 1914 our conception of war was completely unreal. We had vague childish memories of the Boer War, and from these and from a general diffusion of Kiplingesque sentiments, we managed to infuse into war a decided element of adventurous romance. War still appealed to the imagination." [1]

[1] Quoted by D. J. Enright, "The Literature of the First World War," *The Modern Age* (Harmondsworth, Middlesex: Penguin, 1961), p. 157.

The initiation of the war in 1914 came as a profound shock to the British people. In spite of the fear that the expansion of the German navy had caused in 1909, in spite of the Kaiser's fulminations and explicit German threats to Belgium, there were generally amicable relations between Britain and Germany up until the very outbreak of the war. But now, the antagonisms that British people had expressed toward one another were—to an extent—drawn together and directed toward Germany. Caught unprepared, both emotionally and militarily, the nation reacted sharply against those who had taken advantage of and thereby exposed its ambiguities. On August 3, 1914 Edward Grey, Secretary for Foreign Affairs, called for war, and although it came as a surprise to many, there was an immediate and enthusiastic response. "The swing to enthusiastic support for war," A. J. P. Taylor has said, "was not a gradual process; it was a revolution." [2] Even those who had spoken against war, such as Gilbert Murray and John Clifford, found cause for a change of heart.

Barbara Tuchman has described the causes of the war as the consequence of a quarter-century of unrest, the developing attraction of anarchism, the collapse of the aristocratic structure of society, the natural extension of Darwin's depiction of the struggle for existence, personal pique, economic and political forces, and, perhaps most significant of all, the resurgent strength of nationalism. She comments on the latter factor.

Nietzsche recognized the waning of religion as a primary force in people's lives and flung his challenge in these words: "God is dead." He would have substituted Superman, but ordinary people substituted patriotism. As faith in God retreated before the advance of science, love of country began to fill the empty spaces in the heart. Nationalism absorbed the strength once belonging to religion. Where people formerly fought for religion now they would presumably do no less for its successor. A sense of gathering conflict filled the air. [3]

Before 1914 it had been generally expected that if war should come in Europe it would be decided in the first few weeks. When this

[2] *The Trouble Makers* (London: Hamish Hamilton, 1957), p. 129.
[3] *The Proud Tower*, p. 250.

expectation failed, the people and the politicians reluctantly acknowledged that the conflict in which they were engaged would require an unprecedented mobilization. A utilization of the entire productive capacity of the nation was demanded to serve the war effort. So intense and novel were the requirements that there was little sympathy for those who questioned the military involvement or those who wanted to remain pacifists. Every questioner was looked upon with suspicion of treason.[4]

Quickly, the habits of a nation were changed. A journalist reported "we see khaki everywhere." Military searchlights replaced the electric advertising signs in London. Zeppelins were in the air, and boats raced back and forth across the channel. Men were working when ordinarily they would have been at leisure. Lord Northcliffe began an editorial campaign for conscription for military service (which became a reality in May 1916). There was talk of great bloodshed abroad and rumblings of discontent about preparations at home. Organizations to help ward off loneliness for soldiers, their wives, and mothers were formed. In all, a common purpose brought a reknitting of community life and a sense of national identity.

To those to whom was given the task of fighting the war a new spirit was born. If there was a remaining division in the nation's life, it had, for the time being, shifted and could now be said to exist between those who were fighting the war in the trenches and "the others." Such a division momentarily destroyed some of the old social distinctions, encouraged camaraderie across class lines and gave the warriors a sense of having earned whatever the nation could give. The men who had remained at home, even those in key technical jobs, were suspect and often looked upon with contempt and among the contemptibles were young ministers of religion who were not in the trenches. The themes of suffering and death were uppermost in the trench-warrior's mind. The winter of the world was closing in with perishing great darkness.

The horror of the world's winter was soon evident. Paul Nash, the artist, described the war in bitter terms in a letter to his wife.

---

[4] Evidence of this can be found in the story of Bertrand Russell, who was imprisoned on a charge of interfering with recruiting and was deprived of his lectureship at Trinity College, Cambridge.

We all have a vague notion of the terrors of a battle, and can conjure up with the aid of some of the more inspired war correspondents and the pictures in the *Daily Mirror* some vision of a battlefield; but no pen or drawing can convey this country—the normal setting of the battles taking place day and night, month after month. Evil and the incarnate fiend alone can be master of this war, and no glimmer of God's hand is seen anywhere. Sunset and sunrise are blasphemous, they are mockeries to men, only the black rain out of the bruised and swollen clouds all through the bitter black of night is fit atmosphere in such a land. The rain drives on, the stinking mud becomes more evilly yellow, the shell holes fill up with greenwhite water, the roads and tracks are covered in inches of slime, the black dying trees ooze and sweat and the shells never cease. They alone plunge overhead, tearing away the rotting tree stumps, breaking the plank roads, striking down horses and mules, annihilating, maiming, maddening, they plunge into the grave which is this land; one huge grave, and cast up on it the poor dead. It is unspeakable, godless, hopeless.[5]

In the midst of the distress, some commentators remarked about the failure of religion to step onto the battlefield and provide a therapy for the soul. Robert Graves and Alan Hodge commented in retrospect that the British Expeditionary Force was in general irreligious; the men reduced morality to the single virtue of loyalty; no longer did the seven deadly sins bother them; the only thing that counted was that a man be courageous and a reasonably trusty comrade. "God as an all-wise Providence was dead; blind Chance had succeeded to the throne." [6]

Across no-man's-land, some among the enemy also realized that the war had created an impassible gulf in history. Erich Maria Remarque, in *All Quiet on the Western Front,* spoke of the trust that the younger men had until recently held in their elders. "The idea of authority, which they represented, was associated in our minds with a greater insight and a manlier wisdom." Then, with the first sight of death, deep disquietude forfeited the trust; the authorities of the past were set aside. "They surpassed us only in phrases and cleverness. The first

[5] *Outline, An Autobiography and Other Writings* (London: Faber and Faber, 1949), pp. 210-11.

[6] *The Long Weekend: A Social History of Great Britain 1918-1939* (London: Faber and Faber, 1940), p. 15.

bombardment showed us our mistake, and under it the world as they had taught it to us broke in pieces . . . and we saw that there was nothing of their world left. We were all at once terribly alone; and alone we must see it through."[7] Perhaps G. B. Shaw put the point most forcefully in his play *Too True to Be Good* when he described the experience of Aubrey, an ex-chaplain turned thief, who ruminates on his condition as a result of the war.

I stand midway between youth and age like a man who has missed his train: too late for the last and too early for the next. What am I to do? What am I? . . . I have no Bible, no creed; the war has shot both out of my hands. . . .

We have outgrown our religion, outgrown our political systems, outgrown our own strength of mind and character. The fatal word *NOT* has been miraculously inserted into all our creeds.[8]

Yet, in the midst of the blighted ambition, the discouraged spirit, and the disturbed moral sense of the time, there also survived strong hope, and for many there was an anticipation of a future that would be free of war. This was a war to bring wars to an end, a war to make the world safe for democracy, as H. G. Wells first put it. Politicians had said the same thing, ministers had preached it, and many could not forget the high motives with which they had gone into the battle. "This is a straight fight between the mailed fist and the nailed hand," cried Winnington-Ingram, the Bishop of London, who expressed the ideal in its crudest form. J. B. Mozley, in a sermon, maintained in a more sophisticated manner that when Christianity accepts a state as an order of civil life it accepts the methods of state action, including war. In the present situation, therefore, the Christian responsibility was to be faithful to that commitment. For others, however, the war brought anguished assessment of Christian methods and of responsibilities to both friend and foe. For most people the war required participation, but many participated with a heavy heart and with the melancholy awareness that the church and Christian faith had failed in one of

[7] (New York: Fawcett Books, 1962), p. 12.
[8] *The Complete Plays of Bernard Shaw* (London: Paul Hamly, 1956), p. 1167.

its major tasks—that of peacemaker. In addition, there was a gnawing doubt that the outcome of the war would vindicate the optimism and idealism of the social evolutionists. Among these dissenters was J. Ramsay MacDonald who spoke a word of doubt.

I read and listen to the moral flamboyancies of those who tell us that this is the last war, that from it is to date the overthrow of the military castes of Europe, that from the destruction of the Berlin War Office the Peace Temple at the Hague is to come into real being. It is all moonshine. Far more likely is it that this war is the beginning of a new military despotism in Europe, of new alarms, new hatreds and oppositions, new menaces and alliances; the beginning of a dark epoch, dangerous, not merely to democracy, but to civilization itself.[9]

Perhaps the most poignant description of the war, with its hopes and disillusionment, from a religious perspective, was to be found in the writings of an Anglican chaplain, G. A. Studdert-Kennedy. In harmony with the spirit of the time, Studdert-Kennedy was most vexed by the problem of evil. War had etched the reality of evil into the lives of men, and from this fact genuine religion could not shirk. The presence of evil and the presence of God became the commanding themes of his writing and his preaching. As an answer of one to the other, he found the suffering of God, the cross of Jesus Christ. In his earthy style, he expressed his hostility to all weak, escapist religion; a type of religion that he found too often in the trenches.

I wish that chap would chuck that praying. It turns me sick. I'd rather he swore like the sergeant. Its disgusting, somehow. It isn't religion, it's cowardice. It isn't prayer, it's wind. I'd like to shut him up. He probably seldom, if ever, prayed before, and now he substitutes prayer for pluck. I wouldn't mind if he'd pray for pluck, but it's all for safety. I hate this last resort kind of religion; it's blasphemy. . . . There is not, and there cannot be, any connection between Christ and cowardice.[10]

The cruelty, the folly, the waste of war plagued his mind, and the

[9] Lord Elton, *The Life of James Ramsay MacDonald*, p. 258.

[10] G. A. Studdert-Kennedy, from *The Hardest Part* as quoted in *The Best of Studdert-Kennedy* (New York: Harper, 1924), p. 47.

ineptness of the inherited religion to meet the demands of the men in the trenches seared his heart. Only a reclaimed awareness of the meaning of the suffering of God could relate the Christian message to such a time. Yet, even this conviction is one that cannot be piously mouthed by those who stand on the sidelines and encourage the pilgrims; it must express a won faith, an experienced reality. In his poem "Faith," he gave his most concrete expression to this position.

> How do I know that God is good? I don't.
> I gamble like a man. I bet my life
> Upon one side in life's great war. I must,
> I can't stand out. I must take sides. The man
> Who is a neutral in this fight is not
> A man. He's bulk and body without breath,
> Cold leg of lamb without mint sauce. A fool.
> He makes me sick. Good Lord! Weak tea!
>   Cold slops!
> I want to live, live out, not wobble through
> My life somehow, and then into the dark.
> I must have God. This life's too dull without,
> Too dull for aught but suicide.
>
> . . . .
>
> Well—God's my leader, and I hold that He
> Is good, and strong enough to work His plan
> And purpose out to its appointed end.
> I am no fool, I have my reasons for
> This faith, but they are not the reasonings,
> The coldly calculated formulae
> Of thought divorced from feeling. They are true,
> Too true for that. There's no such thing as thought
> Which does not feel, if it be real thought
> And not thought's ghost—all pale and sicklied o'er
> With dead conventions—abstract truth—man's lie
> Upon this living, loving, suff'ring Truth.
>
> . . . .
>
> I see what God has done,
> What life in this world is. I see what you
> See, this eternal struggle in the dark.

I see the foul disorders, and the filth
Of mind and soul, in which men, wallowing
Like swine, stamp on their brothers till they drown
In puddles of stale blood, and vomitings
Of their corruption.

. . . .

I have to choose. I back the scent of life
Against its stink. That is what Faith works out at
Finally, I know not why the Evil,
I know not why the Good, both mysteries
Remain unsolved, and both insoluble.
I know that both are there, the battle set,
And I must fight on this side or on that.
I can't stand shiv'ring on the bank, I plunge
Head first. I bet my life on Beauty, Truth,
And Love, not abstract but incarnate Truth,
Not Beauty's passing shadow but its Self.
Its very self made flesh, Love realised.
I bet my life on Christ—Christ Crucified.[11]

The theodicies of the late nineteenth century had not been elaborate; the prevailing optimism based upon the idea of immanental development had caused interest in the problem of evil to subside. Robert Browning had spoken for the age that crowned evolutionary progress, evil was an extrinsic value that led to a more ultimate good; consequently, while the debilitating power of evil was recognized, it was, in the last analysis, subservient to a good end and therefore not an ultimate reality. The war brought such a view of evil under radical interrogation, and no one raised the questions more insistently than did P. T. Forsyth. In his book, *The Justification of God,* Forsyth accused those who had sanctified human nature and baptized the idea of evolution of having no provisions left that would sustain spiritual life in the midst of war. Only if the cross is kept at the center of faith can faith remain at the center of life in a time of tragedy. The event that gives an abiding foundation for all events is the living action of the Christ as he redeems man and creates a church.

[11] From *The Best of Studdert-Kennedy,* pp. 5-7.

It is Christ, the revelation, and, therefore, the justification of God is not to be found in a visible convergence of all things unto a perfectly happy state, but in the eternal meaning and action of a perfectly holy soul in the profoundest human crisis. . . . The final theodicy is no discovered system, no revealed plan, but in an effective redemption.[12]

The church in the prewar era had failed to be the instrument of God by which peace could be established, Forsyth argued, and now he refused to base his hope upon a sanguine view of what the church would do in the future. To speak of the church's failure was not to speak of her inappropriateness for the task; indeed it was to such activity that she was called. With prophetic force, Forsyth called upon the church to find again her own moral center and thereby become the salt of the earth, the leaven in the world's life. What is needed, he continued, was a movement from anthropocentric, man-centered, humanistic religion to a theocentric faith that stressed the holiness of God and the victory of his righteous purposes.

The world needs what God can do, not what men can do for one another. The themes of love and sympathy both divine and human, had been played hard; but in the concentration upon these qualities there was lost a sense of holiness, of integrity, of the righteousness of God. Christian hope can be reclaimed, and thereby a new hope may be held for the world. But such a hope will not lie in misplaced confidence in an evolutionary process; it will be given in the crisis, in the revolution of redemption. The final theodicy is a gift of God. It is not a rational triumph but the victory of faith. Christ is the final answer of God; the supreme and only viable theodicy is atonement.

Christian theology is governed by a teleology that is guaranteed by soteriology; purpose is established by the fact of salvation. Consequently, hope in the human race and its future is predicated upon the value that God has placed upon man by his incarnate redemptive activity. No doctrine of evolution can deal with the moral situation of the race; no doctrine of gradual ameliorism can deal with the incursion of war, suffering, and death. Only a new creature in Christ is ready to face

---

[12] P. T. Forsyth, *The Justification of God* (London: Latimer House, 1917, 1948), pp. 52-53; cf. also, pp. 48-49, 167-68.

the perplexities of the social order. The war has revealed once for all that the struggle is not between forces, natural events, divergent processes; it is a struggle of wills, of man with man and man with God. And only the creation of a new will can create a new man and a new situation. It is to this fact of redemption that Forsyth pointed and upon which he believed any viable theodicy must be built. If the principle for which he argued is admitted, then, he claimed, the kingdom of God must be recognized as both a present reality and a future hope. As present, it is the ever immediate, firm rich ground upon which every step toward the future is taken. As future, it is final realization of God's intentions for history. Both the present and the future find their coalescence in the "finished" work of the cross of Christ. It is here that God's victory in history is proclaimed. "The evil world will not win at last, because it failed to win at the only time it ever could. It is a vanquished world where men play their deviltries. Christ has overcome it. It can make tribulation, but desolation it can never make." [13]

The exactions of the war were great on everyone—those who remained at home as well as those in the front lines. The demands on those in the trenches were obvious and frightening. But those who had remained in their own country also paid a great price. In addition to the loss of relatives and friends by death there were unsatisfied material needs and renewed internal friction. Abroad in Russia, the Tsar was overthrown by the Bolsheviks, the war with Germany was going badly, and, at home, the Independent Labour Party and the British Socialist Party organized a Popular Front in the United Socialist Council. "Home front" difficulties reached their climax in 1917, which was the worst year of the war for civilians. Food and fuel had become short in supply, and "the queue became a characteristic British institution." [14] Economic unrest turned into political protest. Perhaps more serious political challenge was averted by the fact that in coming to power in 1916 Lloyd George had accomplished a "revolution, British style." [15] He had brought the entire nation under the jurisdiction of the national government in a manner that, even a year before, would have seemed impossible.

[13] *Ibid.*, p. 227.
[14] A. J. P. Taylor, *English History 1914-1945*, p. 88.
[15] *Ibid.*, p. 73.

In 1914 the principles of free trade, free currency, and free enterprise were still sacrosanct to the vast majority of politicians, businessmen, and civil servants, though Joseph Chamberlain had attempted to subvert the first. Now, with the coming of a new cabinet in December, 1916, movements that had been pressing toward strong control of the economy were finally released and enhanced. Asquith was, perhaps, more of an obstacle to centralized control of the war than Lloyd George was an instigator of the forces of collectivism, but the new Prime Minister was the symbol of a strong determination to organize in order to win the war.[16] Whatever the immediate accomplishments of Lloyd George's innovations—and they were responsible for winning the war—their long-range implications were of crucial importance. From the time of the Great War, political and social innovations were predicated upon the assumption that men's hopes resided in social engineering of some kind, in the ordering and arranging of the economic and social forces in such a manner as to redress the imbalances of the previous eras and alleviate the causes of economic distress. In spite of the organization that Lloyd George set up, the unrest continued, then became sharpened through the inconclusiveness of the struggle. The unity that the initiation of hostilities had begun was now dissipated, and by 1918 the ambiguity of a nation involved in an all-out war with a continuing uncertainty about its own internal situation was evident to the most undiscriminating observer. The war, if anything, had become more discouraging, and the summer brought a series of alarming strikes. In June, Parliament passed a bill to give reality to the principle of "one man, one vote" (with the exception of university seats and a second vote for business premises, both of which exceptions continued until 1948). "War," said A. J. P. Taylor, "smoothed the way for democracy."[17] But the conflict continued, and patriotic enthusiasm waned. Then, abruptly, the war closed; from October 30 until November 11, a series of rapid negotiations brought the surrender.

During the struggle two men stood out as national leaders. One was David Lloyd George, the man who, in spite of the disaffection of many of his compatriots, led the nation into effective war mobilization

---

[16] Cf. Arthur Marwick, *The Deluge* (London: The Bodley Head, 1965), pp. 179-80.

[17] *English History 1914-1945*, p. 94.

and who was to be credited with putting his stamp upon the development of central government control in Britain. The other man was King George V, who by his sympathy, courage, and hope gave stability and equilibrium to the nation.

How is one to sum up a war? Especially this war? The costs were staggering. Over one million (one out of every seven in the conscription age) were killed, and probably three times that number were injured or maimed. The financial toll of the war was also great, not only in terms of monies spent and borrowed; but ironically, as would again be the case after the Second World War, some of the ravished countries, such as Belgium, were given a head start by rebuilding their industries, especially textiles, with new equipment and more modern and efficient plants.

But if the price of war was great, David Thomson has reminded us that the price of victory can also sometimes be costly—and once again the major cost is not to be calculated in terms of money.

More intangible, yet real, was the price paid in debasement of values and a sense of moral bankruptcy. The exalting of victory as an end that justified virtually any means was bound to debase moral standards. . . . The mood to encourage "For Victory" was one of militant intransigence—a spirit of ruthlessness and herd-conformity, intolerant of individuality and insensitive to whispers of reason or conscientious scruple.[18]

In the midst of the war John Oman had surveyed its effect and assessed its impact upon the future.

. . . war is ever a kind of apocalyptic and its carelessness of our civilization and all its belongings and its reckless disregard of life and all its securities. Ancient judgments vanish like ancient treasures, and ideas men had thought eternal are discovered to be only the fashion of a departing time. And when this war is over a new age will be upon us also, a better or worse according as we bear ourselves in the material and the spiritual conflict, but certainly another age, and those of us who are not prepared to reconsider all our judgments and help to build a new heaven and a new earth will not be able to

[18] *England in the Twentieth Century* (Harmondsworth, Middlesex: Penguin, 1965), p. 59.

251

retain the old, but will only wander in the new time as shadowy ghosts of a vanished past.[19]

The victory had been won, but with victory came a tide of disillusionment. Lloyd George spoke of making "a fit country for heroes to live in." But within a fortnight after the signing of the armistice, Parliament was dissolved, and the general election that followed was not only distasteful, but the House of Commons that was formed was one "of which no subsequent historian has ever found a good thing to say."[20] The time was one of emotional and intellectual uncertainty. The war had washed away the past; Victoria's and Edward's England was gone forever. A trench had also been dug through England's history.

"After the war," said H. H. Henson, "men must face again the old questions which perplexed them before, but which the strain of the crisis drove from mind. . . . The traditional theology will be again seen to be plainly inadequate to express the truth of religion as they must need perceive it."[21] The war had indeed interrupted but had not obliterated the questions that men had pursued just prior to its commencement. The hostilities struck a mark across time, but England after the war was inheritor of English life before the war; among the legacies that most impressed the postwar era were the problems rather than the confidences of its predecessor.

Strangely enough, the darkness of the midnight, when great empires were beating one another to their knees, issued in a dawn of triumph for idealism; the two powers that emerged from the background to new positions of power were the United States and Russia. The war eclipsed the conflict of rival imperialisms and established new ones. Now succeeding the older empire builders was Woodrow Wilson with his League of Nations, which embodied the idealism (though not the reality) of American democracy. The triumph of communism in Russia was also the establishment of an idealistic, even a utopian, aspiration that called for a radical reordering of the social structure. To speak of this

---

[19] *The War and Its Issues* (Cambridge: The University Press, 1915), pp. 4-5.
[20] Roger Lloyd, *The Church of England 1900-1965*, p. 241.
[21] "The Church After the War," *The Faith and the War*, ed. F. J. Foakes-Jackson (London: Macmillan, 1915), p. 256.

as a dawn is not to speak of the emergence of the perfect political structure, but it is to speak of the burnished streaks that mark the beginning of another day, a day with all its work and toil, as well as its hope and expectation. Perhaps, more exactly, the war brought the end to one ethos and the beginning of new political and economic power structures.

In Britain itself, war was not the only apocalyptic horseman to ride forth. In the summer of 1918 a great influenza epidemic struck and continued through the first three months of 1919. One hundred and fifty throusand people in England and Wales died of the illness. Unemployment followed the war, the economy dropped sharply, the troops were restless for discharge, housing was short, and parts of the Empire, such as Ireland and India, were again petitioning for independence with an importunate spirit.

One of the books that most directly spoke for the questioning spirit in the aftermath of the war was J. M. Keynes' *The Economic Consequences of the Peace*. Keynes had remained an active economic adviser to the government during the war, but, now that it was over, he was ready to fulfill a "solemn pledge" he had made in his own mind to his dissenting friends at Cambridge and Bloomsbury. After vividly describing the personalities and events of the Versailles Conference, he launched an attack on the reparation agreements of that conference. His main argument was that Germany formed the economic center of the continent, and anything that weakened Germany weakened the entire continental economy. The primary failure of Versailles, as he saw it, was very ordinary—namely, human stupidity and selfishness had caused the trouble, and generations would now reap the unhappy consequences. In a distressed voice he closed his book, "We have been moved already beyond endurance, and need rest. Never in the life-time of men now living has the universal element in the soul of man burnt so dimly." [22]

More important than the economic results of the war and the peace conference were the cultural changes that took place. One philosopher rather peevishly argued that little change of significance had transpired.

[22] *The Economic Consequences of the Peace* (New York: Harcourt, Brace & Howe, 1920), p. 279.

"It might have been expected," Alban Widgery wrote, "that the tragic events of the Great War would have aroused British minds from their traditional complacency; . . . It was not so." [23] Widgery then went on to argue that neither Thomas Hardy with his tragic sense of life nor G. B. Shaw with his exposure of hollow shams made any great impression on the British mind; rather, the work of G. K. Chesterton had accomplished its task of making the traditional orthodoxy once again significant. But this judgment was not accurate; for whether the authors he mentioned had any great influence, the sociocultural transformation of 1910-14 and the Great War did. Philosophy and theology would both be forced to adjust to the new situation.

Many British cultural traditions were, as a matter of fact, shattered by the war. One thing seemed certain to most interpreters then and now—the war marked a transition in the British style of life that was even more notable than the transition from Victorian to Edwardian England. It is now time to challenge this thesis, at least in part; for as the case was presented in the first two chapters, a cultural mutation had already taken place prior to the war, and the demand for social reform was everywhere to be heard. The transition of the prewar era, however, was not completed; and, with the intervention of the international hostilities, many of the changes were delayed in effecting their influence until after and with the corroboration of the war. But to point to the importance of prewar activity is not to deny the significance of the conflict itself. The trench warfare in Europe and its reverberations at home created an impassible gulf; a stream of blood had fissured British life.

Some, of course, questioned the significance of the change. In August 1919, W. R. Inge with his characteristic resistence to fads of opinion made an acid evaluation of what had taken place.

The war has caused events to move faster, but in the same direction as before. The social revolution has been hurried on. . . . As regards the national character, there is no sign, I fear, that much wisdom has been learnt. We are more wasteful and reckless than ever. The doctrinaire democrat still vapours about democracy, though representative government has obviously lost both its power

[23] *Contemporary Thought in Great Britain* (New York: Knopf, 1927), p. 15.

and its prestige. The labour party still hugs its comprehensive assortment of economic heresies. Organized religion remains as impotent as it was before the war. But one fact has emerged with startling clearness. Human nature has not been changed by civilization . . . man remains what he always has been—a splendid fighting animal, a self-sacrificing hero, and a bloodthirsty savage. Human nature is at once sublime and horrible, holy and satanic. Apart from the accumulation of knowledge and experience, which are external and precarious acquisitions, there is no proof that we have changed much since the first stone age.[24]

Whether human nature had changed, and it surely had not, the social ritual and cultural sensibility were in a period of transition. The past was set aside in a manner that the rash innovators of a generation earlier had not dreamed. The present was affirmed with all its uncertainties; and yet, nevertheless, with all its anticipations. A poverty stricken working class, a drastically taxed middle class, and an aristocracy that was determined to preserve itself characterized British life. American influences, though often denounced, were especially felt in music (jazz), dance, and recreation. The change in social manners and morals was cause for many a lifted eyebrow and censorious comment: the emancipation of women (1918) brought less social restraint; there was a move toward lighter clothes and shorter hair and skirts; to more open indulgence in liquor, tobacco, and cosmetics, as well as visits to beauty parlors and public houses; to insistence on smaller families and easier regulations for divorce. Men were also affected (could they resist?), and male dress became brighter, more varied, and less conventional. But David Thomson, who mentions many of these transitions, also warns that it must be remembered that in spite of this newspaper-type sensationalism, the more radical changes were limited to a small coterie of society.[25] Even so, the leadership was only an extension of the general tendency of the times; change was in the air.

In terms of the assumptions that permeate a culture, and indeed make a distinctive culture, one of the most important changes that the war years brought was a challenge to *laissez faire* economic theory.

[24] "Our Present Discontents," *Outspoken Essays* (London: Longmans, Green, 1919), pp. 1-2.
[25] *England in the Twentieth Century*, p. 87.

We have already noted the changes that had been precipitated by a new awareness of the corporate nature of society, and these were important ingredients to the ensuing changes. But now it is necessary to note how this corporate awareness worked itself out in terms of the challenge to the cultural assumptions. The breakdown of *laissez faire*, which was epitomized by the collapse of pre-Keynesian theory of self-maintaining full-employment equilibrium, was effected not because the economists had tested their theory against the facts. "The theory collapsed," J. R. Sargeant has argued, "because ordinary men were no longer willing to accept something which experience suggested to be absurd; and Keynes, though not distinguished for intellectual humility, was nevertheless sensitive enough to feel that they might not be wrong." [26] In 1912 Keynes began to express his conviction that *laissez faire* was no longer viable, and in 1926 he brought out his manifesto, *The End of Laissez Faire.* The state must become involved in finance, he argued, and then proceeded to indicate how in specific circumstances this must be accomplished. In 1924 he epitomized his position when he wrote in regard to the matter of foreign investments, "In considering how to do this [i.e. control foreign investments], we are brought to my heresy—if it is a heresy. I bring in the State; I abandon *laissez faire* —not enthusiastically, not from contempt of that good old doctrine, but because, whether we like it or not, the conditions for its success have disappeared." [27] This economic philosophy had its first test in the war, and now it was to become prominent, then dominating in the national economic theory and practice.

Immediately after the war, T. S. Eliot challenged the "romantic" critical tradition in literary studies. This tradition had laid stress on individual inspiration and genius. In an essay, *Tradition and the Individual Talent,* Eliot protested against this mode of interpretation. What must be done, he claimed, is to set literature into the framework of its environment and to recognize the extra-literary influences that affect it, thereby becoming aware of the social nature of artistic achievement. In the words

[26] "Economics: The Would-be, May-be Science," *Crisis in the Humanities,* ed. J. H. Plumb (Harmondsworth, Middlesex: Penguin, 1964), p. 149.

[27] Quoted in Roy Harrod, *The Life of John Maynard Keynes* (London: Macmillan, 1951), p. 348.

of F. R. Leavis, such an approach stressed "not economic and material determinants, but intellectual and spiritual, so implying . . . a different conception of society."[28] And in another lecture, Eliot roundly condemned the translation of the impeccable Greek, scholar Gilbert Murray, not because Murray did not know his Greek, but because he did not know his contemporary language, his contemporary setting.

As a poet, Mr. Murray is merely a very insignificant follower of the pre-Raphaelite movement. As a Hellenist, he is very much of the present day. This day began, in a sense with Tylor and a few German anthropologists; since then we have acquired sociology and social psychology, we have read books from Vienna and heard a discourse of Bergson; a philosophy arose at Cambridge; . . . and we have a curious Freudian-social-mystical-rationalistic-higher-critical interpretation of the Classics and what used to be called the Scriptures.[29]

What the translator must do is bring the living language of the past into the living language of the present, and the present cultural situation is so markedly changed that the language that was adept prior to the war is no longer adequate. Though economic and political determinants were important, Eliot looked upon these more as symptoms of a cultural shift, an understanding of human nature that had been enriched from new sources.

Social customs and stereotyped attitudes that had ceased to carry conviction simply disintegrated, and for many this also included the claims of religion. P. T. Forsyth spoke of the "staggering blow" to faith that the war had dealt, and a study of religious faith among men in the army revealed an appalling ignorance about the sources and nature of religious life. The majority of the men in the service were estranged from the church and highly critical of its practice. This only revealed the general ignorance of religion in the more confident days before the war. But Scott Holland was shocked by the situation. The intellectual aspects of Christianity seemed to have lost their interest; men were no longer concentrating upon the content of the Christian creeds.

[28] F. R. Leavis, *The Common Pursuit* (Harmondsworth, Middlesex: Peregrin Books, 1952), p. 184.
[29] T. S. Eliot, *The Sacred Wood* (London: Methuen, 1920), p. 75.

The report of the chaplains at the Front on the mind of the men in the trenches is severe enough in all conscience. It deals in very plain speech with a mass of the Church's failures. But there is one theme almost entirely lacking. There is no intellectual disturbance, no speculative dispute. . . . [In the *Lux Mundi* era] the trouble was always over the fundamental matters of spiritual belief. It was the dialectical values of the Creed itself that were for ever in debate.

Now, all this seems to have disappeared from the temper and the mood of the typical man at the Front, who represents in the new armies the typical working citizen at home. The central creed hardly ever comes under discussion.[30]

The men on the front had learned to adapt themselves to the situation with a kind of resilience that had been customary in adverse social conditions at home. But there was a restiveness about returning to those same conditions after the war. It was not high spiritual matters that captured their attention; the more mundane matters of food and housing, courtship and marriage, jobs and opportunity were on their minds. They would not return to the old homes and the old cities with quiet spirits.

The theologians we have been concentrating upon represented, for the most part, another era, whereas the war marked a transition point; new issues demanded new responses. But theology was not alone in facing a new situation. Idealism had passed its zenith, optimism was more difficult to come by, economic life found fresh sustenance, new psychological investigations were crowding the old assumptions, poetry and the novel were expressing a new conceptuality. The war had become a chasm between the past and the present, a divider standing in the middle of no-man's-land. Most men were willing to leave the past behind; they were in the present, walking across a new territory, inhabitants of a new age, and above all, explorers.

---

[30] *Creeds and Critics*, pp. 176-77.

XI

CULMINATION AND CHANGE

To look in retrospect and attempt to understand the historical events and the intellectual issues that were intersecting in a particular era requires first of all a careful statement about perspectives. The standpoint that we have assumed is one of sympathetic listening. To be aware of the sensibilities of an age, to see things as those in that era saw them, to get the taste and smell of a time is not easy, especially since such an effort is always threatened by the temptation to press alien considerations. Hence, the question we have kept before us is, How did those in the era understand themselves and why?

A later observer inevitably has the relative advantage of being able to see ends—at least tentative conclusions—as well as beginnings, consequences as well as the initiation of ideas. Not being completely identified with the spirit of an age or living under the aegis of its dominant convictions, he is able to indicate more general perspectives, how ideas took on flesh, and what themes were carried into the future. But, again, it must be emphasized that no observer is in a position to speak a final word of judgment; for an idea, like a grain of wheat, may fall into the ground and die, only to come to life again at some later time bearing much fruit.

Recognizing the reciprocity that exists between a man and his time, I have attempted to set some theological ideas into their context and to see the interplay between intellectual sensibilities and the historical events by which they are formed and which they, to some extent, helped shape. Both sides are important. Circumstances and ideas alike meet their limitations as well as their possibilities. Here there is symbiosis, a living interdependence, mutual need and resistance; theology and society, faith and culture each living with the other with all the tensions of marriage, each struggling with the other, each attempting to understand the other, each with its own integrity, and each dependent upon the other. These have been the ingredients of our study.

As one attempts to gain some overarching perspective on the first two decades of the twentieth century, the first prominent impression is the singular awareness of the transitory nature of the time. The men we have discussed were, for the most part, men whose spirits were tinted by the dye of the age, men who were fully sensitive to and responsive to the present condition of life. To say this is not necessarily to commend them, for the age was one from which it was difficult to escape. Change was rapid and carried people in its wake; social problems were pressing with such urgency that only those who closed their eyes and resolutely refused to acknowledge the piercing shouts were unaffected. The sheer momentum of the transition in the social order tended to direct men's movements and their thoughts. Even so, there were many among those we have been discussing who were not reluctant voyagers or indifferent passengers. Both the practical and theological leaders of the churches were conscious participants in the swirling life of the age. As men of their time, they did not work with a blueprint in hand; rather they were explorers, feeling their way, attempting to get compass bearings, sometimes awkwardly climbing trees to view the land.

The cultural forces at work as the new century began seemed to portend the dissolution of the alignment of Christianity with social-cultural institutions. The remembrance—usually tacit, though sometimes explicit—of socio-religious alliance provoked uneasiness, nostalgia, suspicion, and opposition. Rethinking of the sanctions of political and ecclesiastical life, redefinition of the essentials of Christian commitment, and faithful activity were prime necessities. No longer was it possible for theologians—or simple believers—to draw strength from or find encouragement in the alliance and often the confusion between religious authorities and current conventionalities.

The Edwardians on the whole would have preferred to continue the past, but it was not possible to perpetuate what had been. The forces of change were inexorable, and only the flexible could survive the onslaught. The age had some who dreamed short dreams of utopia. Sometimes they talked of the kingdom of God, but the promised land had only the vague form of "brotherhood" or a "socialistic" society. A few forsook the traditions entirely to launch out into the future. Others surveyed the enigmatic past with keen interest, but few were daunted by it; they respected but did not idolize what had been but was no more. Some, of course, wanted to return to the past, but for the most part these were not men from another age who had become displaced; they were in their place, in their time. The solutions proffered were diverse, the stances different, the remedies varied, as these men lived in the reality of the peculiar situation. The problems as well as the promise of the era were theirs. If the question is asked, of whom are we speaking? one can call the roll. But where should we begin? The order is unimportant: John Clifford, Hugh Price Hughes, Charles Gore and A. M. Fairbairn, J. S. Lidgett, Hastings Rashdall, Alfred Garvie and R. C. Moberly, P. T. Forsyth, Scott Holland, John Oman and William Temple.

To prove the rule, one must also list the exceptions, the two most notable of which were W. R. Inge and H. H. Henson. In a profound sense, of course, these men were also immersed in their era; how could anyone escape it? But they also kept their distance in a way most of their contemporaries did not. W. R. Inge was an early Victorian who lived in a post-Victorian world. He was caustic about that world, but his caustic comment did not lack a cutting edge. Inge wanted to fasten man's eyes upon a better world, a trans-historical world, and a world which, he was convinced, some of their forbears had kept unwearyingly before their attention. Whether the Victorians were as bad as the present generation feared or as good as he thought, he performed a not unimportant service by attempting to measure the temporal against the eternal, or even the present against the past. H. H. Henson was also an alien to his time; he was, he said, a seventeenth-century latitudinarian who was living in the wrong century. He was, and he wasn't. In a fundamental sense he was not at home in the twentieth century; the controversies that swirled around exact delineation of doctrine and that issued in sharply defined parties were strange to his temperament. As a person who did not succumb to the spirit of the age, however, he served that spirit well by his incisive critique. Both of these men, Inge and Henson, were public figures of moment, both were individualists, both were writers of literary excellence, both were gadflies, and, perhaps, both were prophets.

To understand an age one must look both at those who were indigenous to its life and at those who stood at cross-purposes with its spirit. If a study of a particular epoch does not contribute anything else to the understanding of theology, it ought to make clear the context in which theological activity takes place; it ought to reveal the intense struggles, the perplexing uncertainties, the debilitating despair and the resilience of hope. For theology, except in its most truncated and inauthentic expressions, is a way of life. It is not an abstracted reflection upon life; it is life—life lived and thought about in the living of it. Hopefully, some ideas will survive their time, but theology that is written for the future is of no value to the present and probably of little significance for posterity. And here we find the importance of coming to this era as listeners to its internal dialogue.

The undercurrent of the period was the tension that existed between the secular and the sacred. The age was becoming emancipated from its traditional Christian context, and life was becoming thoroughly secular. By secular, in this discussion, is meant the organization of life around some center or centers other than those provided by Christian faith. In western European history, especially from the time of Constantine when Christianity was established as the "official" religion of the Roman Empire, a slow but distinct process was underway: faith in God, as this was embodied in Christian theology and religious rites, became the centripetal force that organized societal and cultural life. This is not to claim that society would not have been organized without these forces nor that in many ways it would have been organized in similar ways by other forces; but it remains historically true that Christian faith and practice were dominant constituting powers in the ordering of Western civilization. Such an informative principle expressed itself in everything from the rituals of daily life to the rhythm of Sabbath days, festivals, and holidays; it influenced economic practices and theories of value; it had political significance in terms of the forms and duties of rulership; philosophy and art lived under its aegis; architecture gave it body and music a voice; the understanding of history as purposeful and natural science as possible were part of its heritage; interpretations of moral duty and the nature of persons were extensions of its life. The permeation of culture by Christianity was thorough.

As the modern age dawned in the seventeenth century, all this began to be challenged in an unprecedented manner. The challenge was issued initially by the spirit of the Enlightenment, a spirit that questioned all absolutes, all received authorities, and the right of religion to play the formative role in civilized life. The rejection of previously reigning sovereigns of thought provoked the question as to what new authority would be accepted; and the history of modern Western civilization can be written as a quest for the principle of authority.[1] But the Enlightenment was a movement of ideas. At times, seemingly, it was epiphenomenal, lacking a body, finding little concrete expression, for, in spite of strong convictions and forceful articulations, the inherited patterns of culture were persistent. Nonetheless, changes were slowly taking place, and perceptive commentators pointed to their appearance: economic considerations were more and more rooted in other than theological or biblical principles; art declared its emancipation; political ideas changed; philosophy refused to remain a servant to theology; utility replaced tradition; technical knowledge replaced faith; science challenged sanctity.

Nevertheless, religious forms and rituals persisted, for the past is never discarded easily. Increasingly, however, there was uneasy tension,

[1] Cf. Thomas C. Mendenhall, Basil D. Henning, and Archibald S. Foord, eds. *The Quest for a Principle of Authority in Europe* (New York: Henry Holt, 1948).

suspicion, and occasionally, open antagonism. Christian form seemed to be without content, rituals were evacuated of their meaning—attractive vehicles that carried nothing. I am speaking of cultural attitudes and dominant moods, not of individuals; for there were still Christian believers, men for whom the rites were the channels of life and for whom the goal of existence continued to be the vision of God. With irregular movement, there was increase and recession, attrition and renewal, but as we come closer to the twentieth century secularization was more and more the reality of life. Other factors reinforced the secularizing tendencies; none, however, was more important than the industrial revolution. New technological advances and increased urbanization seemed to tell against the religious traditions and for the contrary spirit.

Every nation has its own distinctive character. In England each of these happenings had its peculiar expression. The English are a traditional people; the industrialist and the laborer, the school child and his teacher, the politician and the engineer are aware of the national history. Englishmen are also eclectic, lovers of the middle way, believers in the subtle nuance, the delicate balance. Our task is not to judge the virtues or the vices of this peculiar combination of testing and compromise but to note that unlike some European nations, such as France after the Revolution, the English always attempted to retain the past and to acknowledge the impact of the present. Faith and knowledge, science and the Bible, new patterns and old rituals might struggle, but they continued to live together; they were married, and divorce was hard to come by. The distinctiveness of the English situation was precisely in its comprehensiveness, in its inclusion of the divergent elements derived from its Christian past and its secular present. Neither excluded the other, and neither really wanted to exclude the other. Secularization might mean that people did not go to church as much as their forefathers, but it did not mean that they did not want their children to be taught about religion or to participate in religious activities at school. Secularization might mean that people no longer observed as many of the religious rituals as their ancestors, but it did not mean that they rejected baptism, religious marriage ceremonies, or a Christian burial. Secularization might mean that Sabbath observance was no longer rigorous, but it did not mean that there was a general rejection of theism. The situation was mixed, opposites lived together, national life was a blend of traditional authorities and new claimants for power.

Despite the unusual ability of the English to hold antitheses together and to strike a balance between extremes, the tensions present at the close of the Victorian period and during the reign of Edward made reconciliation difficult and at times apparently impossible. By 1910, whether it was desired or not, a cultural transformation was rapidly taking place. There were public demonstrations by dissident groups, labor strikes, theological disputes, social derangement, and foreign agitations; there were also artistic mutation, a new poetry, and new sensibility on the part of novelists.

In the midst of the turbulence the one issue that was pushed most directly into the center was that of the authority that ensures validity to any particular institutional, cultural, or personal style of life. More and more the most widely acknowledged sanction was that which expressed, pleased, or exalted the individual creator or participant. Older traditions of criticism—whether in literature or art—were set aside; institutional forces inherited from the past—whether economic, the House of Lords or the church—were looked upon as dubious legacies or unstable reeds. The free man with a free mind and spirit was eulogized as the savant of the emerging sociocultural milieu.

As Charles Gore saw the problem, the question of the sanctions for Christian faith was intimately connected with the validity of the church, its apostolic succession, sacraments, and creeds. These must be safeguarded if the authenticity of Christian faith was to be preserved. For others, such as the more evangelical party within the church represented by Henry Wace and *The Churchman,* the Scriptures continued to function as the primary sanction for faith and life, although the hermeneutic principles that should govern the interpretation of Scripture were not made clear. Opposed to these more "objective" criteria that establish the authority of Christian faith were those Anglicans who stressed the primacy of religious experience—whether that experience be mystical, of the type described by W. R. Inge; a more personalistic, moral, and intellectual form defended by Hastings Rashdall; a redemptive, pietistic experience stressed by some of the evangelicals; or a sense of encounter with holiness, providence, and love which the writers of *Foundations* argued was to be found at the primary base of religious experience. The older, formerly convincing criteria were falling away; new anchors were being sought with many options being proposed.

Within Nonconformity the issue of authority arose over the critical study of the Scriptures that undercut the traditional identification of authority with the verbal inspiration of the Bible. Since creeds had never been a primary authority among these churches, the loss of biblical authority presented the question of sanctions in a direct and critical manner. By the last decade of the nineteenth century the question of the status of the Bible precipitated a noticeable switch from an insistence upon the authority of the Scripture to the authority of the person of Jesus. This switch was particularly evident in A. M. Fairbairn, who was convinced that biblical criticism had removed the veils from the historical Jesus and that with the clearest vision since the time of the apostles, the believer could look upon Jesus as he actually was. Thus the historical Jesus as the one around whom the Scriptures were fashioned, rather than the Scriptures as such, came to the forefront as the dominant norm. This confidence was shared by the Presbyterian John Oman and the Congregationalist Alfred Garvie, who found a coalescence at this point between biblical criticism and Ritschlianism. Garvie stressed that religious authority came through the experience of redemption, which was effected by the cross. What is of primary importance is that with both Fairbairn and Garvie the theme of Christian experience as response to Jesus, as he is portrayed in the New Testament, was coming to the fore as a cardinal theological principle.

One of the nonconformist theologians who most perceptively investigated the idea of authority was John Oman. The only legitimate authority that Oman would acknowledge was that which was accepted by a person in a free response to a vision that evoked a disciplined obedience. Basing his argument upon his conception of mature human nature as autonomous, self-consciously self-determined, he developed his interpretation of authority as that which draws forth a full and free response from man. There is no valid external sanction that may be imposed upon man; no heteronomous authority can force authentic decision. Beginning with a radical individualism, Oman attempted to relate the individual to a community, and especially to a spiritual community—that is, a community in which there is a shared vision—but his beginning point was so sharply drawn that the question of the cohesion of a body or of authority within a group remained problematic. In a primary sense, Oman built his conception of authority upon a philosophical psychology that stressed the unique, independent integrity of each person, and inevitably his discussion of corporate interrelationship was of subsidiary importance and at times strained.

Another response from within Nonconformity was that of the New Theologians who found sanctions for life and thought in the philosophical and social movements of the day. Established upon a vague idealism or spiritualistic monism and convinced of the ideas of evolutionary development, especially as this expressed itself in social life, these men, led by R. J. Campbell, no longer called upon biblical sources as the control for their theology. The normative guidelines were to be found in socialism as a political ideology and in immanence as a philosophical principle. Upon these two foundation stones they built an interpretation that stressed amelioristic expectation. In a sense, the entire question of authority was removed by the solvent of belief in progress—what should be would be, as the guiding hand of providence worked its will.

In the rise of the New Theology P. T. Forsyth saw a threat to historic Christianity; the foundations that had underpinned the church and its faith from the beginning were now challenged. In agreement with his age, Forsyth did not see any possibility of returning to an infallible Bible; in addition, and unlike many of his contemporaries, he did not see any prospect of returning to a general interpretation of the Jesus of history. Authority is found in the situation of faith, and Christian faith always revolves around its true center, the crucifixion of Jesus. This event constituted a correlation that was initiated by the act of God's self-giving in Jesus and the acknowledgment by the believer of Jesus as Savior. Here was the sure source for authority in Christian experience, a valid center for theological reflection, the foundation of the church, and a point of leverage by which the Christian community could be peculiarly effective in society. Forsyth used the idea of "experience" that was so dear to his time, but he insisted it was experience as formed and transformed by God of which the Christian theologian must speak. For Forsyth, as for few other men of his time,

267

the real question that was at stake was this issue of the sanction of Christian life and thought, and with singleness of eye he rooted the problem of authority in the work of Jesus Christ.

As we have indicated, the question of authority within Anglicanism was especially focused in the doctrine of the church. Even more than Nonconformity, which espoused a more individual form of faith and life and emphasized less the controlling importance of the sacraments, the Church of England struggled with the question of ecclesiastical origins, its orders of ministry, the validity of its sacramental rites and its official relation to the state. Questions about the visible nature of the church were a part of the larger controversy, for if the visible church is the true church then its sacramental life and creedal formulations have an authority that otherwise would not pertain to the church. Hence, the struggle over the validity of the church—its ministry, sacraments, and creeds—was viewed by many, such as Gore, Moberly, and Stone, as being of the essence in the discussion of the foundations for Christian faith. For other Anglicans the locus of authority had so shifted that the church functioned as an extrinsic value for establishing Christian commitment. Lightfoot, Inge, and Rashdall were some of the more important advocates of this position. For these men, faith was rooted in individual experience of the demands of conscience, the mystical presence of God, rational and spiritual enlightenment, or experiences of forgiveness and purposiveness. To state the alternatives in this manner once again runs the risk of oversimplification, for each of these theologians attempted to work out the nuances of interrelationship between the authority of the ecclesiastical tradition and more personal, self-authenticating experience. The point at which a distinction can and must be made is whether the church as a visible expression of the will of God represents the primary sanction for Christian life and faith, or whether it acts in a secondary, corroborative fashion to reinforce what has been authoritatively received elsewhere. Whatever the nuances worked out in regard to the extension of these primary commitments, the basic decision was recognized to be absolutely crucial by those who disagreed.

We have emphasized that both in society as a whole and in the church one of the most prominent problems was that of authority, and we have seen that in neither was it resolved in a commonly agreed upon fashion.

The intellectual leadership of the church recognized the importance of the problem, but they could not offer a solution to the social situation as long as they could not resolve the issue within their own community. As participants in the turmoil of the time, they nevertheless were profoundly affected by the turbulance. Could the faith be established upon sure foundations? Could order in the life of the church foreshadow a contribution to an ordering of society? These were the questions with which they were faced. That they did not find immediate solutions means, in part, that they could not accept easy answers. Men who lived in the spheres of the church and society could not renounce either. What then of the relation of the church with the world? One approach to a viable liaison between the church and the world was that proposed by Charles Gore: establish religious communities [such as the Community of the Resurrection, which he was instrumental in founding] and accept social responsibility as a part of spiritual discipline. Gore labored to bring worship and ethical activity together and attempted to do so by radically stressing both. A result of this approach was a reassessment of the issue of national religious establishment. Should the church any longer attempt to identify with all of the nation, or should the church become disestablished in order to protect her own unique qualities and thereby be enabled to serve society more effectively? However one evaluates this approach, Gore stands out as a person who carried the dual burden with an unusual energy and with clearly defined intention.

Among the evangelicals within the Anglican Church, the emphasis upon personal redemption tended to be individualistic and the theme of salvation a purely personal one. The impact of the gospel upon society was in terms of conversion, so that a redeemed society was one that was composed of redeemed persons. There was, among this group, less sense of the corporate nature of the church or of its mission as a corporate entity. Although a similar strain was to be found in Nonconformity, the impact of social interpretations of the Christian message had modified the radical individualism, especially among the Methodists and the Congregationalists and, to a lesser extent, the Presbyterians. The Baptists, with their evangelical emphasis, retained a conception of the function of the church and of the task of evangelism that made direct engagement with society an ambiguous endeavor. Hugh Price Hughes and J. S.

Lidgett among the Methodists, the New Theologians and P. T. Forsyth among the Congregationalists, John Clifford and J. H. Shakespeare among the Baptists—all, in their variant ways, were representative of the interest in and involvement in this dimension of the church's self-understanding and of her relation to society.

Among the Nonconformists there were two prominent attempts to relate the church and the world. The New Theologians identified the two realms and spoke of the church as witnessing to the spiritual depth of the social process. Others, like P. T. Forsyth and John Oman, tended toward a prophetic role for the church: the church as the community of redeemed persons or persons who shared a common vision were to speak from the vantage point of their acknowledgment of that commitment to the situation of the time. This was not a role of condemnation or a prophecy of doom but a moral stance and a constant reminder that the ultimate reality was not of this world, not even in its most ambitious endeavors. The word of the cross was a word of judgment and a word of redemption, and both words must be spoken with a clear voice.

We have lifted up the fact that the theologians in the first decade of the twentieth century were men of their own time, participants in the intellectual sensibilities that dominated the imagination of their age. Among the concerns that were almost universally embraced was an intense interest in the nature of personhood and the exploration of the meaning of personality. This also was a way of dealing with the problem of authority, for now the issue was internalized and made a part of the discussion of the dignity of the individual person; hence, authority is that which is consciously acknowledged and obeyed. The initiation of this interest, as far as theology was concerned, was to be found in the exploration of the theme of self-development and full maturation by the idealistic philosophers, and especially T. H. Green. Self-fulfillment was a transfer from the doctrine of evolution in nature to the doctrine of evolution or development of the individual person. Hence both the nature of the individual, with special attention paid to his possibilities for full self-realization, and the nature of society, as it interacted with the individual, were of increasing interest. It is not insignificant that both psychology and sociology were becoming distinct disciplines at this period. In England, however, sociology was somewhat slower to develop as a recognized, independent academic discipline than psychology, and part of the reason for this was the high premium that idealistic philosophy placed upon the individual and conscious rationality.

But what are the unique qualities of man? How is the nature of personhood to be most adequately described? It was at this point that idealistic philosophy turned its attention to psychology. It is not surprising that, given the idealistic presuppositions, the psychological description that came out of this era was that which reflected a philosophical perspective rather than an empirical analysis. Further, the interpretation of personality was influenced by the idealistic conviction that reality is cognate with conscious rationality. Given this assumption, personhood at its apex must be described in terms of consciousness, rational ability, freedom to exercise reason, and, finally, the conformity of human personhood with ultimate reality. It was precisely these aspects of personality which were stressed. The spiritual nature of man was an extrapolation from the analogy of being that was held to exist between man and ultimate reality (God); on this basis the themes of conscious awareness, intellectual capacity, and personal freedom were developed. We have attempted to show that such an analysis both grew out of and was congenial to theological interests, as the work of J. R. Illingworth illustrated.

The two most important contributors to the discussion of the nature of personhood from the theological perspective were John Oman and C. C. J. Webb. In both men there was dependence upon the idealistic psychology, but each developed his insights differently. For Webb, religious doctrines found their justification in their satisfaction of the "demands of the religious consciousness," namely, in the experiences of alienation and communion. The incarnation is the cardinal Christian doctrine because it satisfies this dual demand. Webb argued that man, by the exercise of his reason, is able to establish a true description of ideal personality—a description that emphasizes man's intrinsic worth and his need for relationship. Historically the development of the idea of human personality in Western culture was brought to fulfillment by the incarnation and its subsequent demand for trinitarian interpretation. It is upon this ground that both the uniqueness of man as a self and the participation of man in the rational unity of reality was affirmed.

In the thought of John Oman we see somewhat different emphases.

271

Oman resisted many of the Hegelian aspects of idealistic philosophy and insisted that every interpretation of life be built upon the inherent interaction of the givenness of reality and man's apprehension and appropriation of the significance of that which is given. Thus, Oman was concerned with the impingement of the contextual configurations—ranging from individual relations to societal to cosmic factors—upon the one who must appropriate their significance. The theological position that he developed was predicated upon his view of the nature of man. Primarily concerned with the dynamics of personal vision, commitment, and action, Oman interpreted Christian doctrine in the light of these categories.

In several significant ways these two men were alike. Both defined personality in much the same way; both were interested in the mature expression of personhood in Jesus Christ; both were more concerned with persons as individuals than with persons in community. Although each assumed that the concept of good that is shared by all members of a community does have a kind of objective status, the obligation to pursue this common good was assumed rather than shown to flow from the consciousness that it is commonly held. Finally, both were concerned with the ethical implications of man's intrinsic and inalienable integrity. But there were also differences. Webb centered his thought in the Incarnation as this was defined by the Nicene Creed and the trinitarian formulations. Oman, although he spoke of Jesus as the paradigm of full-orbed manhood, did not make a single historical event crucial in his interpretation. The personal context that God has created for man, he argued, is to be found not in a peculiar historical event but in the total arena of life; and the insight that man attains about reality and about himself involves an evaluation of the world as a whole. In terms of why man makes his particular interpretation of life that of moral creaturehood in God's world, there is a second difference. Oman found this conception arising from an evaluation of the significance of the world as a whole, whereas Webb found it adhering to the incarnation. For Webb, it is God's coming in Jesus Christ that affirmed every man's distinctive selfhood and thereby set the norm of maturity. But Webb did not explore the dynamics of the interrelation between man and the incarnate revelation, and at this point Oman's discussion of grace and personality, though set in a more general context, probed more deeply.

The psychological interpretation of human personality constituted the major background against which the person of Jesus Christ was discussed. The Christology of the era was built upon the philosophical interpretation of mature personhood that I have been describing. Once again, there was no one-way traffic in this discussion. The traditional interpretation of Jesus Christ (as in the case of Webb) influenced the discussion of personality, but it is also true that the interpretation of personhood influenced the interpretation of Jesus Christ, and many of the tensions of the era can be viewed in terms of the struggle to bring these two approaches together. Once again, it is necessary to indicate that the centrality of Christology represented an effort to find a sure authority for life.

In *logos* Christology there was a principal dependence upon the theme of God's immanence. The *logos* as creator of the world was present in his creation from the beginning; he remained in his world as its providential guide, and he stands beyond creation as its divine telos. The themes were pervasive: the ubiquity of God's Spirit, the universal revelation of God in his creation, the incarnation as the fulfillment of the past and the adumbration of the future. The evolutionary process was interpreted in such a manner that human personality stood at the apex of the process, and at the pinnacle of human self-realization was the unique person of Jesus. We saw how this interpretation was, in part, also an effort to affirm the dignity of man in contrast to the general evolutionary, naturalistic interpretations, and also that it was of social importance as the kingdom of God was sought in terms of moral means for moral ends. Christ was the creator, sustainer, and consummator.

In the kenotic Christologies one of the primary considerations was the reaffirmation of the full integrity of the human personality of Jesus. Such an emphasis had to take account of the ascription of infallible knowledge to Jesus that had been a part of most previous christological discussion. It also influenced the discussion of the work of Jesus insofar as the integrity of every person had to be maintained even in the face of persistent efforts to interpret grace as an external force that transformed personality. The integrity of the humanity of Jesus and the integrity of every person were the two fundamental realities that must be preserved.

Kenotic Christologies attempted to relate these two by speaking of God's sovereign self-limitation to the confines of human personhood— that is, God was in Christ in a manner appropriate to Jesus' humanity. This meant a renunciation (at least temporally) of such attributes as omniscience, omnipotence, and omnipresence. Laboring under the interpretation of Jesus that had been fostered by the creedal definitions, these men were anxious to preserve the uniqueness of Jesus and to reinterpret his person so as to make the confession of Jesus as Lord compatible with the contemporary understanding of human personality. Thus, in a fundamental sense they were also indebted to this current interpretation, but their primary concern was to insist that even under the conditions of manhood the genuine divinity of Jesus could be maintained and his Lordship and authority affirmed.

William Temple shared this common background, but extending Weston's theme, he stressed the will as the constituting principle of personhood. Others had also emphasized the importance of the will, but Temple's voluntarism was thoroughgoing, and his entire interpretation of Christology was determined by his conviction that the will was the distinctive feature of personhood. This position allowed unusual flexibility in his interpretation of the relation of Jesus to God as well as of Jesus to the believer. But the dependence of Temple upon an idealistic psychology and the question of how distinct his interpretation was from that of the kenoticists were continuing issues that required further exploration. In Temple we found an eclectic figure who drew many different streams together. But, like many of his contemporaries, he gathered the past in order to serve the present.

Our discussion of the first decades of the twentieth century began with the consummation of a style of thought and life that reached its culmination shortly after the new century began. A mode of existence that was radically challenged, then set aside by events that took place shortly before the Great War. Social transpositioning—of the aristocracy, workers, and women—was under way; new legislation foreshadowed radical economic change; new shapes in international and imperial relations were coming into existence and threatening the secured positions of the past; idealistic philosophy lost its position as the dominant intellectual movement; poetry was changing as the Georgians were followed by the war poets and then by the American invasion of Ezra Pound and T. S. Eliot; the novel, under the influence of Virginia Woolf, D. H. Lawrence and, on the wider scene, James Joyce, was striking new pathways; painting was the medium for expression of new sensibilities and social consciousness; in creative activity and criticism, language was in a period of transition—vocabulary, rhythm, and style were all different from the immediate past. And caught in the turmoil of change and exploration were the Christian community and those who would interpret her life.

Every culture obviously influences the theological developments that take place under its aegis. And early twentieth-century England was no exception. What, then, has our listening yielded? We have observed how one particular cultural epoch produced and received its theology. In part, theology was a recipient. The questions with which theology dealt were those that were indigenous to its setting. The intellectual sensibilities were those nurtured by philosophers and politicians, social critics and artists. But theology was also a contributor, and the mainstream felt the influx of a theological current. The era was poignantly aware of unsure moorings, and the changing status of Bible and creeds contributed to the sense of insecurity. With their contemporaries, religious thinkers sounded the depths to find bedrock and studied the stream in order to navigate the rapids. Hence, theology was both influenced by and contributed to the common ethos. The engagement was mutually conditioning as influence was reciprocated. The complexity and the uniqueness of the time were realities that preclude simple conclusions and quick theological generalizations. The instruction we receive is in an increased sensitivity and one that, perhaps, applies to situations other than the period we have studied.

The era was brought to a close by the intervention of armies. The war reinforced the differentiation of the past from the time that followed. By the time of the Armistice it was obvious that many former commitments were being reassessed and some relinquished. In theology, the alliance with idealism was subjected to serious question, and many theologians began to express doubts about the union; social involvement tended to become more significant than doctrinal considerations. In one sense, the concerns that were so dominant immediately before the war—the interpretation of creedal formulations, the transcendence and immanence of God—surrendered to the practical concerns that confronted the church as well as the general culture. England between the World Wars was, like the rest of western Europe, plagued with economic inflation and depression. She was in a period of governmental adjustment, a change of mores and social customs. The pressure of the problems evoked quick reaction and responsive decisions. Theology, like the other forms of literature, was seeking a new style; new sensibilities demanded new conceptualization, new vocabulary, and new modes of expression. What was common to these developments of the interwar years was that they continued to presuppose the issues over which their predecessors had struggled and had been unable to resolve. Setting their feet upon new paths, theologians, with their contemporaries, continued the search for foundations.

APPENDIX A

ROBERT BROWNING
A Man for the Season

One pinch of salt that helped flavor late nineteenth-century England, and one that is sometimes overlooked in theological assessments of the era, was the poetry of Robert Browning. It is difficult to assess fully the influence of Browning because of his subtle pervasiveness, but it is certain that no poet was more widely quoted by theologians and preachers, more idolized by many who turned away from traditional theology but who wanted to retain a sense of the spiritual quality of life, or more accepted by philosophers as sharing their vision of reality. Browning had been something of a stranger to his own time earlier in the century, but by the final decades his popularity exceeded even that of Wordsworth and Tennyson.

Browning made an impact in part because he embodied the characteristics that he eulogized for the age. He praised strength of all types. Physical skill, sexual passion, and keen sensitivity were lauded in his poetry; he honored the strong mind and the strength of creative ability; he expressed a hearty goodwill toward all serious endeavor—whether for good or for evil; and he exalted the capacity for sympathy as well as robust good humor. What he praised he was. To many he seemed to possess in a preeminent fashion all these qualities; and, in addition, he had the

277

ideal, and idealized, love relation with Elizabeth Barrett, which became a symbol of romantic marriage.[1]

In 1883 B. F. Westcott set the stage for ensuing discussions when he delivered a lecture to the Cambridge Browning Society and dealt with the poet's view of life. Two themes were prominent in Westcott's lecture. First, Browning focused his attention upon man, looking for the revelation of God or the Divine to come through the spiritual struggles of man and not through nature or the natural world. Second, he asserted the sovereignty of feeling over knowledge; he stressed man's affective nature; and this, according to Westcott, was the dimension of the human spirit that has the clearest affinity with the heavenly and the eternal. The keynote of his teaching was love, not knowledge.[2]

The importance of these two points is readily evident when one sets them against the background of the late nineteenth century. The emphasis upon the spiritual struggle of man was cognate with the idealistic theme of the unique value of persons and a concentration upon their self-fulfillment. In an age when the biological evolution of every form of life was prominently held, the stress upon the unique value of persons as the apex of that process was congenial to both the philosophical and the theological communities. The second emphasis upon the supremacy of feeling or love, which was in keeping with Wordsworth's romantic approach, was important because it gave priority to experience, to participation and involvement in the delineation of the meaning of life. This was at the time when there was an increased interest in the role of experience in religious life as the foundation upon which theological interpretation must be built.

---

[1] For an assessment of these qualities by an early commentator, see J. T. Nettleship, *Essays on Robert Browning's Poetry* (London: Macmillan, 1868), pp. 4-5. The history of the study of Browning has gone through several distinct stages. The earlier critics who dealt with his work were often awed by his person and achievement; or, if the attitude of awe is an overstatement for some, they were convinced of his first rank among English poets. The most significant of these earlier assessments were those of Mrs. Sutherland Orr, *Life and Letters of Robert Browning* (1891; new ed., revised and in part rewritten by Frederic G. Kenyon, London: John Murray, 1908); and G. K. Chesterton, *Robert Browning* (London: Macmillan, 1903); William Sharp's *Life of Robert Browning* (London: Walter Scott, 1890) is also representative. Since the mid-thirties there has been an effort to develop a revisionist history of Browning's life and achievement: Betty Miller, *Robert Browning: A Portrait* (John Murray, 1952) and Jeannette Marks, *The Family of the Barretts: A Colonial Romance* (London: Macmillan, 1938) indicate this tendency. In the last several years, there have been significant efforts to look at Browning with the desire neither to pay homage nor to prove the earlier portraits false, but to freshly evaluate his poetry and his place in the intellectual tradition. Of special importance are Robert Langbaum, *The Poetry of Experience* (London: Chatto and Windus, 1957) and Hugh Martin, *The Faith of Robert Browning* (London: S. C. M., 1963) and, more lately, Maisie Ward's *Robert Browning and His World: The Private Face* [1812-1861] (New York: Holt, Rinehart & Winston, 1967), the first of a two-volume study. For representative statements, see Boyd Litzinger and K. L. Knickerbocker, *The Browning Critics* (Louisville: The University of Kentucky Press, 1965).

[2] *On Some Points in Browning's View of Life* (Cambridge: J. Palmer, 1883), pp. 6-7.

To both of these themes the idealist philosopher Henry Jones responded in a long, sympathetically critical volume.[3] Jones argued that in Browning's emphasis upon the moral worth of man, his optimism in regard to the triumph of love and the infinite height of the moral horizon of humanity, and his general metaphysical interest he shared the convictions of philosophical idealism. But Jones also criticized Browning on two counts: first, that he did not adequately recognize that rational knowledge is also a part of the divine self-disclosure and that any full-orbed interpretation of the metaphysical foundation of reality must give knowledge as primary a status as the affections: secondly, that Browning did not distinguish carefully enough between Christian optimism, which says that all things work together for good, and pantheism, which says all things are good. Thus, Browning is censured for his agnosticism about the adequacy of knowledge to express reality and for an inadequate theism. But these are developed philosophical doctrines, and while the poet may not be exonerated for failing to deal with them in an adequate fashion, his general spirit was in keeping with the idealistic interpretation of life, and insofar as this is the case Browning was embraced as a significant contributor to the spirit of the age.

Browning was a believer in the idea of evolution, as were many of his contemporaries, even before Darwin was able to demonstrate it with empirical evidence. Once Darwin became prominent some of the earlier scientific descriptions and philosophical discussions became obsolete, but the poetic expression, which allowed more license, sustained its importance. Thus Browning stressed that an understanding of life must embrace the totality of life, that the discipline of man and the progress of man are to be secured only in and through the conditions of complex earthly existence. Hence, Browning did not leave out of account the natural order, although he emphasized the uniqueness of man. The most adequate description of his position is that both nature and man together are manifestations of God's self-revelation, and that this revelation is crowned by Jesus Christ. There was, as G. K. Chesterton insisted, a kind of primal earthiness about Browning's poetry and his evolutionary vision. He embraced all of life, both in practice and in theory.[4]

To many persons, Browning seemed to offer an almost unrestrained optimism, but to others there was no surrender to "idle optimism" in spite of the fact that he held firmly to the cardinal belief that life was moving forward with purpose and that this purpose was the providential will of God. His optimism was rooted in his conviction that love is sovereign and that all evil will be overcome in the triumph of love. But more than an optimist, Browning was a happy man who in his happiness expressed confidence. The position that Browning took in regard to amelioristic development corroborated the attitude of the period in terms of theodicy.

The above themes were usually stressed by Christian interpreters. Others, the most prominent of whom was Mrs. Sutherland Orr, held that Browning was not

---

[3] *Browning as a Philosophical and Religious Teacher* (Glasgow: James MacLehose, 1891).
[4] G. K. Chesterton, *Robert Browning*, pp. 184-85.

a Christian in a strict sense, though he did stress more general religious values. Nonetheless, Mrs. Orr probably made her keenest comment about his approach when she wrote, "The evangelical Christian and the subjective idealist are curiously blended in his composition." [5] And once again the combination of elements we found in the idealist philosophers, though now differently mixed, was repeated. What Mrs. Orr wanted to protest in her biography was the attempt of some Christians to take Browning into their tent as though he was, without reservation, one of their own. What she failed to realize was that the expression of Christian faith was also undergoing change, and that while Browning could not be put into the same bed with orthodox or traditional Christians, especially the Tractarians, there was great commonality between him and many others who were a part of the new theological generation.

It is not surprising, therefore, that at the turn of the century Browning was a prime inspirer of many sermons and was widely used to illustrate theological points. William Temple acknowledged his own debt to Browning as one of the three most important influences in his intellectual development, and in 1904, the year he graduated from Oxford, he published for private circulation an essay on Browning. [6] Silvester Horne, in a remarkable statement, estimated that the influence of Browning upon Nonconformist theology was greater than that of Dale and Spurgeon. [7] Other publications strike the fancy when one reviews the era. In the year 1904 the Reverend Thomas Rain brought out *Browning for Beginners,* and F. Ealand published *Sermons from Browning.* It was not too much for one commentator, Edward Berdoe, to say that Browning had restored him to his Christian faith. So unrestrained was his praise that he introduced his book on Browning by telling the following story. "A student at one of our theological colleges once consulted the divinity lecturer as to the best books on modern theology which he could present to a clerical friend. The answer came promptly and decisively— " 'Give him a set of Browning.' " [8]

Such a valuation was overenthusiastic, perhaps, but it was not completely wrong. Browning was a formative influence, and even if theologians might not universally recommend him as their spokesman, they were not afraid to use him as a major illustrator of their teaching and homiletical endeavors.

To refer to these last books may seem whimsical, but to mention them lifts

---

[5] *Life and Letters of Robert Browning,* p. 354.

[6] For a statement about Browning's influence see, F. A. Iremonger, *William Temple* (Oxford: Oxford University Press, 1948) p. 527. Temple's essay has been reprinted in *Religious Experience,* ed. A. E. Baker (London: James Clarke, 1958). In this essay, he states, "To Browning the climax of history, the crown of philosophy, and the consummation of poetry is unquestionably the Incarnation" (p. 51). Temple compares Browning to Shakespeare as one of the two greatest literary geniuses in English history.

[7] *A Popular History of the Free Churches,* quoted in J. W. Grant, *Free Churchmanship in England,* n. 144.

[8] *Browning and the Christian Faith* (London: George Allen, 1896), p. xiii.

up the point that Browning was a part of the religious atmosphere at the turn of the century. He was taken to be a compatriot by those who were attempting to set theological sails in the winds that swept the era. As no other literary figure, he reinforced or corroborated the idea of evolution, he affirmed the intrinsic value of man and the divine destiny of the human race. And he did it all in a poetic style that could carry the affections and enliven the heart.

In Browning, as in the idealistic philosophers, we have intellectual preparation for theology; for in his work theologians found soil that seemed to offer inexhaustible nourishment for development of the implications of God's indwelling presence, the psychological investigation of the nature of man, and the utilization of a dominant poetic voice in the explication of their interests.

APPENDIX B

QUAKERS IN THE FIRST TWO DECADES

We would neglect an important, although small, Christian body if we did not discuss the Quakers, who represent an indigenous tradition in England. This omission in the main text is due not to an oversight but rather to the fact that during this period Quaker theology was very slight in volume. Theology among the Quakers had always been subservient to practical religious life, and since the time of William Barclay there had been felt little need to make explicit theological reformulations. Warren S. Smith, who has described the Quakers in this era of rapid social, cultural, and religious transition, has commented,

One would suppose that of all the religious sects in the Western world, the Society of Friends would have been best prepared to meet the modern era. They could find no conflict with Darwin. Though they revered the Scriptures, they had never placed the Bible at the center of their faith. They were not predominantly other-worldly and were used to regarding social challenges in a religious light. . . .
Yet Friends were in almost every respect late-comers to this revolution, and, in England at least, furnished no major leadership before the advent of World War I.[1]

This assessment seems just, if one is speaking of the contribution of intellectual reaction among religious groups. Nonetheless, the Friends as a group never lost

[1] "London Quakers at the Turn of the Century," *Quaker History* Autumn, 1964, pp. 94-95.

their rightfully earned reputation for social concern, though some within the society itself felt this dimension was also in need of revitalization.

The most important religious thinker among the Quakers during this period was John Wilhelm Rowntree. Rowntree was born into a Quaker family of long standing and attended Quaker schools, but it was only through a struggle with agnosticism that he came to hold a positive faith himself. Concerned that the Friends were not in the maelstrom of religious and social revolution, he endeavored to awake the church to a new sense of the distinctive contribution it could make. In 1894 a group of younger Quakers began to circulate papers that dealt primarily with theological and educational issues. In 1898, Rowntree took editorial responsibility for this effort and brought out a periodical entitled *Present Day Papers.*[2] In this series, he encouraged the contributions of others and published explanatory comments on contemporary biblical criticism, Quaker theological positions, and the condition of the economically underprivileged.[3] Edward Grubb set the tone for the papers when he stated, "If we fail to give a rational account of ourselves it is not likely that we shall long survive. The spirit of enquiry is awake, and institutions that can only inspire an antiquarian interest cannot maintain their existence."[4] With this dictum in mind, Rowntree undertook the education of the Society so as to insure its continued vitality and contribution.

Although Rowntree contributed only editorial comment to *Present Day Papers,* he was also a spokesman who developed one of the more complete theological positions within the communion; although, in comparison with those we have discussed in the body of the text, this contribution is rather meager. In the major collection of his writings, *Essays and Addresses,* he acknowledges basic dependence upon Edward Caird's *Evolution of Religion,* since it gave hope for taking into account the whole complex nature of man and sought for ways to satisfy the human heart, consequently preparing for engagement with the new time. There were few distinctive emphases in his writings, but he did stress the fact that the doctrine of the Inner Light provided for direct contact with the interests in God's immanent presence and the evolutionary emphases of the time.[5]

In spite of his theological interests, Rowntree was even more concerned that the Quakers make their contribution in the realm of worship. He expressed his vision for his church when he wrote,

If there is one thing that I desire it is that we may not dissipate the spiritual energy of our Society in seeking difference, or conducting controversy on matters theological, but that we may join hands of sympathy over intellectual gulfs, and

[2] *Present Day Papers,* 4 vols., ed. J. Wilhelm Rowntree (London and York: Headley Brothers, 1898-1901).

[3] *Ibid.,* I, 56-57; II, 20, 26-27; III, 195. These are only examples of themes that run through the papers.

[4] *Ibid.,* I, 34.

[5] *Essays and Addresses* (London and York: Headley Brothers, 1905), pp. xxv.

give ourselves to the work of bringing spiritual life and vigor back to our England. What Church more able than we, if only our Meetings for Worship were glowing with warmth, and our silences living silences. We are free from any weight of tradition or ritual, and with our clearer perception of the indwelling nature of the Spirit, ought to strike more easily below class distinction and form to the recognition of the true brotherhood of man—the want of which it seems to me is the cause of much of the materialism of the present day.[6]

The Yearly Meeting of 1895 was the single most significant convocation in the Society during this era. It was called to consider the place of Quakerism in modern society. Concerns for many facets of contemporary life—ranging from slums to justice to capitalism and socialism—were discussed. There was also a recognition of the need for new intellectual interpretation of Quaker beliefs, especially in the light of Darwinian influences upon society.[7] Rowntree, even though he was only twenty-seven years of age at the time, was a leader among the reform group at this meeting and from that point exerted a strong influence until his death in 1905. With his death, a void was left in Quaker theological interest for a generation.

Apart from the more direct theological interests, other concerns were taking definite shape. In 1898 the Socialist Quaker Society was founded. Nine members of the society, including Mary O'Brien, Joseph T. Harris, Thomas Dent, and H. G. Dalton, met in London in April of that year and proposed strategy to acquaint Quakers with the meaning of socialism and means for its implementation. According to Peter d'A. Jones, the theological emphases on the priesthood of all believers, the sacredness of human personality, and the "Inner Light" prepared the way for the democratic and egalitarian political doctrine.[8] From these sources Quaker socialists, who represented only a small portion of the Society, became participants in the larger community of socialist Christians, and their history is intertwined in thought and expression with the movements we have discussed.

Throughout the opening decades of this century, the Quakers, as other church bodies, were struggling to come to terms with their inheritance and their new environment. The leadership of the church was sensitive to the challenges from both directions, and with uncertain success they attempted to acquaint the entire Society with their concerns.

---

[6] *Ibid,* p. xvi.

[7] *Manchester Conference of the Society of Friends, 1895.* See Peter d'A. Jones, *The Christian Socialist Revival, 1877-1914,* p. 370. This is a comprehensive discussion of the Quakers' participation in the socialist movements, esp. pp. 367-89. Cf. also Elfrida Vipont, *The Story of Quakerism Through Three Centuries* (London: The Bannisdale Press, 1954), pp. 229-30. Smith calls this meeting the entrance of English Friends into the modern world, "London Quakers at the Turn of the Century," pp. 104-5.

[8] *The Christian Socialist Revival, 1877-1914,* p. 367.

APPENDIX C

ROMAN CATHOLICISM IN ENGLAND

Roman Catholicism in England in the first decades of the twentieth century lived a separate history. Institutionally, it was intent upon retaining its distinctiveness; it was isolated socially and not politically involved; theologically it was largely bound by conservative continental influences. Only in the individual efforts of a few persons did it reach beyond its own communion and become participant in the general cultural life, including the theological discussions, of the period. Because of this separate existence, we shall look at Roman Catholic developments as running parallel to the mainstream we have been discussing.

From the time of Henry VIII, the history of English Roman Catholicism was closely aligned to the monarchial struggle. By the beginning of the nineteenth century, the church had, as supporter of losing monarchical claimants, dwindled into a small aristocratic minority. In the second and third quarters of the nineteenth century, this inherited strength was given new support by the Irish immigrations and by the growth of the Oxford Movement, which eventuated in the conversion of some of its most prominent leaders, especially John Henry Newman and Henry Edward Manning. As a result of these fresh additions the spiritual life of English Roman Catholicism was rejuvenated.

In 1875, Manning was made a cardinal of the church, and the strength of the continuing tradition was focused in a man who represented the virtue of faithfulness to a received legacy and a strong will to strengthen the internal life of the church. Sharp-featured and ascetic in appearance, Manning carried in his person the determined traditionalist hopes. Contemporary with Manning was John Henry Newman, who followed to the cardinalate in 1879, but, in distinction from his associate, expressed a willingness to live in and help mold the intellectual matrix of the late nineteenth century. An Oxford scholar who possessed a strong love for the university and its mode of life, Newman was a proponent of vital intellectual engagement and full academic participation. If Manning was determined to keep the church true to her past, Newman—while not eschewing the importance of inheritance—was equally set upon relating the truth of the Catholic tradition to the contemporary culture.

Between these two the tension within the life of the church was drawn taut. Most important in indicating the distinction was Newman's attitude toward progressive revelation and his consequent openness toward the future. But a more concrete illustration of the tension can be found in the divergent attitudes toward university education for Roman Catholic youth. Newman was convinced that Roman Catholicism in England needed the enrichment of university intellectual training; as a consequence, he encouraged the establishment of a Catholic College of Oratory at Oxford and negotiated the purchase of land for this purpose. Manning was stoutly opposed to the possible corruption this move might effect—for Oxford was, in the minds of many Roman Catholics, a center of modernism—and moved quickly to open an independent college in Kensington. The Kensington experiment was a failure, however, and after Manning's death, in 1892 (Newman had died two years previously), permission was given for Roman Catholic students to attend Oxford and Cambridge.

During this period, a change in the sociocultural makeup of the Roman Catholic population was also being affected. The indigenous Catholics were from the old aristocracy, which had established place and rank. Now, because of immigrations from Ireland, there were increasing numbers of laborers who were Roman Catholic. As a result, the concentration of Roman Catholics was in the peerage and the labor unions, with only a small middle-class representation.

Nonetheless, by the turn of the century some of the sharp distinctions among Roman Catholics were less pronounced. Catholics increased in number among the professions; converts from the Oxford movement brought in new middle-class persons; the industrial population achieved upward economic mobility; and the slow immigration from Ireland strengthened these moves. On the other side, the strong Irish sentiments of many within the church, plus the anti-Popery current in the general populace, kept Roman Catholics separated from the main flow of English life.[1] Population statistics indicate that by World War I two million per-

---

[1] Cf. David Mathew, *Catholicism in England 1535-1935* (London: Longmans, Green, 1936), p. 234.

sons, or 5 percent of the population, were Roman Catholics, with concentrations in the Southeast and Liverpool.

With the continued tension between the church and the culture, it is not surprising to find the new series of the *Downside Review* attempting to reach across the gap by affirming its place in the national life; hence, its opening editorial comment was an extravagant eulogy of Victoria and assuring Edward VII of "the unfailing loyalty and devotion of English Benedictines to the monarchy." [2]

In 1892, Herbert Cardinal Vaughn succeeded Manning. A continuator of the same tradition, with less rigor and determination, he was nevertheless, responsible for leading the Roman Catholic Church into the twentieth century. A decade later Bishop Francis Bourne was appointed to the See of Westminster, a position that he held until 1935. Our discussion concentrates upon this era, in which Archbishop Bourne was the hierarchical figure whose personality and administrative leadership most affected the Roman Catholic community. Educated in both England and France, his loyalties always remained English and his tastes those of a Londoner. He was elevated to the cardinalate in 1911 and from the vantage point of this new position exercised an increased influence. Dignified in manner and looks, always carrying a profound sense of his spiritual responsibilities, he was conservative in his ideas and administration of church affairs. In his interests, he epitomized the characteristics and the ideals of the dominant stream in English Roman Catholicism.

The attitude of Roman Catholic aristocracy was consistently conservative insofar as there was political activism at all. David Mathew has described them in the following language, "Politically both the older and the newer rich Catholic landowners were markedly conservative in politics. Both sections combined could muster at the end of the Manning period about forty peers, a definite proportion of the Upper House, very respectable in character, solid in quality, seldom erratic, rarely brilliant and politically distinctly inactive." [3]

The political inertia of the peers was matched by that of the country gentry and the struggling squires. But the influx of Irish laborers that had taken place during the first half of the nineteenth century had forced the issue of social concern upon some of the priestly leadership. Awareness of the problems of the poor had been an ingredient in the life of many parish priests since the time of the immigrations, and Cardinal Manning had exhibited an impressive interest in regard to labor questions. In spite of this initiative, Cardinal Vaughn was decidedly disinclined to follow this lead; and the Roman Catholic community as a whole, and particularly within its economically privileged sector, was not actively involved in the "condition of the people" issue. After the turn of the twentieth century, some changes began to take place. At least, minority groups became involved in certain social issues, and in 1909 Father Plater founded the Catholic Social Guild with an educational mission. This group undertook the study of social problems, and in 1922

---

[2] *Downside Review*, vol. I, no. 1, 1901.
[3] *Catholicism in England 1535-1935*, p. 218.

the Guild inaugurated at Oxford a Catholic Worker's College. For the first two decades of the present century, however, this remained a subordinate interest; the church was feeling the strain between establishing its own inner life and its unique mission.

At the same time, Charles Lindley Wood, later Lord Halifax, was attempting to seal a relation between the Roman Catholic Church and the Church of England. The national hierarchy resisted this move, but Lord Halifax, with undaunted energy, followed his vision of the organic unity of the two churches. From the time Lord Halifax met the French Vincentian, Fernand Portal, in 1890, the two worked in tandem to achieve the commonly held goal. In 1895 Portal was called to Rome, and, after consultation, Leo XIII published the apostolic letter *Amantissimae voluntatis* on April 14, in which he addressed "the English who desire the Kingship of Christ in the unity of faith." The letter spoke specifically of "reconciliation and peace" and encouraged a patient search for unity.

For a moment there was hope on the part of Lord Halifax that a significant step had been taken toward full unity, and to serve this hope Portal established the *Anglo-Roman Review* in Paris in December, 1895. The whole matter of Anglican orders was taken under consideration by the Papacy and a historical commission was charged with the study. Cardinal Manning remained negative and the commission report was divided. On September 13, 1896, the Pope sent the bull *Apostolicae Curae* in which he declared Anglican orders invalid. The vivid expectations were annulled.

Through the succeeding years, down to the conversations at Malines, Belgium, in 1921, Lord Halifax tenaciously pursued the grail and exhibited integrity, resourcefulness, and faithfulness to the cause of union.[4] In spite of the initial failure, Halifax and Portal provided courageous ecumenical endeavor at the turn of the century.

As the twentieth century opened, however, a number of facets of intellectual tension were becoming unmistakeably apparent within the church itself. A few liberal Roman Catholics were pressing for new freedom—especially theological freedom. Leaders such as Lord Acton had been restive for a generation. Taking their lead from European theologians, Britishers were developing new perspectives of their own. By 1901, the evidence of challenge was becoming clear, and the English Bishops issued a joint Pastoral Letter against growing liberal tendencies. The leader of the "Modernists," as they were called, was Father George Tyrrell, a member of the Society of Jesus. Tyrrell, a man of mystical temperament, became chief spokesman for and an unrelenting exponent of the Modernist movement. A later Roman Catholic historian has described Tyrrell as "a man of brilliant endowment and deep spirituality, but unbalanced and easily influenced, too ready to

---

[4] Cf. the biography by J. G. Lockhart, *Charles Lindley Viscount Halifax 1839-1885,* I, and esp. *1885-1936,* II (London: Geoffrey Bles, 1935-36) for a thorough account of this remarkable man and the ecumenical effort he made.

make the latest theory the measure of truth." [5] Consonant with his own change of attitude, Tyrrell at first moved slowly, but then with increasing strength into a critical stance and finally to direct challenge. From the probing of his earliest works, he gradually took a position that questioned both the doctrinal position as well as the authority of the church.

The year 1907 was a time of unusual ferment in Roman Catholicism, as it was in Nonconformist theology. In that year Pius X issued two condemnations of the Modernist movement. On July 3 the decree *Lamentabili sane* catalogued the condemned and now proscribed errors of the Modernists; two months later, on September 8, the Pope sent the Encyclical *Pascendi dominici gregis*. In this latter statement, the Pontiff made plain that he was not attempting to judge the internal disposition of the souls of those who teach Modernist doctrines, but he did condemn their teaching. The issue was clear-cut—"the security of the Catholic name is at stake;" and those who hold these views are "animated by a false zeal of the Church . . . put themselves forward as reformers of the Church." Accused of curiosity and pride, of immodesty and agnosticism, and of being in revolt against the magisterium of the church, the Modernists stood condemned. In their system they had achieved "the synthesis of all errors." "Undoubtedly, were anyone to attempt the task of collecting together all of the errors that have been broached against the faith and to concentrate into one the sap and substance of them all, he could not succeed in doing so better than the Modernists have done." [6]

As prescriptions against the Modernists, the Pope instituted a number of concrete actions: scholasticism was made the basis of the sacred sciences ("i.e. that which the Angelic Doctor has bequeathed to us"); anyone tainted with Modernism was to be excluded from directorships or professorships of seminaries or universities; diligence must be exercised in selecting candidates for Holy Orders; Bishops were to prevent the writings of the Modernists to be read when they were published— even if the books had the *Imprimatur;* also they were to prevent, where possible, the publication of such books, and published books were to have an *Imprimatur* that was preceded by *Nihil obstat* and the name of the censor; restriction was placed on secular priests as editors of papers or periodicals; limitations were placed on congresses and public meetings; in every diocese a "council of viligance" was to be established in order to enforce these "commands" and "prescriptions" in writings and social institutions; and, in one year from this date and every three years thereafter, Bishops of all dioceses were to furnish a "diligent and sworn report" that these instructions were being carried out. The Modernists had challenged the magisterial authority of the church, and the hierarchy responded with all its strength.

[5] E. L. Watkin, *Roman Catholicism in England from the Reformation to 1950* (London: Oxford University Press, 1957), p. 216.

[6] *All Things in Christ: Encyclicals and Selected Documents of St. Pius X,* ed. Vincent A. Yzermans (Glen Rock, N.J.: The Newman Press, 1954), p. 117.

James A. Magner has claimed that the Modernist movement caused a serious setback in the spontaneous development of Catholic thought. By pushing too fast, he argued, the process of creative development was not only stymied but also completely cut off for the time being.

> The Church has lost some of the prestige which it enjoyed under Leo XIII. In its bosom discouragement has seized a number of the intellectual or social workers. Denounced, tracked down and villified by the press of occult power . . . many withdraw forever from the lists, who might have fought useful battles for the triumph of the Christian cause. This uneasiness was unfortunately felt in many theological seminaries, in religious scholasticates, in university centers. . . . our young men have no longer the sacred fire of intellectual work, and it is well-nigh impossible for professors to rekindle it.[7]

In England, Tyrrell was the one who most directly felt the suppression that *Pascendi gregis* enforced. But there was immediate response in many of the newspapers and magazines.[8] *The Nation* on September 21 expressed no surprise, knowing "the ruling spirit of Vatican," but affirmed that the new spirit would endure. *The Tablet,* a Catholic paper, responded positively a week later, and although it continued to present Tyrrell's responses and letters, it affirmed, "The judgment of the Apostolic See will be received here, as by Catholics throughout the world, with glad obedience, and with a deepened sense of gratitude to the Holy Father for the signal and timely service which in the discharge of his august office he has rendered." The *Times* on November 2 and the *Guardian* on November 20 ran editorials that were critical of the Roman Catholic position, and throughout Tyrrell himself carried on a large and pugnacious correspondence attacking the Vatican as having learned nothing and Pius X as too old to learn.

The man who caused the uproar was distinctive. Born in Ireland, and possessor of Irish red hair and an Irish temper, Tyrrell arrived in England in 1879 (pro pitiously) on the Feast of All Fools. Shortly thereafter he converted to the Roman Catholic Church. In his moving and provocative autobiography, Tyrrell described his further movement into the priesthood and his joining of the Society of Jesus.[9] Whatever the evaluation made of his activities in restrospect,[10] the story of his life

---

[7] "The Catholic Church in Modern Europe," *The Catholic Historical Review,* April, 1937, p. 8.

[8] The best collection of materials on this response was compiled by Maude D. Petre and presented to Cambridge University Library. This collection contains articles for the years 1906-14 and remains unpublished.

[9] Cf. M. D. Petre, *Autobiography and Life of George Tyrrell,* 2 vols. (London: Edward Arnold, 1912). The first volume is Tyrrell's own account down to the year 1884; the second volume is Miss Petre's supplementation and completion of the account.

[10] J. Lewis May, for instance, even though sympathetic and even commendatory of Tyrrell's character, sees him as always having been a wild, untamable creature who never could have found a place in the Jesuit structure and claims that Tyrrell should have with candor recognized this also. See *Father Tyrrell and the Modernist Movement* (London: Burns, Oates and Washbourne, 1932).

as a Jesuit was one of an intense struggle that finally issued in a distressed realization of his own incapacity to fit into the Order in any normal manner. He was reacting against the imposition of ecclesiastical authority; he felt deep aversion to many of the explicit doctrinal formulations of the church; he carried on a personal struggle for freedom of thought and writing; and he increasingly supported, and was supported by, others among the Modernists—especially those in France.

As a man of Enlightenment dispositions, Tyrrell was questioning contemporary expressions of authority even as he searched for new foundations; for him the problem was not Catholicism but the present character of Roman Catholicism. Taking himself to be paradigmatic of the predicament of modern man, he cried for freedom to explore the meaning of faith in the twentieth century, and he asked his church to give to him and his compatriots this opportunity.

Because of his inability to accept the authority of *Pascendi gregis* and in a struggle to publish materials that the Order had declined to allow, he was dismissed from the Society of Jesus, and on October 22, 1907, Rome deprived him of the sacraments—a sentence virtually amounting to excommunication. From this point on, there was constant writing and constant battling. But the struggle was short, and on July 12, 1909 he died. "When Tyrrell died," says M. Loisy, "it may be said that Modernism, considered as a movement of overt resistance to the absolutism of Rome, died with him. . . . Tyrrell had been in these latter years the leading apostle of the movement. He was not a savant, but he was endowed with a great mind, a great soul, a great heart, and with the enthusiasm of a martyr." [11]

Catholicism, Tyrrell believed, as a continuator of the truth of Christian faith, was of prime importance, but "Romanism" or "Vaticanism" was disruptive of that dominant tradition and had, by its present misuse of authority, made it impossible for those who stood in the line of the Catholic tradition to come into valid relation with the modern world. The major culprit, according to his analysis, was an ossified theology—that is, theology that attempted to maintain intact a set of inherited dogma, that refused to recognize the legitimate maturation of faith, that focused its attention exclusively upon he past and, withal, enforced its opinions by the exercise of absolutist hierarchical power. From Tyrrell's point of view, all these claims and assertions were wrong. Theology, if it is to be valid, must recognize its fragmentary, fallible character; it must become related to the practical needs of the religious life, such as prayer; it must become future-oriented so as to envision and realize its possible transformative maturation; and it must free itself from its close and unhealthy alliance with ecclesiastical power.

Positively, Tyrrell was interested in resetting the priorities: religious experience was prior to theology; consequently theology must always be in the service of and contributory to living religious awareness. In agreement with those who found religion to be a common ingredient in universal human history, he attempted to

---

[11] Quoted in May, *Father Tyrrell and the Modernist Movement,* p. 262.

place Catholicism within this matrix and argued that it had its central place because it offered the most hope for the practical development of the awareness of God. The theme of development led Tyrrell to one of the crucial points of his contention; namely, it offered hope for solving the dilemma of the exercise of authority.

The misunderstanding that had enveloped Romanism was over its attachment to a fixed and unalterable deposit of faith and its claim that intellectual assent to these formulations was the only valid criterion for the establishment of Christian faith. Against this view, Tyrrell became oriented toward the future, and he argued for an understanding of the necessary development of the seeds of religious life that was found in all awareness of God and emphatically so within the true Catholic tradition. In short, authority must be understood not as something that reaffirms the past with an inflexible attitude but, rather, as the reach of man's innate awareness of God for its proper fulfillment. Authority, therefore, was to be understood in pragmatic terms, in terms of how it contributed to the self-fulfillment of man's religious capacity. Hence, authority should be neither restrictive nor designed in a negative fashion so as to frustrate maturation; as valid, authority should be directing, encouraging, releasing, guiding. Ecclesiastical sanctions should be administered not so as to prevent growth but so as to support faith in its search for completion. In the last analysis, authority, as Tyrrell conceived it, must function internally, in companionship with man's personal quest for maturation and with respect for each individual's intrinsic integrity, for in this manner the inheritance from the past could serve as preparer for a freer, more adequate future. This was the issue that primarily estranged Tyrrell and the hierarchy. If it could be resolved, then there would be no need to concentrate upon the symptomatic expressions of his concrete theological explications.[12]

When Tyrell died, the Anglican A. L. Lilley praised him in an obituary in the *Commonwealth* for July 7, 1909: "He has gone from us; and yet he is not gone, he is here, a part of the world's stress in the days that are coming through a darkness we cannot yet wholly penetrate towards a light which he saw and spent his life preparing us to see."

From the side of Catholic theology there were responses that defended the Pope's action. One of the most important replies was provided by the Jesuit Father Sydney F. Smith. For a number of years Smith wrote regularly for the Catholic periodical *The Month,* and through the first two decades of the twentieth century he was a leading Roman Catholic theological spokesman. It may be claimed

---

[12] For the direct discussion of this issue see *Medievalism: A Reply to Cardinal Mercier* (London: Longmans, Green, 1908) and *Christianity at the Crossroads* (Longmans, Green, 1909). Two authors have given a good description of Tyrrell's theological development: John Ratte, *Three Modernists: Alfred Loisy, George Tyrrell, William L. Sullivan* (New York: Sheed and Ward, 1967) and Alec R. Vidler, *The Modernist Movement in the Roman Church* (Cambridge: Cambridge University Press, 1934).

that his articles in *The Month* are as close to a systematic statement of Catholic thought as one can find in England in the first two decades. Raised in a vicarage near Sandwich, he was converted to Catholicism at the age of 21 in 1864; in 1891 he joined the staff of *The Month*. Throughout his active writing career he was interested in the defense of the Church and served as a reference person for the Roman Church's condemnation of Anglican orders in *Apostolicae Curae*. He had little sympathy with schemes of social reform, but he was a fair commentator and a careful critic.[13]

In an article in the November, 1907 issue of *The Month,* Smith responded to *Pascendi gregis* and offered an answer to the Modernists. Epistemologically, he said, Modernism was Kantian and not Thomistic; and in this it erred, for the human intellect is under no limitation to trust all that lies beyond the world of appearances as unknowable. Moreover, doctrine affirms that Jesus used miracles and fulfilled prophecies to proclaim his divine Sonship. Faith has been misinterpreted by the Modernists. Rightly understood, "faith is the assent given to propositions the truth of which is certified to us not directly by the light of our personal reasoning, but indirectly, and on the testimony of God which we can absolutely trust." As a consequence, the dogma of the Catholic Church is true beyond all doubt and is affirmed by the Church, reason, and the Holy Spirit. The Modernists, in contrast, rely exclusively upon religious sentiment as the test for dogma. In opposition to the new tendencies, Catholicism must once again make clear its foundation in the authority of tradition and Scripture. It must reassert its origin in Jesus' commission, and it must reinforce its conviction that the sacraments are not only signs but are the imparters of grace. In stating this position, Smith was returning to the classical positions of the church and argued that they were still valid for the present day.[14]

If Father Tyrell represented the radical element within English Roman Catholicism and Father Smith represented the continuing conservatism that was characteristic of the mainstream within the church, the most prominent mediating figure of the era was Baron Friedrich von Hügel. No other man of the era was more eulogized by people of varied backgrounds and divergent interests. Charles Gore, in reviewing *The Mystical Element in Religion,* remarked, "This is a work by perhaps the most learned of living men."[15] And R. J. Campbell considered this book the single most important influence that entered his life at that period.[16] Walter M. Horton, in surveying the era, evaluated von Hügel as the single most important theologian of the period in England.[17] Whatever the judgment by contemporaries and chroniclers of the time, this man was the most significant figure in Roman Catholic theology in England.

[13] See, "The Late Father Sydney Smith, S. J.," *The Month* (August, 1922), pp. 97-101.
[14] Cf. also his "What is Modernism," *The Month* (March, 1908), pp. 284-85.
[15] *Church Quarterly Review,* Oct., 1911, p. 89. Cf. Maisie Ward, *The Wilfred Wards and the Transition* (London: Sheed & Ward, 1934), II, 300-301.
[16] *A Spiritual Pilgrimage,* p. 241.
[17] *Contemporary English Theology* (New York: Harper, 1936), p. 43.

Born in Florence, Italy, in May 1852, of a Scottish mother and a German father, von Hügel moved to England with his family in 1867. He was educated by private tutors and never attended any formal school. With his cosmopolitan background, it is not surprising that he became a master of several contemporary languages as well as a good linquist in Hebrew, Greek, and Latin. Because of a religious crisis that he experienced at the age of eighteen, he turned his attention for the rest of his life to religious thought. In the succeeding years, he became a friend of many of the major Roman Catholic thinkers on the continent and developed a wide range of friends among Anglicans as well as Roman Catholic leaders in England. In 1873, he married Lady Mary Herbert, daughter of Sidney Lord Herbert of Lea, with whom he had three daughters. In all, he published five books, two of them in the period with which we are concerned—*The Mystical Element in Religion* in 1909 (which was his most important study) and *Eternal Life* in 1912.

The insatiable hunger that the Baron had for religious knowledge and religious living was matched by his deep commitment to his friends. After reading Tyrrell's *Nova et Vetero,* a book he praised to friends, he contacted its author, and the two became extremely close friends. Certainly, in their early friendship Tyrrell felt encouraged by von Hügel's interest but was later distressed by the Baron's unwillingness to follow the lead of ideas to their logical conclusion. But von Hügel was devoted to the church and never thought of his own theological explorations as moving beyond the accepted boundaries of his communion. And, indeed, he evidently made some effort to persuade Tyrrell to take a less precipitous course. When, in 1927, he wrote the preface to the second edition of *The Mystical Element in Religion,* he looked back upon this friendship and sighed, "Father Tyrrell has gone, who had been so generously helpful, especially as to the mystical states, as to Aquinas and as to the form of the whole book, for so many years, long before the storms beat upon him and his own vehemence overclouded, in part, the force and completeness of that born mystic."[18] As with many rich friendships, the road was uneven and often diverged, but a constancy of concern and continual efforts to reach one another across wide chasms remained a part, and the sustaining part, of the fellow feeling.

In addition to his personal qualities, von Hügel's religious thought remains an important historical legacy. In many ways, the Baron was a man of his own hour—his interests and his assumptions were dominated by the mind-set of the era, and it may be claimed that his influence was rooted in the fact that he was so endemic to the time. Even so, he stood out from his time with his clear insistence upon the transcendence of God, and by using this theme as the touchstone for his theological interpretation. Thus, when one turns to *The Mystical Element in Religion,* he is

[18] (London: J. M. Dent & Sons, 1927), p. vii. For an account of this friendship through their correspondence, see M. D. Petre, *Von Hügel and Tyrrell: The Story of a Friendship* (New York: E. P. Dutton, 1937).

immediately aware of its deep enmeshment in its own milieu, even as it strains at some of the arbitrary boundaries that seemed to seal the thought of the period.

The central chapter of this work is the second, in which von Hügel expresses the key concepts of his position; and it is this chapter which became, immediately, the most influential. With his penchant for triads, he analyzes the three fundamental constituents of all religion: institutionalization, creedal or critical formulations, and mystical apprehension. Religion finds its vitality precisely in the interaction and mutual conditioning of these elements. The institutional aspect refers to the rites, rituals, and polity that shape a religious tradition with its identifiable communities; the critical dimension lifts up the intellectual interpretation, which may be found in creeds and constructive theology; the mystical aspect points to the interior, personal experiences that express the unitive formation of the soul with God. In these three dimensions we have religion's way of living, of thinking, and of being. Throughout the book, there are references to historical and psychological expressions of these aspects, often in a highly schematized manner. But, wherever concrete religion takes its form, von Hügel contends, it does so through the interplay, tension, and common enrichment of these cardinal constituents.

Philosophically, the most significant stress in this book, as well as in his succeeding work, is his emphasis upon the priority of God in all religious knowing. In the preface to his second edition he reemphasized this position, for now with increased clarity, he claimed, he was convinced that religion could not even be conceived as extant without the impingement of the Object of Religion upon human apprehension, so that "the reality of the Object (in itself the Subject of all subjects) and its presence independently of all our apprehension of it—that its Givenness is the central characteristic of all religion worthy of the name."[19] This position he designated "critical realism."

Because of this priority of God in religious knowing, von Hügel argues,

> For Religion is ever, *qua* religion, authoritative and absolute. What constitutes religion is not simply to hold a view and to try to live a life, with respect to the Unseen and the Deity, as possibly or even certainly beautiful or true or good: but precisely that which is over and above this,—the holding this view and this life to proceed somehow from God Himself, so as to bind my innermost mind and conscience to unhesitating assent.[20]

This statement has one basic qualification—namely, men, because they are creatures who live with multiple capacities and in multilateral relationships, have many interests that range beyond the immediate experience of God. Hence, they must find their own independence and explore the dimensions of their autonomy.

---

[19] *The Mystical Element in Religion* (London: J. M. Dent & Sons, 1908), I, xvi. See esp. Maurice Nidoncelle, *Baron Friedrich von Hügel* (London: Longmans, Green, 1937) for the best study of von Hügel's thought, and this in spite of his unconvincing reconstruction of the relation of von Hügel to Tyrrell and the Modernist movement.

[20] *Ibid.*, I, 46.

Such development is legitimate when man recognizes that "all life sustains itself only by constant, costing renovation and adaptation of itself to its environment, the religious life, as the most intense and extensive of all lives, must somehow be richest in such newness in oldness, such renovative, adaptive, assimilative power." [21]

One of the most distinctive qualities of the Baron's position was his effort to maintain a comprehensive, or what he more correctly calls a "synthetic," view of man. As a result, he stressed the various inter-relationships among the institutional, intellectual, and mystical components within religious experience. Moving beyond the more narrow confines of the essential religious experience, he then attempted to relate this basic dimension of man's life to the wide range of ethical responsibilities. [22] As in the case of some of his non-Roman contemporaries, especially Gore and Forsyth, he stressed the fact that religion cannot be reduced to morality; and this stress was made in the light of the historical efforts to do so, such as Kant, as well as the present tendencies of some Christian socialists. [23] Von Hügel was concerned to stress, as a consequence of his statement of the primacy of God's transcendence, the fundamental place of man's relation to God; it is in this relationship that religion comes to birth and is nourished in life. But he also insisted that there is a mutual involvement of religion and morality, for while religion transcends all other spheres of life, it also belongs to and affects every sphere. The relation of religion to morality is one of interaction, so Troeltsch is quoted positively,

We can but keep a sufficient space open for the action of both forms, so that from their interaction there may ever result the deepening of Humane Ends by the Christian Ethics, and the humanizing of the Christian End by the Humane Ethics, so that life may become a service of God within the Cultural Ends, and that the service of God may transfigure the world. [24]

For von Hügel, there is an ontological and axiological hierarchy in which God as Being and as Creator has the primacy. But the created order reflects its Creator, so that every man has an innate moral sense as well as a thirst for God. The highest moment of full-orbed human experience arises when the moral sense is combined with the religious sense. In such a situation the love of goodness and the love of God become coimplicates, and the human being reaches toward maturation.

At this point, von Hügel's doctrine of development becomes important, for he attempts to relate the priority of God's revelation to man's fragmented receptivity, and the completeness of the religio-moral complex to man's slow maturation. Hence,

---

[21] *Ibid.*, I, 47.

[22] *Ibid.*, II, 259-60. von Hügel concludes his study of St. Catherine with an exploration of these interrelationships.

[23] *Ibid.*, II, 260-61.

[24] *Ibid.*, II, 273-74.

the fixed point of revelation in religious experience is the fixity of a fountainhead from which flow the waters of life, waters that touch everything on the bank as they pass. "The fixity, in a word, will be conceived and found to be a fixity of orientation, a definiteness of affinities and of assimulative capacity." [25] The revelation that inaugurates the religious life is inexhaustible, and its richness is to be ingredient to the complex of human relationships and all the practical applications of life.

The question of authority for von Hügel is answered by the proper assignment of values. The life that is ordered so that its basic commitment is to the worshiping love of God and its consequential commitment is to its fellows lives under the aegis of this authority. The Roman Catholic Church, for him, possessed a different sort of authority—one that performs a supportive and nourishing role. This particular historical expression of institutionalization and intellectual interpretation provides a richness of possibility for the ordering of life and the interpretation of the meaning and implications of that order. Hence, the Baron remained faithful to the Roman Catholic Church because of his debt and his hope for the nourishing of the mystical experience.

With von Hügel we come to the close of the era we are considering. For a moment, the Church had reasserted its authority over its votaries, but seeds planted in the era foreshadowed a time when reassessment would again have to be made. For the time being, at least, the challenge of George Tyrrell had been repelled, as Father Sidney Smith represented the inherited attitudes that were to be maintained. Von Hügel was a mediating figure who thought afresh even as he acknowledged the authority of the Church and its hierarchy. As the era came to a close, Roman Catholicism may be seen as struggling to keep a steady course along previously charted routes; but the sea was increasingly stormy.

[25] *Ibid.*, I, 72.

SELECTED BIBLIOGRAPHY

History, General

Adams, W. S. *Edwardian Portraits*. London: Secker and Warburg, 1957.

Appleman, P., Madden, W. A., and Wolff, M. (eds.). *1859: Entering an Age of Crisis.* Bloomington: Indiana University Press, 1959.

Benson, E. F. *As We Are*. London: Longmans, Green, 1932.

————. *King Edward VII*. London: Longmans, Green, 1933.

Binyon, C. C. *The Christian Socialist Movement in England*. London: S. P. C. K., 1931.

Booth, Charles (ed.). *Life and Labour of the People in London*. 17 vols. London: Williams, Norgate, 1889-1903.

Clark, G. Kitson. *The Making of Victorian England*. London: Methuen, 1962.

Cowherd, R. G. *The Politics of English Dissent*. London: Epworth Press, 1919.

Dangerfield, George. *The Strange Death of Liberal England 1910-1914*. New York: Capricorn, 1935.

————. *Victoria's Heir*. New York: Harcourt, Brace & Company, 1941.

Ensor, Robert. *England 1870-1914* (Oxford History of England). Oxford: Clarendon Press, 1936.

Halévy, Elie. *A History of the English People in the Nineteenth Century: Imperialism and the Rise of Labour 1895-1905.* Translated by E. I. Watkin, Vol. V. London: Ernest Benn, 1929.

_____. *A History of the English People in the Nineteenth Century: The Rule of Democracy 1905-1914.* Translated by E. I. Watkin, Vol. VI. London: Ernest Benn, 1934.

Hall, W. P. and Albion, R. G. *A History of England and the British Empire.* Boston: Ginn, 1946.

Laslett, Peter. *The World We Have Lost.* London: Methuen, 1965.

Marwick, Arthur. *The Deluge: British Society and the First World War.* Boston: Little, Brown, 1966.

Masterman, C. F. G. *The Condition of England.* London: Methuen, 1909. (Reissued 1959 with introduction by J. T. Boulton.)

Mendenhall, Thos. C., Henning, Basil D., and Foord, Archibald S. *The Quest for a Principle of Authority in Europe.* New York: Henry Holt, 1948.

Pankhurst, E. Sylvia. *The Suffragette Movement.* London: Longmans, Green, 1931.

Taylor, A. J. P. *The Trouble Makers.* Bloomington: Indiana University Press, 1958.

_____. *English History 1914-1945* (Oxford History of England). Oxford: Clarendon Press, 1965.

Thomas, Neville P. *A History of British Politics from the Year 1900.* London: Herbert Jenkins, 1956.

Thomson, David. *England in the Nineteenth Century: 1815-1914.* Harmondsworth, Middlesex: Penguin Books, 1950.

_____. *England in the Twentieth Century.* Harmondsworth, Middlesex: Penguin Books, 1965.

Thompson, E. P. *Making of the English Working Class.* London: V. Gollancz, 1965.

Tuchman, Barbara. *The Proud Tower.* New York: Macmillan, 1962.

History, Economic

Ashworth, W. *An Economic History of England 1870-1939.* London: Methuen, 1960.

Beer, Max. *History of British Socialism.* London: G. Bell, 1921-23.

Court, W. H. B. *British Economic History 1870-1914.* Cambridge: The University Press, 1965.

Cunningham, W. *Socialism and Christianity.* London: S. P. C. K., 1909.

Harrod, Roy. *The British Economy.* New York: McGraw-Hill, 1963.

Keynes, J. M. *The Economic Consequences of Peace.* London: Macmillan, 1919.

_____. *The End of Laissez Faire.* London: Hogarth Press, 1926.

Pigou, A. C. *Alfred Marshall and Current Thought.* London: Macmillan, 1953.

Stern, W. M. *Britain Yesterday and Today.* (Outline Economic History from mid-18th Century.) London: Longmans, Green, 1962.

Webb, Sidney and Beatrice. *The History of Trade Unionism.* London: Longmans, Green, 1902.

_____. *The Decay of Capitalist Civilization.* New York: Harcourt, Brace, 1923.

History, Ecclesiastical

Allchin, A. M. *The Silent Rebellion: Anglican Religious Communities.* London: S. C. M., 1958.

Beck, G. A. (ed.). *The English Catholics 1850-1950.* London: Burns and Oates, 1950.

Binyon, G. C. *The Christian Socialist Movement in England.* London: S. P. C. K., 1931.

Clark, Henry Wm. *Liberal Orthodoxy: A Historical Survey.* London: Chapman's Hall, 1914.

Cruikshank, M. *Church and State in English Education: 1870 to the Present Day.* London: Macmillan, 1963.

Davidson, R. T. (ed.). *The Five Lambeth Conferences.* Compiled under the direction of the Most Reverend Randall T. Davidson, Archbishop of Canterbury. London: S. P. C. K., 1920.

Davies, Horton. *The English Free Churches.* London: Oxford University Press, 1952.

Davies, Rupert Earl (ed.)., *John Scott Lidgett: A Symposium.* London: Epworth Press, 1957.

Davies, Rupert Earl, and Rupp, G. *A History of the Methodist Church in Great Britain.* London: Epworth Press, 1965.

Davies, Rupert Earl. *Methodism.* London: Epworth Press, 1963.

Edwards, Maldwyn L. *Methodism and England.* London: Epworth Press, 1943.

The Evangelistic Work of the Church. (The report of the Archbishop's Third Committee of Enquiry.) London: S. P. C. K., 1918.

Gairdner, W. H. T. *Edinburgh 1910.* Edinburgh: Oliphant, Anderson and Ferrier, 1910.

Glover, Willis B. *Evangelical Nonconformists and Higher Criticism in the Nineteenth Century.* London: Independent Press, 1954.

Grant, John Webster. *Free Churchmanship in England: 1870-1940.* London: Independent Press, 1962.

Johnson, Humphrey J. T. *Anglicanism in Transition.* London: Longmans, 1938.

Knox, Wilfred L. *The Catholic Movement in the Church of England.* New York: Gorham, 1925.

Knox, Wilfred L., and Vidler, Alec R. *The Development of Modern Catholicism.* London: Philip Allan, 1933.

Lilley, Alfred L. *Modernism: A Record and Review.* London: Isaac Pitman & Sons, 1908.

Lloyd, Roger. *The Church of England 1900-1965.* London: S. C. M., 1966.

Mathew, David. *Catholicism in England 1535-1935.* London: Longmans, Green, 1936.

Mudie-Smith, R. (ed.). *The Religious Life of London.* London: Hodder & Stoughton, 1904.

Newsome, David. *Godliness and Good Learning.* London: John Murray, 1961.

O'Conner, John J. *The Catholic Revival in England.* New York: Macmillan, 1942.

Ollard, S. C. *A Short History of the Oxford Movement.* London: Mowbray, 1915.

Payne, E. A. *The Free Church Tradition in the Life of England.* London: S. C. M., 1944.

_____. *The Baptist Union: A Short History*. London: Carey Kingsgate Press, 1958.

Selbie, William Boothby. *Nonconformity, Its Origin and Progress*. London: Williams & Norgate, 1912.

Spinks, G. S. *Religion in Britain Since 1900*. London: Andrew Dakers, 1952.

Stewart, H. L. *A Century of Anglo-Catholicism*. London: J. M. Dent & Sons, 1929.

Sykes, Norman. *The English Religious Tradition*. London: S. C. M., 1953. Revised 1961.

Tatlow, Tissington. *The Story of the Student Christian Movement*. London: S. C. M., 1933.

Underwood, Alfred Clair. *A History of the English Baptists*. London: Baptist Union Publications, 1947.

Vidler, Alec R. *The Modernist Movement in the Roman Church*. Cambridge: University Press, 1934.

_____. *A Century of Social Catholicism 1820-1920*. London: S. P. C. K., 1964.

_____. *20th Century Defenders of the Faith*. London: S. C. M., 1965.

Wearmouth, Robert F. *The Social and Political Influence of Methodism in the Twentieth Century*. London: Epworth Press, 1957.

Autobiography and Biography

Asquith, H. H. *Memories and Reflections*. 2 vols. London: Cassel, 1928.

Bell, G. K. A. *Randall Davidson: Archbishop of Canterbury (1903-1928)*. 3rd ed.; London: Oxford, 1952.

De La Bedoyère, Michael. *The Life of Baron von Hügel*. New York: Scribner's, 1952.

Bennett, Arnold. *The Journals of Arnold Bennett*, ed. Newton Flower, 3 vols. London: Cassell, 1932-33.

Bowra, C. M. *Memories, 1898-1939*. Cambridge: Harvard University Press, 1967.

Campbell, R. J. *A Spiritual Pilgrimage*. London: Williams & Norgate, 1916.

Dark, Sidney. *Five Deans*. (J. Colet, J. Donne, J. Swift, A. P. Stanley, W. R. Inge). London: Jonathan Cape, 1928.

Elias, Frank. *The Rt. Honorable H. H. Asquith*. London: James Clarke, 1909.

Elton, Godfrey E. *The Life of James Ramsay MacDonald*. London: Collins, 1939.

Forster, E. M. *Goldsworthy Lowes Dickinson*. London: Edward Arnold, 1934.

Fox, Adam. *Dean Inge*. London: John Murray, 1960.

Garvie, A. E. *Memories and Meanings of My Life*. London: Allen & Unwin, 1938.

Haldane, R. B. *Autobiography*. London: Hodder & Stoughton, 1929.

Harrod, H. R. F. *The Life of John Maynard Keynes*. New York: Harcourt, Brace & World, 1951.

Henson, Herbert Hensley. *Retrospect on an Unimportant Life*. 3 vols. London: Oxford University Press, 1942-1950.

Holland, Henry Scott. *A Bundle of Memories*. London: Wells Gardner, Darton, 1915.

Horton, Robert F. *An Autobiography*. London: Allen & Unwin. 1918.

Hughes, Dorothea P. *The Life of Hugh Price Hughes.* London: Hodder & Stoughton, 1904.

Illingworth, Agnes L. *The Life and Work of John Richardson Illingworth.* London: John Murray, 1917.

Inge, W. R. *Diary of a Dean: St. Paul's 1911-34.* London: Macmillan, 1949.

Iremonger, F. A. *William Temple.* Oxford: Oxford University Press, 1948.

Jacks, L. P. *The Confession of an Octogenarian.* London: Macmillan, 1942.

Jones, Thomas. *Lloyd George.* Cambridge: Harvard University Press, 1951.

Keynes, J. M. *Two Memoirs.* London: Rupert Hart-Davis, 1949.

Lloyd George, David. *War Memories of David Lloyd George.* 6 vols. London: I. Nicholson & Watson, 1933-36.

Lockhart, J. G. *Charles Lindley Viscount Halifax 1839-1885.* Vol. I. London: Geoffrey Bles, 1935.

_____. *Charles Lindley Viscount Halifax 1885-1934.* Vol. II. London: Geoffrey Bles, 1936.

Lyttleton, E. *The Mind and Character of Henry Scott Holland.* London: Mowbray, 1926.

Matheson, Percy Ewing. *The Life of Hastings Rashdall.* London: Oxford University Press, 1928.

Masterman, Lucy Blanche. *C. F. G. Masterman: A Biography.* London: Nicholson, 1939.

Masterman, N. C. *John Malcolm Ludlow: The Builder of Christian Socialism.* Cambridge: University Press, 1963.

Micklem, Nathaniel. *The Box and the Puppets.* London: Geoffrey Bles, 1957.

Montague, C. E. *Disenchantment.* London: Chatto and Windus, 1922.

Moorman, J. R. H. *B. K. Cunningham.* London: S. C. M., 1947.

Muggeridge, Kitty and Adam, Ruth. *Beatrice Webb: A Life.* New York: Knopf. 1968.

Muirhead, John Henry. *Reflections by a Journeyman in Philosophy.* London: Allen & Unwin, 1942.

Murray, Gilbert. *An Unfinished Autobiography.* London: Allen & Unwin, 1960.

Newman, John Henry. *Apologia pro Vita Sua.* London: Sheed & Ward, 1946.

Orchard, W. E. *From Faith to Faith.* London: Putnam, 1933.

Paget, Stephen. *Henry Scott Holland.* London: Murray, 1921.

Petre, Maude D. *Von Hügel and Tyrrell; The Story of a Friendship.* London: J. M. Dent, 1937.

Porritt, Arthur. *The Best I Remember.* London: Cassell, 1922.

Prestige, G. L. *The Life of Charles Gore.* London: William Heineman, 1935.

Roberts, R. E. *H. R. L. Sheppard: His Life and Letters.* London: John Murray, 1942.

Russell, Bertrand. *My Philosophical Development.* London: Allen & Unwin, 1959.

_____. *Portraits from Memory.* New York: Simon & Schuster, 1956.

Selbie, W. B. *The Life of Andrew Martin Fairbairn.* London, 1914.

Sitwell, Edith. *Taken Care of.* New York: Atheneum, 1965.

Thompson, J. M. *My Apologia.* Oxford: Alden Press, 1940. (Printed for private circulation only.)

Tyrrell, George. *Autobiography and Life of George Tyrrell.* 2 vols. Edited and arranged by Maude D. Petre. London: Longmans, Green, 1912.

Ward, Mrs. Humphrey. *A Writer's Recollection.* London: Collins, 1918.

Ward, Maisie. *Gilbert Keith Chesterton.* New York: Sheed & Ward, 1943.

Webb, Beatrice (Potter). *My Apprenticeship.* London: Longmans, Green, 1926.

Welland, Dennis. *Wilfred Owen.* London: Chatto and Windus, 1960.

Wilkinson, John T. *Arthur Samuel Peake, 1865-1929.* London: Epworth Press, 1958.

Literature and Art

Bowra, C. M. *The Background of Modern Poetry.* Oxford: Clarendon Press, 1946.

Chesterton, C. K. *Poems.* London: Burns & Oates, 1915.

————. *Robert Browning.* London: Macmillan, 1903.

————. *Orthodoxy.* London: Fontana Books, 1961 (originally published in 1908).

Ellmann, Richard (ed.). *Edwardians and Late Victorians.* New York: Columbia University Press, 1960.

Galsworthy, John. *The Forsyth Saga.* London: William Heinemann, 1922.

Henderson, Archibald. *George Bernard Shaw, Man of the Century.* New York: Appleton-Century, 1956.

Jones, Henry. *Browning as a Philosophical and Religious Teacher.* Glasgow: James MacLehose, 1891.

Marriott, Charles. *Modern Movements in Painting.* London: Chapman & Hall, 1920.

Martin, Hugh. *The Faith of Robert Browning.* London: S. C. M., 1963.

Morrell, Roy. *Thomas Hardy: The Will and the Way.* Oxford: University of Malaya Press, 1965.

Nettleship, John T. *Essays on Robert Browning's Poetry.* London: Macmillan, 1868.

Sackville-West, Violet. *The Edwardians.* London: Hogarth Press, 1931.

Stone, Wilfred. *The Cave and the Mountain: A Study of E. M. Forster.* Palo Alto: Stanford University Press, 1966.

Wells, Herbert George. *An Englishman Looks at the World.* London: Cassell, 1914.

Williams, Raymond. *Culture and Society 1780-1950.* London: Chatto & Windus, 1958.

Wilson, Edmund. *Axel's Castle.* New York: Scribner's, 1931.

Woolf, Virginia. *The Hogarth Essays.* London: Hogarth Press, 1924.

Theology, Primary Sources

The Atonement in Modern Religious Thought. (Originally published in *The Christian World,* winter, 1899-1900. Contributors include: R. J. Campbell, P. T. Forsyth, Silvester Horne, R. H. Horton, A. Harnack, Marcus Dods, W. F. Adeney, F. W. Farrar.) London: James Clarke, 1900.

Bethune-Baker, James Franklin. *The Miracle of Christianity*. London: Longmans, Green, 1914.

_____. *The Faith of the Apostles' Creed*. London: Macmillan, 1918.

Campbell, R. J. *The New Theology*. New York: Macmillan, 1907.

_____. *Christianity and the Social Order*. London: Chapman & Hall, 1907.

_____. *New Theology Sermons*. London: Williams & Norgate, 1907.

Carpenter, Joseph Estlin. *The Historical Jesus and the Theological Christ*. London: Philip Green, 1911.

_____. *Studies in Theology*. London: J. M. Dent, 1903.

Church and Faith (Protestants in the Church of England) Edinburgh and London: Blackwood, 1899.

The Church Congress, Report of, Cambridge, 1910. C. Dunkley, editor. London: Allen & Sons, 1910.

Clifford, John. *Socialism and the Teachings of Christ*. London: Fabian Society, 1898.

Contentio Veritas. (H. Rashdall, W. R. Inge, H. L. Wild, C. F. Burney, W. C. Allen, A. J. Caryle) London: John Murray, 1902.

Davidson, Randall. *The Testing of a Nation*. London: Macmillan, 1919.

Fairbairn, A. M. *Studies in Religion and Theology*. London: Hodder & Stoughton, 1910.

_____. *The Place of Christ in Modern Theology*. London: Hodder & Stoughton, 1893.

_____. *The Philosophy of the Christian Religion*. London: Hodder & Stoughton, 1902.

Figgis, J. N. *The Gospel and Human Needs*. London: Longmans, Green, 1909.

_____. *Civilization at the Cross Roads*. London: Longmans, Green, 1912.

Foakes-Jackson, F. J. *The Faith and the War*. London: Macmillan, 1915.

Forsyth, P. T. *The Person and Place of Jesus Christ*. London: Independent Press, 1909.

_____. *The Cruciality of the Cross*. London: Independent Press, 1909.

_____. *Theology in Church and State*. London: Hodder & Stoughton, 1915.

_____. *The Church and the Sacraments*. London: Independent Press, 1917.

Gardner, Percy. *A Historic View of the New Testament*. London: A. & C. Black, 1901.

_____. *The Growth of Christianity*. London: A. & C. Black, 1907.

_____. *Evolution in Christian Doctrine*. London: Williams & Norgate, 1918.

Garvie, A. E. *Studies in the Inner Life of Jesus*. London: Hodder & Stoughton, 1907.

Glazebrook, M. G. *Faith of a Modern Churchman*. London: John Murray, 1918.

Glover, T. R. *The Jesus of History*. London: S. C. M., 1917.

_____. *Jesus in the Experience of Men*. London: S. C. M., 1921.

Gore, Charles. *The Church and the Ministry*. London: Longmans, Green, 1888.

_____ (ed.). *Lux Mundi*. London: John Murray, 1890.

_____. *The Incarnation of the Son of God* (Bampton Lecture 1891) London: John Murray, 1891.

_____. *Dissertations on Subjects Connected with the Incarnation.* London: John Murray, 1895.

_____. *The Basis of Anglican Fellowship: An open letter to the clergy of the diocese of Oxford.* London: Mowbray, 1914.

_____. *The New Theology and the Old Religion.* London: John Murray, 1908.

_____. *The Philosophy of the Good Life.* London: John Murray, 1930.

Gregory, Benjamin. *The Holy Catholic Church, the Communion of Saints.* (Delivered originally in 1873 Fernley Lecture) London: Wesleyan Methodist Book Room, 2nd ed., 1885.

Gwatkin, Henry Melvill. *The Bishop of Oxford's Open Letter. An Open Letter in Reply.* London: Longmans, Green, 1914.

Hatch, Edwin. *The Organization of the Early Christian Churches.* (Bampton Lectures 1880) London: Rivingtons, 1888.

_____. *The Growth of Christian Institutions.* London: Hodder & Stoughton, 1887.

Headlam, Arthur Cayley. *History, Authority and Theology.* London: John Murray, 1909.

Henson, H. H. *The Relation of the Church of England to the Other Reformed Churches.* Edinburgh: Blackwood, 1911.

_____. *Cross-Bench Views on Current Church Questions.* London: Edward Arnold, 1902.

Hibbert Journal. L. P. Jacks (ed.). *Supplement 1909: Jesus or Christ.* London: Williams & Norgate, 1909.

Holland, H. S. *Henry Scott Holland: A Selection from His Writings.* B. M. G. Reardon (ed.). London: S. P. C. K., 1962.

_____. *Miracles.* London: Longmans, Green, 1911.

_____. *Logic and Life.* New York: Scribner's, 1882.

_____. *Creeds and Critics.* London: Mowbray, 1918.

Horton, Robert Forman. *Inspiration and the Bible.* London: T. Fisher Unwin, 1888.

Hügel, Baron Friedrich von. *The Mystical Element in Religion.* London: J. M. Dent, 1908.

Illingworth, J. R. *Personality Human and Divine.* (Bampton Lectures) London: Macmillan 1894.

_____. *Divine Immanence.* London: Macmillan, 1898.

_____. *Divine Transcendence.* London: Macmillan, 1911.

Inge, W. R. *Christian Mysticism.* London: Methuen, 1899.

_____. *The Philosophy of Plotinus.* 2 vols. (Gifford Lectures 1917-18) London: Longmans, Green, 1923.

_____. *Christian Ethics and Modern Problems.* London: Hodder & Stoughton, 1930.

Knox, R. A. *Some Loose Stones.* London: Longmans, Green, 1913.

Lacey, Thomas A. *Unity and Schism.* London: Mowbray, 1917.

Lidgett, John Scott. *The Spiritual Principle of the Atonement.* London: Charles H. Kelly, 1898.

_____. *The Fatherhood of God.* Edinburgh: T. and T. Clark, 1902.

_____. *Apostolic Ministry*. London: Robert Culley, 1909.

_____. *God, Christ, and the Church*. London: Hodder & Stoughton, 1927.

Matthews, C. H. S. (ed.). *Faith or Fear*. London: Macmillan, 1916.

Matthews, W. R. *The Problem of Christ in the Twentieth Century*. Oxford: Oxford University Press, 1950.

Moberly, R. C. *Ministerial Priesthood*. London: John Murray, 1897.

_____. *Atonement and Personality*. London: John Murray, 1901.

Nichols, John Broadhurst. *Evangelical Belief*. London: The Religious Tract Society, 1899.

Oman, John Wood. *Vision and Authority: Or the Throne of St. Peter*. London: Hodder & Stoughton, 1902.

_____. *The Church and the Divine Order*. London: Hodder & Stoughton, 1911.

_____. *The War and Its Issues: An Attempt at a Christian Judgment*. Cambridge: University Press, 1915.

Pathways to Christian Unity: A Free Church View. (Arthur Black, G. S. Darlaston, W. E. Orchard, William Patson, J. H. Squire, Maleston Spencer) London: Macmillan, 1919.

Quick, Oliver C. *Essays in Orthodoxy*. London: Macmillan, 1916.

_____. *The Testing of Church Principles*. London: John Murray, 1919.

Rashdall, Hastings. *Philosophy and Religion*. London: Duckworth, 1909.

_____. *Conscience and Christ*. London: Duckworth, 1916.

_____. *The Idea of Atonement in Christian Theology*. (Bampton Lectures 1915) London: Macmillan, 1919.

_____. *God and Man*. Oxford: Basil Blackwell, 1930.

Rawlinson, A. E. J. *Dogma, Fact and Experience*. London: Macmillan, 1915.

Relton, Herbert M. *A Study in Christology*. London: S. P. C. K., 1922.

Sanday, William (ed.). *Different Conceptions of Priesthood and Sacrifice*. (Report of a conference held at Oxford, December 13-14, 1899.) London: Longmans, Green, 1900.

Sanday, William. *Christologies Ancient and Modern*. Oxford: Clarendon Press, 1910.

_____. *Bishop Gore's Challenge to Criticism*. London: Longmans, Green, 1914.

_____. *The Meaning of the War for Germany and Great Britain*. Oxford: Clarendon Press, 1915.

_____. *The Position of Liberal Theology*. (A friendly examination of the Bishop of Zanzibar's open letter entitled "The Christ and His Critics.") London: The Faith Press, 1920.

_____ and Williams, N. P. *Form and Content in the Christian Tradition*. London: Longmans, Green, 1916.

Spens, Will. *Belief and Practice*. London: Longmans, Green, 1915.

Streeter, B. H. (ed.). *Foundations*. London: Macmillan, 1912.

_____. (ed.). *The Spirit*. London: Macmillan, 1919.

Temple, William. *The Nature of Personality*. London: Macmillan, 1911.

_____. *Religious Experience*. London: J. Clarke, 1958.

Thompson, J. M. *Miracles in the New Testament*. London: Edward Arnold, 1911.

Towards Reunion. (Church of England & Free Church Consultation 1818-19.) London: Macmillan, 1919.

Tyrrell, George. *A Much-Abused Letter.* London: Longmans, Green, 1906.

_____. *Oil and Wine.* London: Longmans, Green, 1907.

_____. *Medievalism. A Reply to Cardinal Mercier.* London: Longmans, Green, 1908.

_____. *Christianity at the Crossroads.* London: Longmans, Green, 1909.

Vine, C. H. (ed.). *The Old Faith and the New Theology.* London: Sampson Low, Marston, 1907.

Warschauer, Joseph. *The New Evangel.* London: James Clarke, 1907.

_____. *Jesus: Seven Questions.* London: James Clarke, 1908.

_____. *Problems of Immanence.* London: James Clarke, 1909.

Webb, C. C. J. *Group Theories in Religion.* London: Allen & Unwin, 1916.

Westcott, B. F. *Christus Consummator.* London: Macmillan, 1886.

Weston, Frank. *The One Christ.* London: Longmans, Green, 1914.

_____. *The Christ and His Critics.* London: Mowbray, 1919.

Williams, Charles. *The Principles and Practices of the Baptists.* London: Kingsgate Press, 1903.

Wordsworth, John. *The Ministry of Grace.* London: Longmans, Green, 1901.

Philosophy, Primary Sources

Alexander, Samuel. *Space, Time and Deity.* London: Macmillan, 1920.

Balfour, Arthur J. *The Foundations of Belief.* London: Longmans, Green, 1894.

Bosanquet, Bernard. *The Principle of Individualism and Value.* London: Macmillan, 1912.

_____. *The Value and Destiny of the Individual.* London: Macmillan, 1913.

_____. *The Meeting of Extremes in Contemporary Philosophy.* London: Macmillan, 1921.

Bradley, F. H. *Ethical Studies.* Oxford: Clarendon Press, 1876, 1927.

_____. *Appearance and Reality.* London: Swan Sonnenschein, 1897.

Caird, Edward. *The Critical Philosophy of Immanuel Kant.* 2 vols. Glasgow: James MacLehose, 1889.

_____. *The Evolution of Religion.* 2 vols. Glasgow: James MacLehose, 1894.

Caird, John. *The Fundamental Ideas of Christianity.* Glasgow: James MacLehose, 1899-1904.

Collinwood, R. G. *Religion and Philosophy.* London: Macmillan, 1916.

Ewing, A. C. *Idealism: A Critical Survey.* London: Methuen, 1934.

Green, T. H. *The Works of the Thomas Hill Green,* ed. R. L. Nettleship. 3 vols. London: Longmans, Green, 1885.

Haldane, Richard B. *The Pathway to Reality.* 2 vols. (Gifford Lectures 1902-3.) London: John Murray 1903, 1904.

Hügel, Baron Friedrich von. *Essays and Addresses on the Philosophy of Religion.* 2 vols. London: J. M. Dent, 1921, 1926.

James, William. *Varieties of Religious Experience.* London: Longmans, Green, 1902.

Laird, John. *Problems of the Self*. London: Macmillan, 1917.

Lodge, Oliver. *The Substance of Faith Allied with Science*. London: Methuen, 1907.

McDougall, William. *Outline of Psychology*. London: Methuen, 1923.

_____. *Social Psychology*. London: Methuen, 1928.

McTaggart, John Mc. Ellis. *Some Dogmas of Religion*. London: Edward Arnold, 1906.

Moore, G. E. *Principia Ethica*. Cambridge: University Press, 1903.

Personal Idealism. Henry C. Sturt (ed.). Philosophical essays by eight members of the University of Oxford. (Stout, Schiller, Gibson, Underhill, Marett, Sturt, Russell, Rashdall) London: Macmillan, 1902.

Pringle-Pattison, A. (Seth). *Hegelianism and Personality*. Edinburgh: William Blackwood & Sons, 1887.

_____. *Man's Place in the Cosmos*. Edinburgh: Blackwood, 1897.

_____. *The Idea of God in the Light of Recent Philosophy*. (Gifford Lectures 1912-13) New York: Oxford University Press, 1920.

Ritchie, D. G. *Darwin and Hegel*. London: Swan Sennenschiem, 1898.

Schiller, F. C. S. *Humanism*. London: Macmillan, 1912.

Ward, James. *Naturalism and Agnosticism*. 2 vols. London: Macmillan, 1909.

Webb, C. C. J. *God and Personality*. London: Allen & Unwin, 1919.

_____. *Divine Personality and Human Life*. London: Allen & Unwin, 1920.

Wilson, John Cook. *Statement and Inference*. Oxford: Clarendon Press, 1926.

Philosophy and Theology: Secondary Sources

Akers, Samuel L. *Some British Reactions to Ritschlianism*. Scottdale, Pa.: Mennonite Press, 1934.

Bertocci, Peter A. *The Empirical Argument for God in Late British Thought*. Cambridge: Harvard University Press, 1938.

Brilioth, Y. *The Anglican Revival: Studies in the Oxford Movement*. London: Longmans, Green, 1933.

Carpenter, James Anderson. *Gore: A Study of Liberal Catholic Thought*. London: Faith Press, 1960.

Dakin, Arthur H. *Von Hügel and the Supernatural*. London: S. P. C. K., 1934.

Davies, Horton. *Worship and Theology in England, 1850-1900*. Princeton, N. J.: Princeton University Press, 1962.

_____. *Worship and Theology in England, 1900-1950*. Princeton, N. J.: Princeton University Press, 1965.

Elliott-Binns, L. E. *English Thought 1860-1900: The Theological Aspect*. New York: Seabury Press, 1956.

Emmett, Cyril. *Conscience, Creeds and Criticism*. London: Macmillan, 1918.

Ewing, A. C. *The Idealist Tradition: From Berkeley to Blanshard*. New York: The Free Press, 1958.

Garvie, A. E. *The Ritschlian Theology*. Edinburgh: T. and T. Clark, 1899.

Geoghegan, William D. *Platonism in Recent Religious Thought*. New York: Columbia University Press, 1958.

Grensted, L. W. *A Short History of the Doctrine of the Atonement.* Manchester: Manchester University Press, 1920.

Griffith, Gwilym Oswald. *The Theology of P. T. Forsyth.* London: Lutterworth, 1948.

Healey, F. G. *Religion and Reality: The Theology of John Oman.* Edinburgh: Oliver & Boyd, 1965.

Hearnshaw, L. S. *Short History of British Psychology 1840-1940.* London: Methuen, 1964.

Horton, Walter M. *Contemporary English Theology.* New York: Harper, 1936.

Inge, William. *The Platonic Tradition in English Theological Thought.* London: Longmans, Green, 1926.

Jones, Henry. *The Life and Philosophy of Edward Caird.* Glasgow: MacLehose, 1921.

Jones, Maurice. *The New Testament in the Twentieth Century.* London: Macmillan, 1924.

Lawton, John Stewart. *Conflict in Christology.* (A study of British and American Christology from 1889-1914) New York: Macmillan, 1947.

Lester-Garland, Lester V. *The Religious Philosophy of Baron von Hügel.* London: J. M. Dent, 1933.

Mackintosh, H. R. *Doctrine of the Person of Jesus Christ.* New York: Scribner's, 1912.

Major, H. D. A. *English Modernism.* London: H. Milford, 1927.

Metz, Rudolf. *A Hundred Years of British Philosophy.* New York: Macmillan, 1938.

Mozley, John K. *Ritschlianism, an Essay.* London: Nisbet, 1909

Muirhead, J. H. *Contemporary British Philosophy* (First series). London: Macmillan, 1924.

_____. *The Platonic Tradition in Anglo-Saxon Philosophy.* London: Allen & Unwin, 1931.

Neill, Stephen Charles. *The Interpretation of the New Testament, 1861-1961.* London: Oxford University Press, 1964.

Passmore, J. A. *A Hundred Years of Philosophy.* London: Duckworth, 1957.

Ramsey, A. M. *From Gore to Temple* (American title: *An Era in Anglican Theology*). London: Longmans, Green, 1960.

Reckitt, M. B. *Maurice to Temple.* London: Faber and Faber, 1947.

Richter, Melvin. *The Politics of Conscience: T. H. Green and His Age.* London: Weidenfeld & Nicolsen, 1964.

Rodgers, John Hewitt. *The Theology of P. T. Forsyth.* London: Independent Press, 1965.

Schilpp, P. A. (ed.). *The Philosophy of C. D. Board.* New York: Tudor, 1959.

_____. (ed.). *The Philosophy of G. E. Moore.* New York: Tudor, 1952.

Sorley, William Ritchie. *A History of English Philosophy.* Cambridge: University Press, 1920.

Warnock, G. J. *English Philosophy Since 1900.* London: Oxford University Press, 1958.

Webb, C. C. J. *A Century of Anglican Theology.* Oxford: Basil Blackwell, 1923.

_____. *A Study of Religious Thought in England from 1850.* Oxford: Clarendon Press, 1933.

Welleck, R. *Kant in England.* Princeton: Princeton University Press, 1931.

White, Alan R. *G. E. Moore, A Critical Exposition.* Oxford: Basil Blackwell, 1958.

Widgery, Alban G. *Contemporary Thought of Great Britain.* New York: Knopf, 1927.

Wood, H. G. *Belief and Unbelief Since 1850.* Cambridge: Cambridge University Press, 1955.

Wolheim, Richard. *F. H. Bradley.* Harmondsworth, Middlesex: Penguin Books, 1959.

INDEX

313